THE BOOK OF
BERGH APTON

A Rural Ride in Norfolk

GEOFFREY I. KELLY

HALSGROVE

First published in Great Britain in 2005

British Library Cataloguing-in-Publication Data.
A CIP record for this title is available from the British Library.

Frontispiece photograph: *Neville Jermy* (left) *and Arthur Smith hoeing sugar beet at Washingford House farm in the 1980s.*

ISBN 1 84114 418 5

HALSGROVE

Halsgrove House
Lower Moor Way
Tiverton, Devon EX16 6SS
Tel: 01884 243242
Fax: 01884 243325
E-mail: sales@halsgrove.com
Website: www.halsgrove.com

Printed and bound in Great Britain by CPI, Bath.

CONTENTS

ACKNOWLEDGEMENTS

We express our thanks to all who have generously searched out and loaned photographs and images, and who have helped with information on both photographs and captions: Peter Annis, John Avery, Valerie Athow Baker, Paris Back, Ann Ball, Judith Barber, Roger Barcham, Albert Burgess, Ron Cain, Colin Carver, John Clemence, Barry and Richard Cushing, Tony Davy, Bob Debbage, Janet Dew, the Dye family, Ruby Eastell, Albert Eirera, Ronnie Farrow, Sharon Finn (Australia), Roy Flowerdew, Albert Forder, Alison Freeman, John and Sally Garrett, Margaret Halford, Graham Harber, Ann Harris, Seejay Harrison, Judith Holmes, Fiona Hubbard, Olive Hudson, Joel Hull, Chris Johnson, Colin Keeler, Bob Kerry, Lorie Lain-Rogers, Sigi Legge, Sally Leigh, John and Joy Lester, John Ling, Fred and Violet Littlewood, Joyce Loyd, Nick Macartney, John Madden (Canada), Bruce Marsh (Canada), Philippa Millington, Timothy O'Riordan, Mike Page (aerials), Kevin Parfitt, Ashley Price, the late Jim Rayner, Josephine Riley, Stuart Roper, Arthur Royall, Evie Sayer, Sandy Schröder, Eric Seeley, Derek Secker, Trevor Sillett, Ena Smith, Martin Snellgrove, Anna Stratton, Bernie and Di Webb, Alan and Vera Weddup, the late Hugh Wilkinson (Canada) and Michael and Jill Willcox.

We also thank sincerely those who offered photographs that we have, for one reason or another, been unable to use. Inevitably there will be some whose help we have omitted to acknowledge. To them, too, we give our grateful thanks but with apologies for the omission. Their reward, we hope, will be the quality of the product.

And, finally, thanks to Milton Harris of Town Farm, the first chairman of Bergh Apton Local History Group, who proposed that this book be written, and to the residents of this and neighbouring parishes, together with members of Bergh Apton Local History Group, who have helped in its research: Stephanie Crome, Linda Davy, Bob Debbage, Roy Flowerdew, Chris Johnson, Lorie Lain-Rogers, John Ling, Dennis Moye, Phyllis Ride and David Skedge. We would also like to give our thanks to the Parish Council, the Tenwinter Trust and to Bergh Apton Community Arts Trust (BACAT) for their financial support and encouragement.

Sandy Schröder's map of the parish of Bergh Apton, 1994.

GLOSSARY

It is hoped that *The Book of Bergh Apton* will be a source of abiding interest for a wide range of readers. Bergh Apton has had a long and fascinating history, dealt with at length in this text; but, by the nature of things, some of the words and terms used in it that are familiar to historians may not be so to others. While a number of such words and terms are explained in the narrative, usually in the context of their first appearance, the following listing should also be helpful:

advowson: the right to present to the living (see below) of a parish i.e. recommend a member of the clergy for the tenure of a rectory or vicarage.

agistment: taking in livestock to feed upon one's land for a fee.

armigerous: entitled to bear a coat of arms.

ashlar: blocks of cut stone.

baffle entry: an entry to a house facing the side of a chimney.

bressumer: a beam spanning a fireplace.

brick-skinned: clay- or timber-framed building clad with an outer skin of brick.

capital: the top of a pillar.

carucate: an area of land, approximating to 120a.

catslide: a roof extending beyond the main range of a house in an unchanged pitch to span an adjoining outhouse.

champaign: historically countryside in which the farmland was generally found in large fields divided into strips prior to Inclosure (see below), and which still possesses an open character.

copyhold: a form of tenure, abolished by the 1922 Law of Property Act, in which land and/or buildings were held at the will of the lord or lady of a particular manor. See also Court Baron (below).

corbel head: decorative terminal on a hoodmould.

cordwainer: a boot- and shoemaker, generally also skilled in other work with leather.

Counter-Reformation: the movement in the reign of Mary Tudor in which many of the religious changes which took place during the Henrician Reformation (see below) were reversed.

Court Baron: (later called Court General): a session of the manorial court at which major issues were dealt with, such as transfers of copyhold (see above) property.

Court Leet: a session of the manorial court concerning the maintenance of good order within the area of the manor's jurisdiction.

daguerreotype: the earliest practical form of photographic print, invented in 1839 by Louis Daguerre.

demesne: the heart of a manorial estate, usually comprised of a hall or manor-house and a home farm, sometimes with such features as a dovecote, mill, park and warren.

diapering: a lozenge pattern formed by the use of burnt (dark-coloured) bricks amongst the usual red ones of a wall.

dog-iron: an iron placed by a hearth to support a burning log.

English bond: brickwork consisting of alternating courses of headers and stretchers.

essoin: having a reasonable excuse for one's non-appearance at a manorial court presented by a fellow tenant.

fee simple: freehold which bore no encumbrances.

Feoffees: trustees invested with the tenure of a specific estate.

flat-keyed: recessed mortar in a brick wall with a vertical (not angled) face.

frankpledge: a system whereby heads of households were bound in groups of ten, each responsible for the good behaviour of the others.

furlong: in the sense of an area of land, a section of a usually unenclosed field with a length of one furlong (220yds).

gault: a form of clay burnt to produce pale greyish, often described as white, bricks.

glebe: the territorial endowment of a rectory or vicarage, enjoyed by the incumbent as his freehold.

gentrification: a term used in respect of the modernisation of an existing, vernacular house (for a definition of which, see p.78) with architecturally designed features.

guilloche: a pattern composed of curved lines.

hayward: a person historically chosen at a manorial court who had responsibility for the good maintenance of hedges and fences within its area of jurisdiction for the term of one year.

Henrician Reformation: the religious changes, most notably the break with Rome, brought into being during the reign of Henry VIII.

hipped: a roof with all four sides pitched to a ridge.

hoodmould: projecting stonework above a window or door to throw off rain (often decorative).

hundred: in the sense of an administrative unit, a division of a county comprised of a varying number of parishes.

Inclosure: this variant of the word 'enclosure', with its well-known meaning, is consistently used in respect of Acts of Parliament and consequent Awards in which, briefly, hitherto common land within a parish was mostly divided up between the existing

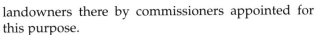

landowners there by commissioners appointed for this purpose.

Inquisitio Eliensis: a survey of lands belonging to, or claimed by, the Abbot of Ely about the time of the Domesday Book, 1086.

Inquisition Post Mortem: an inquisition held after the death of a person holding lands directly or indirectly from the Crown, at which the identity of the legal heir was declared and his or her right to inherit stated.

lay subsidy: A tax levied on non-ecclesiastical persons, at a rate for country residents for one-fifteenth (or sometimes less) of the value of their moveable items and, in some cases, wages.

livery: in respect of landholding, one was granted livery of an estate after having inherited it and become of age.

living: in the ecclesiastical sense, the tenure of a rectory (as at Bergh Apton) or a vicarage by a priest.

louvre: a slatted aperture in a window or door.

mediety: a half-share of a living (see above).

meslin: mixed corn, usually wheat and rye.

messuage: a house and its appurtenances.

mullion: a vertical divider in a multi-light window.

ousterlemain: a device by which an estate was granted to an heir who had become of age.

outliers: lands within the jurisdiction of a manor, but lying at some distance from its core area.

outshut: an outhouse, attached to the main body of a house.

patera: a small dish.

perch: a measure of length, equalling 5.5yds and an area being this unit squared. An acre is comprised of 4 roods, a rood of 40 perches.

planchered: ceiled-over, not open to the rafters.

plough (team): in the context of early-medieval times, a plough together with the oxen which drew it.

quarter: in the context of a measure of corn, 640lb dry weight.

quickset: a hedge formed by planting cuttings of, for the most part, whitethorn, which had the propensity to grow quickly.

quoin: corner stone.

recognizance: a legal bond.

refenestrate: having earlier windows replaced.

rendell: a sheaf of flax.

reveal: the angled surface of a wall or window-frame that increases available light.

rood: a measure of land comprising one-quarter of an acre.

sequestrator: the controller of a vacant living (see above), principally for the benefit of the creditors of the previous incumbent.

socage: tenure of land, often that of a manor, mostly in return for a regular financial payment and/or the provision of goods.

terrier: a written description of land, mostly used in the context of glebe (see above) terrier.

tie-beam: a beam that connects two rafters or other timbers to prevent them from spreading apart.

Y-tracery: masonry in the form of the letter 'Y'.

ABBREVIATIONS (used in references)

ANF: Archdeaconry of Norfolk
a.r.p.: acre(s), rood(s), perch(es)
BACAP: Bergh Apton Community Arts Programme
BACT: Bergh Apton Conservation Trust
BALHG: Bergh Apton Local History Group
ESRO: East Sussex Record Office
HER: Historic Environment Record(s)
IE: Inquisitio Eliensis
MSS: manuscripts
NCC: Norwich Consistory Court
NMAS: Norfolk Museums and Archaeology Service
NPR: Norwich Probate Registry
NRO: Norfolk Record Office
TNA: The National Archives
£.s.d.: pounds, shillings, pence

INTRODUCTION

To mark the new millennium the residents of Bergh Apton made plans to celebrate this event with the production of a history of the village. In 1997 Milton Harris of Town Farm, Bergh Apton, suggested I submit proposals for a parish history to the Parish Council. Shortly afterwards, under the aegis of the Bergh Apton Local History Group (BALHG), detailed plans for the production of this book, were formalised.

Bergh Apton folk are proud of their parish, which in particular possesses an impressive number of houses dating from between the sixteenth and the eighteenth centuries. In conjunction with this current research, and in respect of commissions carried out over the last 20 or so years, many householders have warmly welcomed me into their cherished homes – to all of you, I offer my thanks for your hospitality. Locally, a great deal of useful material is held by Bergh Apton Parish Council, BALHG archivists, and in the Parish Church of SS Peter and Paul. The Norfolk Record Office in Norwich, and the Norfolk Studies and Reference Libraries at Gildengate House, Norwich, (now relocated within the Norwich Millennium Library), were useful sources of information, while details of prehistoric finds were mostly provided by the Norfolk Museums and Archaeology Service (NMAS), at Union House, Gressenhall. Further afield, sources were checked at the Family Records Centre, London; The National Archives (formerly the Public Record Office), Kew; the Bodleian Library, Oxford, and at the East Sussex Record Office, Lewes. Thanks are due to all concerned. The photographic material used to illustrate the text has been separately acknowledged on p.4. Acknowledgments are also made to the repositories in which the extensive source material for Bergh Apton is located.

Central to the history of Bergh Apton is that this post-Reformation civil and ecclesiastical parish was formed from the hitherto, generally distinct, parishes of Bergh and Apton. This matter will be considered in detail in due course; however, when appropriate, given the historic boundary between Bergh and Apton, which is in part precisely and in other parts approximately known, certain references have been made to each of these in isolation.

This history has not been compiled with a view to publication as a purely academic work, and consequently the text has not been overburdened with citations; on the other hand, it is only proper that essential ones should have been given. As for the format of the text, dates throughout are given in New Style (Gregorian calendar) with the beginning of the year dating from 1 January, rather than in the Old Style (Julian calendar) 25 March which obtained prior to 1752. To avoid confusion, a certain amount of standardisation with regard to the spelling of personal and place-names, particularly in medieval and early-modern times, has been deemed appropriate; however, the spelling of surnames follows original sources. References to the River Chet should be taken to include its headstream, the Well Beck. With regard to obsolescent units of square measure, readers may wish to be reminded that an acre is comprised of 4 roods, a rood of 40 perches (a.r.p.). Similarly it should be recalled that, until 1971, the pound sterling comprised 20s., and each shilling comprised 12d.(£.s.d.). Metric equivalents for imperial units have not been included in the text.

Clearly, it would have been impractical to include everything discovered concerning the story

The author Geoffrey Kelly on the bonnet of his father's car outside Holly Cottage, The Street, in 1948.

of Bergh Apton within the covers of this book. For the most part, material left out is lodged with representatives of BALHG and consequently forms the basis of a permanent archive for the benefit of future students of the parish.

This book could in no way have been produced without the loyal and assiduous efforts of members of BALHG: they must be offered not only my own heartfelt thanks but also those of the parish as a whole. In any case, I would wish to absolve BALHG members from any responsibility for errors – hopefully, few in number – such as may be found in the text. To this, John Ling has kindly contributed two appendices: the first on the war memorial, with biographical details of those named thereupon; the second on the Village Hall.

I count myself privileged as an outsider to have been invited to write *The Book of Bergh Apton*. At least I can claim to have known this fascinating village for just about all of my life, for when I was but a few weeks old in 1944 my mother moved from my Hardwick birthplace to become sub-postmistress of Brooke and it was Brooke-based postmen who delivered the mail to the larger part of Bergh Apton. Later, when I was aged four, my father took a photograph of me perched upon the bonnet of his car in The Street in Bergh Apton. Little did I know then that in 1982, as a consultant historian, I would be commissioned to research the first of a number of properties in the village; or that I would return another 20 years later to write a comprehensive account of Bergh Apton.

Geoffrey I. Kelly
Frettenham, Norfolk
2005

An aerial view of Church Meadow Lane, looking north to its junction with Threadneedle Street and Mill Road, taken in December 2004. (MIKE PAGE)

Chapter I

The Bergh Apton Landscape

Bergh Apton is a Norfolk parish extending to 1,988 acres, situated some 7 miles south-east of the city of Norwich. Its latitude is 52 degrees 34 minutes north, and its longitude 1 degree 24 minutes east. The landscape is gently undulating, typical for south Norfolk, but there is a relatively steep slope from the north side of the valley floor of the River Chet in the south-west and south of the parish rising to an altitude of about 120ft. At its lowest point, where the River Chet ceases to mark the shared parish boundary with Sisland and enters Thurton, the land is about 15ft above mean sea level.

Territorial Divisions

For the longer part of its documented history, Bergh Apton, together with the villages of Brooke and Howe, lay within a detached part of the Clavering Hundred; Loddon Hundred separated this from the main portion of the Clavering Hundred. The hundred originated in Anglo-Saxon times and was used as a territorial division for the majority of English counties. However, the boundaries of individual hundreds changed somewhat over the first few centuries of their existence. In the eleventh century, Apton was intimately associated with what is now the adjoining, discrete parish of Alpington. At that time the villages of Bergh and Apton were variously described as being first in Loddon and then in Henstead Hundreds but, by the thirteenth century, Bergh and Apton were regarded as lying in the Clavering Hundred. By the twentieth century, hundreds (or pairs of hundreds) had ceased to exist as local government units for most practical purposes, saving Poor Law Unions, and the frequently coextensive Rural Districts often adopted their names; however, the name Clavering – as a component of the Loddon and Clavering Rural District Council – effectively became obsolete when this body's appellation was simplified as Loddon Rural District Council in 1935. As a consequence of the Local Government Act of 1972, Bergh Apton has been a parish within South Norfolk District Council since 1 April 1974.

Water Sources

Nowhere in Bergh Apton does the Upper Chalk, lying as a dip-slope beneath this parish, outcrop; however, it forms the aquifer which provides the source of virtually all the water required for modern domestic, agricultural and commercial use. In the

Chet Valley, early 1980s. Taken from Bergh Apton's church tower, this view to the south-east shows the roofs of Hall Farm and its barns just visible above trees bordering the churchyard.

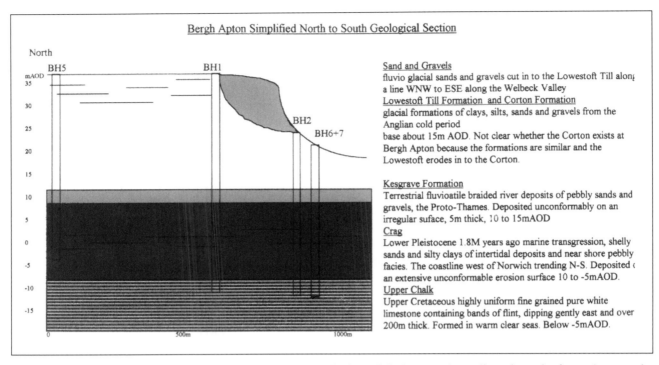

A geological cross-section of soil layers, drawn by Joel Hull of Norfolk County Council to show the formations on the north side of the Chet Valley. BH1, 2, 5, 6 and 7 were boreholes, sunk to monitor the water quality.

days before technology permitted water extraction from such a deep reserve, the needs of Bergh Apton folk and their livestock would have been met from the River Chet, its tributary the Little Beck, and from ponds, ditches, shallow wells and, indeed, rainwater tubs and the like.

The Norwich Crag

The oldest deposit to outcrop at Bergh Apton is the Norwich Crag, an unconsolidated mixture of shelly sands and gravels, laid down by the sea that covered eastern Norfolk about 1,800,000 years ago, prior to the initial advance of the glaciers of the Quaternary ice age. This formation is only visible at ground level in a narrow band running by the Chet Valley for a few hundred yards below Bussey Bridge.

Drift Deposits

Virtually all of Bergh Apton was covered by drift during the overall period of the ice age. However, it must be borne in mind that it was by no means throughout the whole of this period that the land that would become this parish was covered by ice. The sequence of events during the ice age remains a source of some dispute in geological circles. However, it seems most likely that while four distinct advances of the ice shaped the surface of most of Norfolk, it was only during one or two of these that Bergh Apton was actually covered by a glacial blanket. Over much of central, southern and south-eastern Norfolk the sheet(s) laid down a deposit of

An ammonite found by John Lester of Mill Road, Bergh Apton, in 1965.

chalky and sandy clay, sometimes called boulder clay, but locally more usually referred to as Lowestoft till. After the end of the ice age the Lowestoft till was weathered to form a heavy soil, which, until the clearances first initiated in Neolithic times, became thickly forested. This material covers the largest part of Bergh Apton.

The sands and gravels deposited by the melting ice aligned on a band from west-north-west to east-south-east to the north side of the Chet Valley, from near Wellbeck Bridge to Bussey Bridge. Here we find, particularly to the west of Bergh Apton church, lighter soils that were successively favoured by Bronze-Age, Romano-British, and pagan-Saxon man. An area covered by similar, although even more extensive sandy deposits, lies within Bergh Apton and extends into neighbouring Thurton. It approximates to the pre-Inclosure White Heath, which was

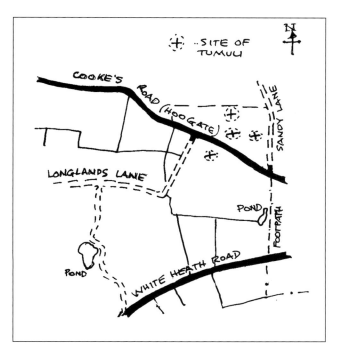

Fig.1.1. The location of the White Heath tumuli according to the Ordnance Survey map of 1908. They were also known as Hoos, after which Hoogate (later Howgate) took its name.

also occupied by Bronze-Age man. This is evident by the tumuli to be found in the area. One other geological feature is easily identified. A distinct although irregularly shaped band of sandy clay runs generally eastward from Bergh Apton House to the Thurton parish boundary and is broken at one point by a lobe of Lowestoft till.

Peat Extraction and Flooding

Narrow bands of peat flank the River Chet and its headstream the Well Beck, together with its tributary the Little Beck. This peat was laid down about 2500BC, the approximate time at which the early-Bronze-Age succeeded the Neolithic period. Moreover, it is of the kind that was widely extracted in east Norfolk and north-east Suffolk in medieval times. Those excavations subsequently flooded to create the Broads; however, there is no evidence of any such extraction having occurred as far upstream as Bergh Apton. The Chet Valley hereabouts has rarely flooded to any considerable extent in modern times; however F. Blomefield and C. Parkin mention a declaration in an otherwise unspecified Inquisition of 1658 that 592 acres of Bergh Apton were 'subject to be drowned'.[1]

Human Occupation of Bergh Apton

Upon what are for the most part drift deposits, the landscape of Bergh Apton with which we are familiar today has essentially been fashioned by mankind:

indeed, the story of human occupation has been documented here in a continuous sequence from the mid-eleventh century. There are hints encapsulated in archaeological evidence that this locality had also been settled for much of the time back through the Bronze Age, to the Neolithic period – albeit certain finds dating from the Palaeolithic and Mesolithic cannot be taken as providing evidence for continuous settlement. From the fourteenth century onwards there was a dynasty of absentee lords of Bergh Apton's principal manor. The absence of a single landowning family dominating the other resident landowners permitted the rise to relative prosperity of numerous yeoman farmers, along with members of the lesser gentry. Their prosperity remains apparent in the substantial houses that they built or rebuilt in late-Tudor and Stuart times, which stand in numerous localities within the parish.

Hillside Farm, 2002.

White House Farm in the late 1980s. This was the home of farmer Fred Hemmant, a well-known horseman and steam engine enthusiast who died in 1990. The photograph shows the early farmhouse (on the left) and the Victorian extension (on the right).

The stables at Sunnyside, c.1960. This was once the site of a holding farmed by Aaron Rope before he moved to Holly Lodge Farm. He was the father of Leonard and Hubert Rope who were killed in the First World War.

Farming Systems

Whereas there are early references in deeds and in court book entries to fields – meaning common or open fields, comprised of strips in separate owner-ship yet requiring co-operative management – such fields had ceased to form the major landscape element of this parish by the sixteenth century. Indeed, there are hints that such fields may never have been formed entirely of strips, but had always been a mixture of such features with some intrusive closes. Certainly, no evidence has been forthcoming which would indicate that Bergh Apton as a whole – or Bergh and Apton as distinct villages – had had the well-documented two or (more often) three field system, associated with much of Midland England and also with the light (or relatively light) soil region of west-central and northern Norfolk. Writers from late-Tudor times remarked upon Norfolk, other than its Fenland and Broads regions, as divided between an extensive champaign open countryside. In other words, it is a sheep–corn zone and a long-enclosed and well-wooded district generally associated with the heavy (or relatively heavy) soils of southern and east-central Norfolk. We must turn to consider how the landscape of Bergh Apton reflected the broad features associated with this latter region, and indeed continues to display them. From the inclosure of the early-medieval period to the first decade of the nine-teenth century, a form of husbandry is found that is mirrored throughout much of lowland England.

It would appear from the evidence of wills and probate inventories from the late-medieval period, as well as the very nature of the surviving yeoman farmhouses and farmsteads, that Bergh Apton folk, like those in most villages elsewhere in the wood–pasture zone of Norfolk, found that its soils were such as favoured the development of mixed farming. The emphasis was on dairying rather than an overwhelming concentration upon arable husbandry. The latter was associated with sheep flocks that were folded upon open fields between harvest and spring sowing. Given that the farming pattern which evolved in the wood–pasture zone tended – and one is driven to some generalisation – to give middling men a good livelihood, but did not favour the agglomeration of great wealth such as is ultimately manifest in the survival of prodigy houses and great estates in the sheep–corn zone, the yeoman farmers of Bergh Apton, beyond the type of farm-house just mentioned, left their mark on its landscape in the following ways.

Piecemeal Inclosure of Open Fields

First, as any such open fields as had existed in the Middle Ages did not suit a farming economy with an emphasis on the pastoral, they were gradually swept away by piecemeal inclosure from the fifteenth century. Lords of the (capital) Manor of Bergh Apton were absentee landlords; so as long as the succession of stewards honestly forwarded to their masters' coffers the dues from the free, copy-hold and leasehold tenants, and kept the peace – at least, primarily, to the seventeenth century – through the medium of the manorial court, there was little or no seigniorial interference in the devel-opment of husbandry. This meant that when the time came for the parliamentary Inclosure of the parish in the first decade of the nineteenth century, the proceedings of the commis-sioners in Bergh Apton were mostly concerned with the extinguishing of common pasture, as opposed to that of the common fields of sheep–corn zone parishes.

A Non-Nucleated Settlement Pattern

Wood–pasture husbandry led to the development of a non-nucleated settlement pattern, such as we see in Bergh Apton today – except for the concentration of post-Inclosure building upon the former Apton Heath (Fig.2.1, p.15). The village does not exhibit the feature of housing grouped in one particular area, often closely associated with the church and manor-house, such as is typical of sheep–corn villages as they existed up to and often beyond the time their open fields were extinguished – Anmer, Harpley and Rougham provide examples of such villages in Norfolk. Bergh Apton, as a non-nucleated parish, has features that exist – or existed – with regard to its settlement, which should be detailed further. Not unnaturally, ready access to the River Chet and its flanking meadows with some common pasture was of great value; consequently, there survives a chain of valley-edge farmsteads from Hillside Farm in the west extending 2¼ miles to Rose Cottage Farm in the east.

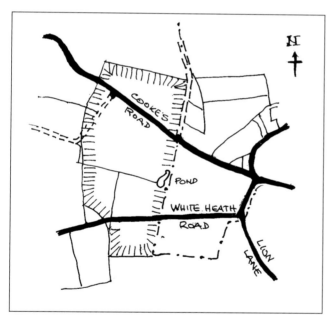

Fig.1.2. Common pasture of the village pre-1806 – White Heath.

Ancient Isolated Farms

The desirability of immediate access to the common pastures to the north of Bergh Apton, particularly Apton Heath and White Heath, was a factor which led to the development of settlement by the edge of these; however, when these commons were extinguished by the Inclosure Award of 1806, smaller farms hereabouts, particularly those which had previously been downgraded to labourers' cottages, tended to be demolished in the century or so which followed. Hence, this particular feature of Bergh Apton's overall settlement pattern remains less apparent today – the most obvious surviving example being Bergh Apton Manor.

Twisting Roads

Allied to Bergh Apton's non-nucleated settlement, are its many roads that tend to twist and turn about the parish – this very much a feature of the pre-Inclosure highways here.

The Changing Landscape

The landscape of Bergh Apton evolved but slowly, at least until the Inclosure Award of 1806; indeed, truly rapid evolution was only manifested over approximately 40 years following the end of the Second World War. This particular period witnessed much grubbing up of hedges, many of which would have been ancient, and the amalgamation of fields. Towards the end of the twentieth century, some reconstitution of hedges and planting of trees, either individually or so as to form small plantations, has partly countered the grubbing up and felling that had previously occurred.

Looking over Bergh Apton from the top of the church tower, it can be viewed as a cohesive amalgam of settlement, trees and hedgerows, farmland and valley, a happy place. As the following chapters reveal, it has suited sojourners and settlers, and grown gently, as it were, to assume its present face over the passage of many centuries.

The Bergh Apton Hedgerow Survey

This survey is being carried out by the Bergh Apton Conservation Trust at the time of writing and has four main phases:

The first phase was completed in 1998 and comprised a physical survey of the parish to plot existing hedgerows and woodland. The results of this are depicted as overprint on the six inches to one mile (1:10,560) Ordnance Survey of 1905, which is used as a base map. The data indicated are: hedgerows existing in 1905 and 1998; hedgerows existing in 1905 but not 1998; hedgerows existing in 1998 but not in 1905; woodland existing in 1904 and 1998; woodland (including orchards) existing in 1905 but not 1998; woodland existing in 1998 but not 1905; and ponds existing in 1998.

The second phase consists of a detailed survey of 30m (100ft) sections of existing hedgerows. This survey commenced in 1999 and is expected to be completed by about 2009, after which sections of the parish will be covered on an annual basis. The surveyors are using standard recording sheets acquired from the Norfolk Hedge & Boundary Survey. These sheets provide for the following basic data to be entered for each length of an individual hedge: names of trees and shrubs, climbers and ground flora; hedge condition and height; adjacent and boundary features.

The third phase (still ongoing in 2005) involves a comparison of existing hedgerows and woodland

Bergh Apton Conservation Trust replanting an area of ancient boundary hedge in 1999. This is locally known as the 'Tenwinter' hedge, as it is situated on the border between Bergh and Thurton, on land given to the village by Christopher Tenwinter in 1599. Left to right: *Jenny Rolfe, Frances Hubbard* (partially hidden), *John Ling and Hilary Ling* (partially hidden).

with those which existed at various times over the last 120 years or so, to show how these features of the village landscape have changed. Evidence of past hedgerows and woodland has been gathered from maps and aerial photographs, acquired for the benefit of the project in particular and thus for the benefit of the parish and wider public in general. The sources acquired are: the 1:2,500 Ordnance Survey of 1881–84, noted for accurately indicating the positions of all roadside, hedgerow and isolated trees, and the full revisions of this (albeit not indicating such trees) at the same scale of 1905, 1926 and 1971; the Royal Air Force aerial photographs of 1946 (mentioned above). Crown/Ministry of Defence copyright applies to these photographs, which are held by the Norfolk Museums and Archaeology Service at Union House, Gressenhall, and which is licensed to copy the same.

The aim of the fourth phase is to replant former hedges, particularly those marking the parish boundary or which would serve as wildlife corridors. To this end in the spring of 1999, BACT replanted a piece of neglected hedge forming part of the boundary with Thurton.

As above, replanting of another section of the ancient boundary hedge in 1999, with Lorie Lain-Rogers in action.

References

[1] F. Blomefield and C. Parkin, *An Essay towards a Topographical History of the County of Norfolk*, 2nd edn, (London, William Miller, 1805–1810).

Chapter II
Palaeolithic to Iron Age

The Lower-Palaeolithic Period

It is to the Lower Palaeolithic that we must cast our minds back in order to note the first tangible evidence of man's handiwork in Bergh Apton – that is to maybe in excess of 400,000 years ago. The artefact concerned was in the form of an incomplete hand axe[1], found by John Lester[2] in November 2000 upon what had been (until the Inclosure Award of

Above left: *An incomplete hand-axe from the Lower-Palaeolithic period with the dimensions 86mm x 63mm x 31mm.* (JOHN LESTER COLLECTION)

Above right: *The upper side of a baby mammoth tooth found by John Lester in the area of Apton Heath.*

1806) Apton Heath. It would not have been wrought by an ancestor of anyone alive today, but by a member of that extinct branch of the human family known as *Homo erectus*.

A further axe, found c.1959 by one Palmer on Hempland Close (as this field was named on maps of 1806 and 1841), has not been ascribed to any particular period of the Palaeolithic on the NMAS database,[3] and may have been fashioned by a member of our own human species, *Homo sapiens*, albeit the branch thereof then evolving into Neanderthal man. A large round flake tool, perhaps worked about the same time, found in Bergh Apton by John Lester according to a list drafted by BALHG, does not appear on the database given to me by the NMAS. John Lester was also the discoverer (c.1980, on the pre-Inclosure Apton Heath, south of Mill Road) of a tooth identified by Norwich Castle Museum staff as that of a baby mammoth; if this creature had not died from natural causes, it may well have been slain by Palaeolithic hunters who frequented this locality.

The Mesolithic Period

The Mesolithic period followed the final retreat of the ice about 10,000 years ago, and lasted until about 4000BC. John Lester has found a flint arrowhead and various blades from this time on the former Apton

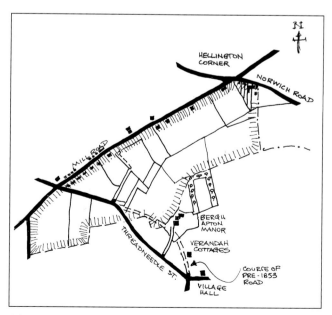

Fig.2.1.   *Common pasture of the village pre-1806 – Apton Heath, showing later field boundaries and buildings.*

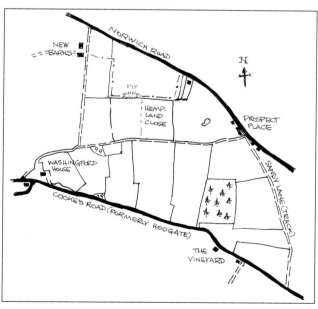

Fig.2.2.   *Hempland Close, where a Palaeolithic axe was found in 1959.*

15

Heath.[4] Until about 4000BC, the ancient men who left their mark upon Bergh Apton in the form of their lost or abandoned tools would have been wandering hunter-gatherers.

John Lester with a few of the artefacts he has picked up while field walking in the Apton Heath area over a period of nearly 50 years.

The Neolithic Period

During the Neolithic period, which extended between about 4000 and 2500BC, the hunter-gatherers generally ceased to wander and formed settled, farming communities. Evidence of their existence in Bergh Apton has been found in the form of a polished flint axe, found in 1961 by J. Waters on the edge of the gravel pit to the west of Town Farm (Fig.3.1, p.20), and by a jade axe, found in a beet field adjoining Bergh Apton School by E.D. Loades in 1971.[5] According to the BALHG list, John Lester has also found two small axe heads (of which one was intact), a considerable number of arrowheads, and a scraper, the latter from the churchyard path area. None of these have yet been entered into the NMAS database.

Bronze-Age Man in Bergh Apton

Four barrows (otherwise known as tumuli), which are now recognised as dating from the Bronze Age – approximately 2500BC to 800BC – were first recorded on White Heath, Bergh Apton, c.1830 (Fig.1.1, p.11). Three of these lay in a field to the north side of Cooke's Road and another on the opposite side of this highway.[6] The Revd C.R. Manning of Diss, writing in 1854, who was then re-examining these features in the company of the Revd Dr William Beal

of Brooke, mentioned that 'more than twenty years ago, Mr William Utting, a solicitor at Thurton, had caused some of the barrows to be opened'. Manning continued by describing an urn that his own investigation had brought to light. This stood upside down upon the natural ground level within one of the barrows, but actually lay nearly 4ft below the top of this barrow. Unfortunately this urn, which was 14.5in. tall by 11.5in. wide at its lip, disintegrated as it was being uncovered. Furthermore, it was found to contain a mass of burnt human bones.[7] Sadly, all the barrows described above were ploughed out by the early-twentieth century; however, their sites remain visible in aerial photographs.

Interestingly, deed evidence reveals that Cooke's Road was known as Hoogate or Howgate from the sixteenth to the eighteenth century (Fig.1.1, p.11). This would derive from 'the way to the hills', meaning barrows; such features were regarded with some veneration by our forebears, and in this and other cases in Norfolk had their existence reflected by road or hundred names, as in the case of the Forehoe Hundred.

In 1914, a Mr Chambers found a Bronze-Age beaker, 4.75in. tall, in a gravel pit at Sunnyside.[8] About one mile to the south-west of White Heath, westward of Town Farm, a gravel pit was first opened up during the 1940s. Here, in 1948, 12 pottery sherds were found, considered to date from the Bronze Age. These pieces were too fragmentary to be identified as having been used for domestic or funerary purposes.[9] In the same gravel pit in 1950, an urn was located and found to have been inverted over the cremated remains of a child aged about five.[10]

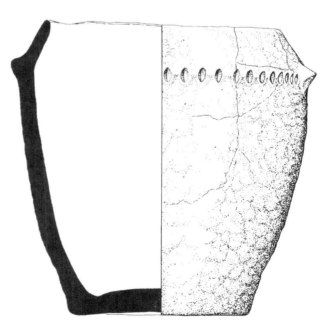

The beaker pot found in the Parish Pit in 1914.

Arrowheads dating from the Mesolithic and Neolithic periods. (JOHN LESTER COLLECTION)

A barbed and tanged Neolithic arrowhead.
(JOHN LESTER COLLECTION)

A jade axe found by E.D. Loades in 1971.

A Neolithic hand-axe.
(JOHN LESTER COLLECTION)

This hand-axe dates from the Bronze Age.
(JOHN LESTER COLLECTION)

The Parish Pit on Sunnyside where a Bronze-Age beaker pot was found in 1914.

John Lester found a barbed and tanged flint arrowhead of the Bronze Age on the surface of the field to the north side of Town Farm c.1970.[11] According to the NMAS database,[12] a Bronze-Age spear fragment was found prior to 1987 by the south side of the gravel pit, west of Town Farm, latterly used as a landfill site until its final closure as such in 1983.

Iron-Age Settlers

The Iron Age succeeded the Bronze Age and is generally taken to close with the Roman invasion of Britain in AD43. According to the NMAS database (as supplied to the writer in 2004), nothing has been found in Bergh Apton dating from this period, although *An Historical Atlas of Norfolk*[13] does mention that Iron-Age pottery has been found in the parish. This would not be surprising, given that this vicinity found favour with settlers both prior to, and following, this period. All the same, further confirmation of this matter would be welcome, while one looks with some confidence to the discovery of Iron-Age artefacts here in future.

References
[1] NMAS: HER 35852.
[2] Of Mill Road, Bergh Apton who has seasonally field walked the area for nearly 50 years.
[3] NMAS: HER 10327.
[4] NMAS: HER 10306.
[5] NMAS: HER 10435–6.
[6] Yet another barrow lay a little further to the east in the adjacent parish of Thurton; it was apparently this, and not one of those in Bergh Apton as stated in certain Victorian directories, in which a sword was found.
[7] Revd C.R. Manning, 'Notice of the Examination of some British Barrows in the Parish of Bergh Apton' in *Norfolk Archaeology* (Norwich, Norfolk and Norwich Archaeological Society, 1859), vol.5.
[8] NMAS: HER 10314.
[9] Barbara Green, *East Anglian Archaeology – The Anglo-Saxon Cemetery at Bergh Apton, Norfolk* (Gressenhall, Norfolk Archaelogical Unit, 1978), vol.7.
[10] *Ibid.*
[11] NMAS: HER 10314.
[12] HER 24171.
[13] Peter Wade Martins (ed.), *An Historical Atlas of Norfolk*, 2nd edn, (Norwich, Norfolk Museums Service, 1994) p.33.

Chapter III

Roman to Pagan-Saxon Times

The Roman Occupation

By the end of the first century AD, the Roman occupiers established the town which they named *Venta Icenorum* at what is now Caistor St Edmund, 5 miles to the west-north-west of Bergh Apton. During the third century AD, they erected a fort at what was then the northern bank of the Broadland estuary as it emptied into the North Sea at modern Caister-on-Sea, 15 miles to the north-east of Bergh Apton. In the following century, not long before the Roman military abandoned England, a further, larger fort was built by the southern bank of the Broadland estuary, at what later became known as Burgh Castle, 11 miles east-north-east of Bergh Apton. The subject of this history thus lay in an area in which there was considerable Roman, and Romano-British activity: consequently, it should come as no surprise that artefacts from this period should have been located here.

Evidence of Romano-British Life

The gravel pit to the west of Town Farm (Fig.3.1, p.20) was not only the site of a number of Bronze-Age finds (as detailed in the previous chapter). Roman material dating from the second and third centuries AD was also unearthed there in 1932 and 1955. The finds included pottery, roof and flue tiles, burnt daub with comber decoration, painted wall plaster, a bone pit, a copper alloy patera handle, animal bones and oyster shells, plus a coin of Carausius AD286–293.[1]

Aerial photo of the gravel pit in 1977, including Hall Farm (top left), *Valley Farm* (extreme top right) *and Town Farm* (right foreground), *with the school and Parish Church* (upper centre). (NORFOLK MUSEUMS AND ARCHAEOLOGY SERVICE; PHOTO BY DEREK EDWARDS)

The view north-west from the church tower, towards the site of some Roman finds (on the extreme left of picture).

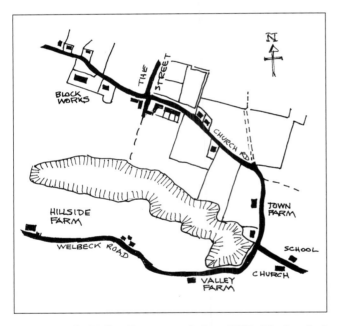

Fig.3.1. The Valley Farm gravel pit, c.1977. The hatched area defines its greatest extent.

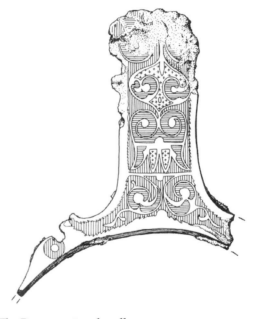

The Roman patera handle. (NICK ADAMS, ASSISTED BY SUE WHITE; NORFOLK ARCHAEOLOGY & ENVIRONMENT)

David Dymond has observed that while Roman sites and roads in Norfolk have been discovered over many generations, and indeed continue to be discovered, '[i]t is more than likely that the great mass of evidence for Romano-British life has yet to be found'.

A Roman Road?

For my part I proffer the suggestion that a section of Roman road in Bergh Apton may have been aligned approximately east-south-east from The Street, past the site of Apton church, across White Heath, to leave the parish between Beech Farm and Thurton Hall.

Continuing along the same alignment, it would have crossed the modern A146 at the Six Crossways, Thurton, and then that part of Langley Park lying within the parish of Chedgrave. The course suggested for the most part corresponds to existing roads and tracks (Fig.3.3, p.24). It is tempting to suppose a Roman road might be identified given the amount of material unearthed at the Bergh Apton site. This would have been the most convenient southern land route between *Venta Icenorum* and the mouth of the Broadland estuary, thus allowing for a necessary ferry or ferries to the east, given this estuary and its Waveney arm would have been too deep to ford hereabouts.

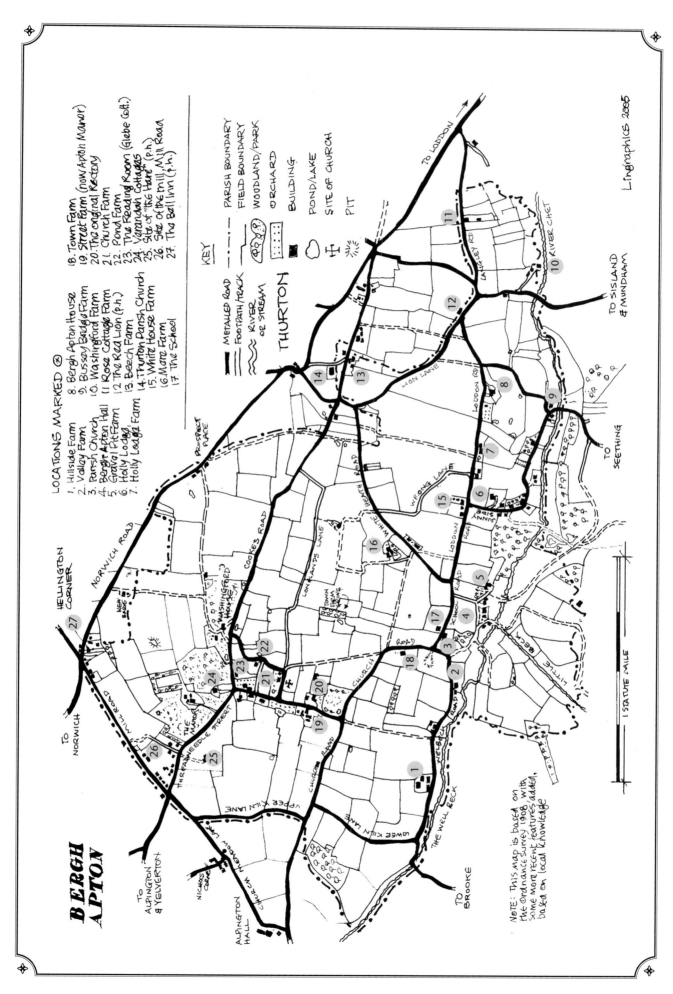

BERGH APTON

THURTON

LOCATIONS MARKED ⊗

1. Hillside Farm
2. Valley Farm
3. Parish Church
4. Bergh Apton Hall
5. Gravel Pit Farm
6. Holly Lodge
7. Holly Lodge Farm
8. Bergh Apton House
9. Bussey Bridge Farm
10. Washingford Farm
11. Rose Cottage Farm
12. The Red Lion (p.h.)
13. Beech Farm
14. Thurton Parish Church
15. White House Farm
16. Mare Farm
17. The School
18. Town Farm
19. Street Farm (now Apton Manor)
20. The original Rectory
21. Church Farm
22. Pond Farm
23. The Reading Room (Glebe Cott.)
24. Verandah Cottages
25. Site of "the Hare" (p.h.)
26. Site of the mill, Mill Road
27. The Ball Inn (p.h.)

KEY

— · — · — PARISH BOUNDARY
- - - - - - - FIELD BOUNDARY
🌳🌳🌳 WOODLAND/PARK
ORCHARD
■ BUILDING
POND/LAKE
✝ SITE OF CHURCH
PIT

━━━━ METALLED ROAD
- - - - FOOTPATH/TRACK
～～～ RIVER or STREAM

NOTE: This map is based on the Ordnance Survey 1908 with some more recent features added, based on local knowledge.

Lingraphics 2005

1 STATUTE MILE

Some of the Finds from the Bergh Apton Gravel Pit Archeological Dig

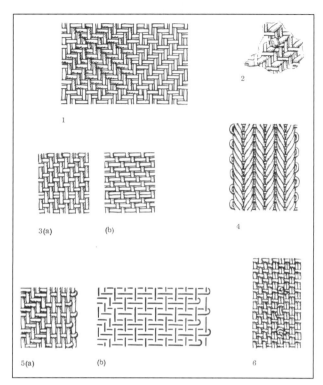

Types of woven material, traces of which were evident as impressions in metal artefacts in the pagan-Saxon graves.

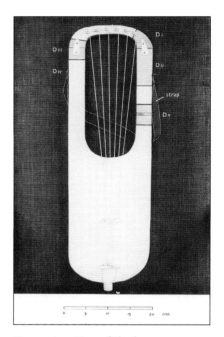

Reconstruction of the lyre.

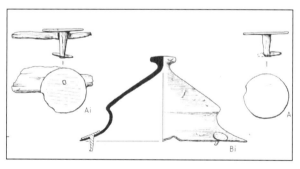

A pagan-Saxon shield boss (a raised, decorative central feature).

WE ARE GRATEFUL TO NORFOLK ARCHAEOLOGY & ENVIRONMENT FOR ALLOWING US TO REPRODUCE THE ILLUSTRATIONS PICTURED ON PP.22–23, WHICH WERE DRAWN BY NICK ADAMS, ASSISTED BY SUE WHITE.

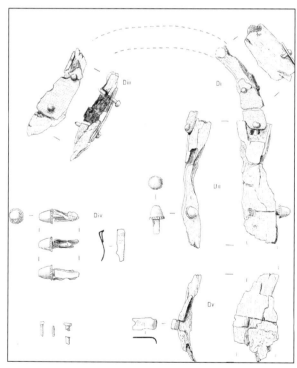

A drawing that illustrates the lyre fragments found. It would have been played by a 'scop', a pagan-Saxon minstrel or storyteller.

Barbara Green, *East Anglian Archaeology – The Anglo-Saxon Cemetery at Bergh Apton, Norfolk* (Gressenhall, Norfolk Archaelogical Unit, 1978), vol.7.

Some of the Finds from the Bergh Apton Gravel Pit Archeological Dig

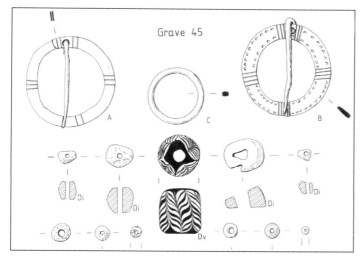

Two pagan-Saxon brooches, a bangle and beads.

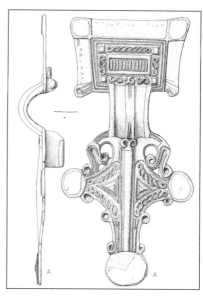

A square-headed brooch made from gilded copper alloy, showing the subtle variations in design achieved by pagan-Saxon craftsmen.

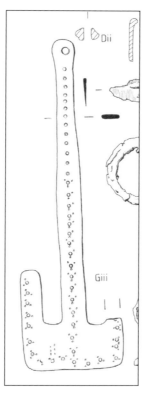

A pagan-Saxon girdle hanger (a lady's decorative belt ornament).

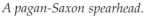

A pagan-Saxon spearhead.

Another pagan-Saxon square-headed brooch, made from gilded copper alloy.

Barbara Green, *East Anglian Archaeology – The Anglo-Saxon Cemetery at Bergh Apton, Norfolk* (Gressenhall, Norfolk Archaelogical Unit, 1978), vol.7.

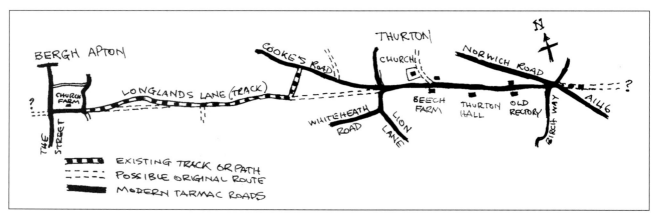

Fig.3.3. The present-day course of what may have been a major Roman highway.

There has been earlier conjecture concerning Bergh Apton during this period.

There is a tradition that a battle was fought here, one force occupying White Heath, whilst the enemy was placed on Barnes Heath; and it is not improbable that this spot was the scene of an engagement between the Romans and the Iceni. The churchyard stands in the centre of the site of a Roman camp, of about the same area as those at Tasburgh and Caister.[2]

A Roman key handle found by Albert Eirera in 2004.

However, as with my suggestion as to the possible Roman road, no solid evidence has appeared to support the statements just quoted; in any case it is no longer believed that the camp at Tasburgh was established by the Romans.[3]

Pagan-Saxon Times

The gravel pit site westward of Town Farm has certainly provided a rich source of information concerning the early settlement of Bergh Apton. Beyond what was discovered here and detailed in the text, fresh finds in 1973 were to be made on the eve of a formal archaeological investigation. All of this concerned a date closely approximating to AD600, the pagan-Saxon period.

The initial finds of 1973 amounted to five copper alloy objects and an iron spearhead; these were to prove small beer compared with what was subsequently to be uncovered. In this immediate vicinity, 63 inhumation burial pits were located, of which, while but 28 contained human bones, as many as 58 yielded grave goods. The latter included a range of metal objects including spearheads, a sword and, most exciting of all, the remains of a lyre.[4] All of this concerned a date closely approximating to AD600, the pagan-Saxon period. This investigation, of necessity restricted in scope, is confidently believed to have uncovered but a section of the cemetery.

References

[1] Barbara Green, *East Anglian Archaeology – The Anglo-Saxon Cemetery at Bergh Apton, Norfolk* (Gressenhall, Norfolk Archaelogical Unit, 1978), vol.7.

[2] William White (Limited) (*sic*), *History, Gazetteer and Directory of Norfolk*, 5th edn (Sheffield, William White Limited (*sic*), 1890) p.201.

[3] John A. Davies and others, *East Anglian Archaeology –* *The Iron-Age Forts of Norfolk* (Gressenhall, Norfolk Museums Service, 1991), vol.54.

[4] For a fully detailed account, reference should be made to Barbara Green, *East Anglian Archaeology*, vol.7. In any case, NMAS: HER 24171 includes the following finds prior to 1987, from this site and period: a sleeve clasp, brooch and an unidentified item, all of bronze.

Chapter IV

The Eleventh Century

The documented history of Bergh Apton is more or less continuous from the mid-eleventh century: a rare distinction for a Norfolk village, although one should say 'villages' through to the mid-sixteenth century because until then Bergh and Apton were essentially distinct ecclesiastical parishes and often so treated for lay purposes. The overall descriptions of 1086 (including the references back to 1066) indicate a settled population of different groupings of men, including a few slaves, and a mixed agricultural economy.

The story of eleventh-century Bergh and Apton is revealed by three distinct groups of documents: a charter; two wills; and the (Little) Domesday Book with the associated *Inquisitio Eliensis*.

A Royal Charter

In a charter, which can only be dated to between 1042 and 1066, King Edward (the Confessor) confirmed the privileges and lands that Ely Abbey enjoyed in Bergh

Part of a late-Saxon stirrup strap found in Bergh Apton by Albert Eirera in 2001.

and Apton.[1] How long this abbey had possessed them, or their precise location, cannot be ascertained; however, they may in part relate to the bequests in the first of the two wills to be dealt with below.

Aelfric's Will

In either 1042 or 1043, given internal evidence, Aelfric Modercope[2] made his will 'before he went across the sea'. It is not known where this testator lived. The relevant section of his will translates from the Old English as follows:

I grant the estate at Bergh to St Etheldreda's [Ely Abbey] with all the rights with which I acquired it, both woodland and open land. And I grant Thurwineholm with Loddon and Fuglholm with Bergh. And the sheep are to be divided into two parts, half for Loddon and half for Bergh.[3]

It is possible to make some comments concerning the location of the land in Bergh bequeathed to Ely Abbey by Aelfric. The woodland was probably not in the Chet Valley, otherwise it would more likely have been described by the testator as carr (i.e. wetland woodland, often of alders). The open land, too, is likely to have been on the higher ground, and for at least some of the year would probably have had the sheep folded upon it. Fuglholm means 'the birds' meadow', and hence probably lay in the Chet Valley.

Edwin's Will

A yet more revealing will was that of Edwin, a thegn of Edward the Confessor. A will not readily dated but apparently written prior to the Norman Conquest through which Edwin lived, moreover, as a consequence of which, he was either deprived of his property, or had it descend to a possible Norman son-in-law of which intriguing possibility, more in due course. It is known that his sister, Wulfgyth, made her will about 1046, and that his nephew, Ketel, made his prior to 1066. We do not know where Edwin lived, although save for two carucates (about 240 acres) at Blyford, Suffolk, all of his property as revealed by his will and in the Domesday Book lay in Norfolk. The relevant section of his will translates from the Old English as follows:

And I grant to St Etheldreda's [Ely Abbey] the estate at Bergh south of King's Street, except the northern

An aerial view of the Parish Church of SS Peter and Paul, Bergh Apton, and the school, shortly after the school's closure in 1981 and its conversion into two dwellings. (NORFOLK MUSEUMS AND ARCHAEOLOGY SERVICE; PHOTO BY DEREK EDWARDS)

The place in Apton where St Martin's Church stood, 2004. The remains of the church were finally cleared in 1834.

Church Farm, the house, 2004.

The track and hedge that run along a double-banked ditch that defines the border between the ancient settlement of Bergh and its neighbour Alpington, 2004.

enclosure at Appelsco. And half the turfpit is to belong to Apton, and a way to it two rods [11yds] broad. And ten acres south of the street to Bergh church. And ten acres north of the street to Apton church.[4]

As for the location of places in Bergh and Apton mentioned in Edwin's will, some valid comments may be offered. References to streets in Anglo-Saxon times often related to Roman roads, and hence within the context of Bergh Apton the King's Street may be taken as supporting my view as to the existence of such a road. From the specific name 'King's Street', we might infer a highway of more than local significance.

The suffix 'sco' to Applesco means wood, and may relate to one at Alpington as much as to one at Apton.[5] Interestingly, while the wood known as Kiln Grove in historic Bergh was not planted until the early-nineteenth century upon an enclosure of 23 acres within the significantly named Appleton Furlong[6], its north-western edge not only marks the boundary with Alpington but possesses an early feature, a double-banked ditch (Fig.4.1).

As for the turf pit, the fact that half of it was to belong to Apton, together with means of access – presumably leading from an existing road – may mean that the testator at the time of writing his will had not decided to bequeath the other half, or maybe the other half was not his property. Turves in Norfolk were usually cut from waterlogged ground, hence the well-known origin of the Broads; however, as Apton did not enjoy the benefit of a valley such as that of the Chet at Bergh, its turf pit may have been situated in a damp hollow. Indeed, a not unlikely location for at least that part of the turf pit lying in Apton would be the northern edge of a field called Toft Pit Close (Fig.4.2, p.28) on the Inclosure Award Map of 1806; the hollow which exists there extends northward into an adjacent field in the parish of Hellington, which in Edwin's time may well have been in the hands of another owner.

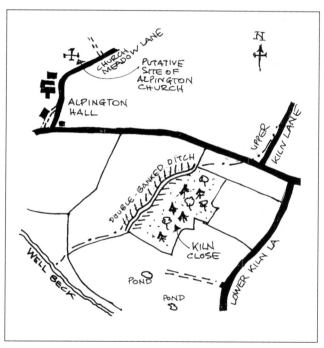

Fig.4.1. The double-banked ditch on the boundary between Bergh Apton and Alpington. The adjacent Kiln Close (later Kiln Grove) is discussed in Chapter IX, p.69. Also shown is the site of the putative Alpington church discussed in Chapter V, p.32.

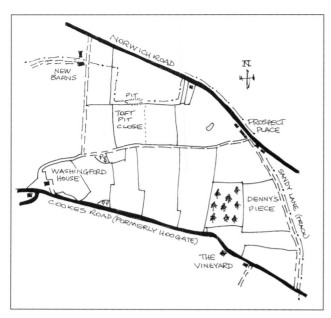

Fig.4.2.   Toft Pit Close.   The hollow on its northern boundary may be the site of a turf pit mentioned in the Will of Edwin, a thegn of Edward the Confessor.

The ten acres apiece left to Bergh and Apton churches may indicate the core of the glebe with which each of these parishes had been endowed, to which brief reference was to be made during the reign of Edward I (1272–1307) and more fully described from 1613, when the earliest surviving terrier was drafted.   More significant is the mere mention of these two churches: that of Bergh doubtless upon its clearly early-existing site – early, given the 'hump' on which it stands, likewise nearby Thurton – and that of Apton presumably upon the site which was essentially cleared in 1834.

A valid aside: the site chosen for the original church at Bergh may even have inspired the name of this parish (or vill, as one should say with regard to early-medieval times); thus the Old English 'beorh', meaning 'hill', rather than 'bur(g)h', meaning 'fortified place'.

St Ethelbert's Church, Thurton, 2004.

The Little Domesday Book and The *Inquisitio Eliensis*

We turn to what was recorded concerning Bergh Apton at the time of the Domesday Survey, 1086. The counties of Norfolk, Suffolk and Essex were not included in what is regarded as the Domesday Book proper, but in an associated, simultaneously compiled, and, indeed, more detailed volume known as the Little Domesday Book.   In addition, about the same time, a subsidiary source was compiled, the *Inquisitio Eliensis*.[7]

All the sources mentioned in the last paragraph agree that as a consequence of the Norman Conquest, the lands of Edwin passed to Godric the Steward (otherwise Godric Dapifer).   It is known from the *Inquisitio Eliensis* and other sources listed[8] in respect of the estate Edwin held in 1066 at Little Melton, that his wife was named Ingrid; moreover, as the same sources reveal that Godric's wife was also named Ingrid, there is an intriguing possibility that the latter was Edwin's daughter, and that Godric came to enjoy Bergh and other estates through his marriage as much as through the post-Conquest redistribution.

The Little Domesday Book has but one reference to Bergh *qua* Bergh (although for Washingford, see below).   Under the head of Tortuna (Thurton) in Loddon Hundred, it described six free men whom Godric the Steward has with 20 acres, and then (1066) as now (1086) one plough(team).   This entry further described a Torp – that is Thorpe by Haddiscoe, in Clavering Hundred – in which there were a further six free men having 13 acres and possessing one plough(team), and also eight smallholders.   They were stated as belonging to Bergh, together with all customary dues, and where they were assessed.

The *Inquisitio Eliensis* replaces the latter entry by one for Bereh, that is Bergh, though listing it in Henstead Hundred.   According to the Hundred Rolls of the thirteenth century, Bergh Apton was in a detached portion of Clavering Hundred; however, in 1086 a number of Norfolk Hundreds had yet to acquire their long-standing boundaries.   The entry concerned translates from the Latin as follows:

St Etheldreda [Ely Abbey] held Bergh before 1066 with four carucates [about 480 acres] of land.   Always [that is both in 1066 and 1086] 10 villagers and five smallholders.   Now [that is additionally in 1086] two villagers and five smallholders.   Now two slaves. Always two plough[teams] belonging to the lordship, and one belonging to the men.   Now one mill, and woodland for 16 pigs.   Then [1066] four head of cattle, always two riding-horses.   Twelve free men belong to this manor who are in Loddon Hundred.   They have 40 acres of land; always one plough[team]; while there are also 11 smallholders, one acre of meadow and two and a half plough[team]s.   Also eight free men in Henstead Hundred, who have 40 acres of land; always one

The garden wall at Church Farm in 2004, showing a dressed (worked) stone, probably taken from St Martin's Church.

plough[team]. Also one free man at 40 acres of land; always half a plough[team]. The value then £2 and now £4. Now Godric the Steward holds under St Etheldreda from his predecessor, Edwin.

One element of Bergh was indeed fully described in the Little Domesday Book, that is Wasingaford, albeit under the head of Loddon Hundred – clearly the same Washingford that survived as an independent manor into the twentieth century. Its entry translates as follows:

In Washingford one free man [who had been] of Edwin holding 30 acres, and two smallholders. The jurisdiction is in the Hundred. And under him [the aforesaid free man], six free men [who had been] of the same [Edwin] are holding 16 acres. Then as now two plough[teams], four acres of meadow and one mill.

The records compiled in 1086 do not refer unambiguously to Apton, which we know existed then thanks to Edwin's will; they have generally been taken as referring to neighbouring Alpington. The name Apton is considered to relate to Api's vill or farm, that of Alpington to Alhmund's vill or farm. On the other hand, Apton may have originated as a reduced form of Alpington, in which, with a number of other places as revealed by the Little Domesday Book, Edwin had property that he did not mention in his will. Given the following description of Appletona in the Little Domesday Book, together with variants as given in the *Inquisitio Eliensis*, and bearing in mind the question which arises about the true ecclesiastical status of Alpington in the Middle Ages, it can be concluded that Appletona subsumed both Alpington and Apton as far as the scribes of 1086 were concerned. Thus this description translates as follows:

Edwin held Appletuna in the reign of King Edward as two carucates [about 240 acres]. Then as now eight smallholders and one slave. Then as now, one plough[team] on the demesne [home farm of the manor],

Washingford Farm on the River Chet, 2004. This is the site of the water-mill mentioned in the Little Domesday Book.

half a plough[team] belonging to the men, and six acres of meadow. Woodland for 12 pigs [IE states six], and four hives of bees. Then as now, one horse, five head of cattle, 60 sheep and eight pigs; and eight and a half sokemen* [IE omits], 40 acres of land, and one and a half plough[team]s [IE omits]. Also two free men of Edwin, the predecessor of Godric [omitted by IE], 40 acres of

land and an acre of meadow. Then as now, one plough[team]. It was then worth £2 and now £3 [IE gives then £1.10s. and now 10s.]. IE adds: one league in length and one league in width [that is about one and a half miles square], and renders 13 pence in tax [that is out of the 240 paid by the entire Hundred]. This land St Etheldreda [Ely Abbey] ought to have by exchange with Bergh.

As regards the question as to whether at least some of 'Appletuna' related to Apton, should we be able to regard the dimensions given under the former name in 1086 as being approximately accurate, it would give an area of about 1,440 acres – and this would be close to the total obtaining today for Alpington with the Apton element of Bergh Apton.

In the Little Domesday Book there is another entry in respect of 'Appletuna' that has to be taken into consideration, given the possibility that it relates in some manner to Apton. Listed under Loddon Hundred, as one of the holdings of Roger Bigot (Sheriff of Norfolk and Suffolk) we find: 'In Appletuna 30 acres of land in demesne and one smallholder. The whole then and now worth £1.10s. The jurisdiction is in the Hundred.'[9]

Washingford Farm, 2004. The mill leat, running towards the camera, carried the water away from the mill and back into the River Chet.

Eleventh-Century Mills

Mills in the eleventh century would invariably have been water-mills: that at Washingford probably occupied the site on the River Chet straddling the boundary with Sisland which was to obtain until at least 1841,[10] while the mill at Bergh was probably situated to the south of Bergh Apton Hall, within the approximate area of the Bergh (with Apton) demesne.

References
[1] P.H. Sawyer, *Anglo-Saxon Charters*, (London, Royal Historical Society, 1968).
[2] The second part of his name is a nickname, rather than a surname as we would understand it today.
[3] D. Whitelock, *Anglo-Saxon Wills*, (Cambridge, Cambridge University Press, 1930).
[4] *Ibid.*
[5] I treat with the matter of the relationship between Apton and Alpington later in this history.
[6] Court book, deed and map evidence.
[7] A survey of lands belonging to or claimed by the Abbot of Ely in the three counties just mentioned, plus Cambridgeshire, Hertfordshire and Huntingdonshire.

The text of the *IE* is about 90 per cent identical with that of the Little Domesday Book; however, as will be revealed, the former contains information of relevance to Bergh Apton which was not set out in the latter.
[8] See H.A. Doubleday and Lord Howard de Walden (eds.) *Complete Peerage* (London, St Catherine Press, 1936), vol.9, p.412.
[9] While research I have carried out into property in Alpington leads me to suppose that Roger's holding, as just noted, merely related to land in that parish as such, it would appear from points to be considered in the next chapter that he and his successors to this land also had some interest in Apton church.
[10] Tithe Apportionment.

*Tenants holding land within the estate concerned.

Chapter V

The Twelfth and Thirteenth Centuries

The Munchensy Family

Henry I (1100–1134) granted the fees (manorial estates) which Godric the Steward had enjoyed to the Munchensy family.[1] The genealogy of this family is insufficiently clear as to whether Hubert the grantee was the one recorded by the Little Domesday Book in 1086, or his son and namesake who would himself appear to have died between 1115 and 1120. Certainly the younger Hubert held Bergh at some time, while at his death his eldest son and heir was Gilbert. The latter had died by 1130, and was succeeded by his next younger brother, Hubert de Munchensy.

Hubert apparently died between 1159 and 1166, and Warin died in possession of Bergh by 1162, hence it would appear that the latter had held this particular fee and others belonging to Godric the Steward for but a short time.

Warin Lord Munchensy married Agnes, daughter of Payn FitzJohn. Warin was to leave Bergh in the possession of his widow. More particularly, in 1185, by which time Agnes had married Haldinald de Bidun and been widowed for a second time, she held Bergh 'of the church of Ely', and was aged about 60 (hence clearly much younger than her first husband); moreover, as a widow, her holding was further subject to the disposal or gift of the then king, Henry II. Agnes appears to have died in 1190 or 1191.[3]

Sir William de Munchensy, elder surviving son of Agnes, inherited Bergh. In an undated deed he granted land previously held of this manor by one Gilbert de Karleman to Ralph de Bradeker at an annual rent of 1s. This deed is of interest as a witness was Richard de Wassingford[4], who if not Lord of Washingford had presumably taken his surname from an association with it.

Sir William de Munchensy married Aveline, daughter of Roger de Clare, Earl of Hertford, by 1186, and by whom he had two sons, William and Warin. These sons were minors when their father died between 1201 and 1204. The elder son, William, died about 1208, only a short time after he came of age.[5]

Warin Lord Munchensy gave King John 2,000 marks (£1,333.6s.8d.) for the right to enter into his inheritance, including Bergh, on 23 December 1213. Warin first married Joan, youngest daughter of William Marshal, 4th Earl of Pembroke, shortly after the latter's death in 1219; his son by Joan, John, died without issue in 1247, having predeceased him and leaving as his own heir his sister, also Joan. The latter was to marry Henry III's half-brother, William de Valence, later in 1247.[6]

Warin Lord Munchensy, lord of Bergh, next married Denise, widow of Walter Langton and daughter of Nicholas de Anesty, about 1234. She bore him his son William, who was a minor when his father died in 1255. Bequests in the latter's will were said to amount to the enormous sum of not less than 200,000 marks (£133,333.6s.8d.). The widowed Denise subsequently married Robert (or Richard) Butyller, whom she outlived. She must have lived to a great age for the medieval period, as she did not die until 1304.[7]

William de Munchensy, son and heir of Warin by his second wife, was a minor when his father died and was placed under the wardship of his half-brother-in-law, William de Valence. When he came of age in 1256, he was admitted to his lands in Norfolk – including Bergh – Essex, Kent, Gloucestershire and Northamptonshire. He took the side of Simon de Montfort during the latter's rebellion against Henry III, but was in due course fortunate enough to have been pardoned by that monarch. William married an Amice, who bore him but one known child, their daughter Denise. William died during military operations at Dryslwyn Castle, Carmarthenshire, in 1287.[8]

Denise de Munchensy, heir to her father William, was a minor when he died, and in the following year the wardship of her lands was granted to her grandmother, Denise, and her father's other executors. She married Hugh de Vere, a yeoman to Edward I, in 1290, and, having become of age, was granted livery of her lands in 1297.[9]

Apton and Alpington

Other than the fact that the lordship of Bergh extended into Apton, far less is known concerning the latter in the twelfth and thirteenth centuries. Blomefield noted that its Church of St Martin was a rectory in the patronage of the Vaux family. This statement, together with Blomefield's further remark that Robert de Vaux held land under Roger Bigot, provides a link with the short entry in the Little Domesday Book with regard to the land in 'Appletuna' held by the latter.[10] Given the confusion which stems from the available eleventh-century evidence concerning the respective identities of Apton and Alpington, and the failure of primary-source material to refer to any church which Alpington may have had – that is other than the Ordnance Survey having noted 'site of church' 200yds north-east of Alpington Hall, and the name 'Church Meadow Lane' for the adjacent road – it can

31

Alpington Hall, 2004.

The northern end of Church Meadow Lane in Bergh Apton, 2004. It runs into Alpington and past the site of the putative Alpington church.

Farm buildings at Alpington Hall, 2004.

be argued that Alpington as constituted within its present-day boundaries may never have had a church of its own: should any reader discover proof that it did, I would be the first to acknowledge it.

As for Ordnance Survey indications of sites of antiquities, those on the large-scale sheets of the nineteenth century have in some instances proved to be incorrect. No excavation has ever taken place on the purported site of Alpington church, while the few pieces of masonry found thereabouts may merely have come from a long since demolished farm building. No church at Alpington was listed in the Norwich Diocesan Taxation of 1254, nor in the Taxation of Pope Nicholas in 1291, nor have records of institutions to a living at Alpington been discovered prior to the Reformation, nor any wills of incumbents, nor any inventories of church goods. Certainly from the Reformation, Alpington parishioners have used Yelverton Parish Church; however, from the close relationship between Alpington and Apton which clearly obtained in the eleventh century, it may be that inhabitants of the former have treated the church of the latter as their own during at least the earlier Middle Ages.

The Patronage of Apton Church

Blomefield noted that after being in the patronage of the Vaux, Apton church passed in that respect by the heiresses of that family to the Nerefords and Lord Roos. In addition, in 1223/4, Robert de Nereford's claim to the advowson of Apton was accepted over that of one Roger le Pavilly, and in this respect five acres of land were granted to Robert and his heirs. In the reign of Edward I (1272–1307), the rector of Apton had a manse with ten acres of glebe; it was then valued with Bergh, the lord of which was its patron. It is time to consider Blomefield's statements in detail.

Robert de Vaux certainly held land under Roger Bigot in 1086 at Ashby St Mary, Carleton St Peter, Claxton and Thurton, according to the Little Domesday Book, although he was not named in respect of Bigot's 30 acres in 'Appletuna'. As for the immediate succession from Robert, it is not possible to clarify this from the genealogies, but it should be noted that it was his grandson and namesake who founded Pentney Priory during the reign of Stephen (1134–1154). The latter Robert's son, William, and grandson, Robert, both flourished during the reign of Henry II (1154–1189). The last-named Robert de Vaux's son, Oliver, died between 1244 and 1249, while Oliver's son, John, died in 1287, leaving two daughters by his wife, Sybil.[11]

In 1288, Petronilla, elder daughter and co-heir of John de Vaux, married William de Nereford. The latter was the son of Piers de Nereford, one who had been born by 1224 and who died by 1262.[12] William de Nereford died in 1302 and his wife in 1326.[13]

Maud, younger daughter and co-heir of John de Vaux, married Sir William de Roos, but it is not known when. The latter died in 1316, apparently having outlived his wife. Thus, the dates given for this couple, and for William and Petronilla (above), might be taken as accommodating Blomefield's

Staff at The Rectory in the 1920s. The gardener on the right is Alfred Boggis but the other gardener and the cook are unknown.

statement that their apparent joint holding of the patronage of Apton passed at some time during the reign of Edward I to the lord of Bergh. This on first sight appears to be contradicted by a further statement of Blomefield:

In the reign of Edward I [1272–1307], William Lord Munchensy was patron of [Bergh] church; the rector then had a manse, with 14 acres of land, and held it with Apton, and a mediety of the church of Holveston; there was also a vicarage erected out of the profits of the rectory, belonging to the fee of the prioress of Carhow [i.e. Carrow], endowed with 30 acres of land, and valued together at 26 marks [£17.6s.8d.].

I consider that Blomefield's statements with respect to the churches of Bergh and Apton in the reign of Edward I can be reconciled if we accept that these two livings were then combined, but that it was not until shortly after the death of William Lord Munchensy in 1287, and after the respective marriages of the de Vaux sisters, that the actual patronage of Apton passed into the hands of William's heirs

Livings and Lordships

With regard to both Apton and Bergh having a manse – dwelling for the priest – during the reign of Edward I, in addition to the glebe each possessed, it is interesting to note that Bergh Apton Rectory, as it had been documented by the body of evidence for the (combined) parish from the sixteenth century until it ceased to serve as such in 1959, lay within the historic bounds of Apton. Maybe the early, distinct manse of Bergh stood near its – now Bergh Apton – church.

The first known rector of Bergh and Apton was Simon de Liston, whom Blomefield recorded here in 1285/6. In the same year, James was vicar, the only instance in which a vicar was mentioned with regard to Bergh and/or Apton. James clearly owed his position to the Prioress of Carrow, while in any case William Lord Munchensy endowed this priory with two parts of the tithes of his demesne land at Bergh Apton valued at £1.6s.8d. annually. Ralph de Walpole, Bishop of Norwich (1288–99), and his successor John Salmon (1299–1325), confirmed this latter grant. At some time between 1325 and the Reformation, it was compounded for 12 quarters of wheat.[14]

As for the lordship of Washingford, Blomefield recorded that William de Washingford held it in 1256/7.

The Lay People of Bergh and Apton

As for the lay people of Bergh and Apton, no names emerged from the records in the twelfth century, and but a few in the thirteenth century. On 12 July 1202,

On Gosbalds field, looking east towards White Willows, 2004.

Thomas son of Roger, Geoffrey the brother of Thomas, and Huelin their sister, together conveyed to Richard Gerbald a tenement of 15 acres with appurtenances in Apton. In exchange, the three siblings received five acres and appurtenances in Apton, to be held of Richard, his heirs and the heirs of these, by free service and an annual payment of 15s., with the proviso that foreign service valued at 20s.3d. could be demanded.[15] That the surname Gerbald (and later modifications of it) has had a resonance within the Apton element of Bergh Apton down to the present day is noted at the end of the next chapter.

The next record encountered of such a lay person concerned Geoffrey Gunnild of Bergh in 1260 when on 1 June, according to the Patent Rolls, William Len of Yelverton, chaplain, was found not guilty of the mayhem of the said Geoffrey.

References

[1] According to H.A. Doubleday and Lord Howard de Walden (eds.) *Complete Peerage* (London, St Catherine Press, 1906), vol.9, pp.411–2.

[2] *Ibid.*, p.412.

[3] *Ibid.*, p.419; Francis Blomefield, *An Essay towards a Topographical History of the County of Norfolk* (London, William Miller, 1806), vol.10, pp.96–9.

[4] Blomefield, *op. cit.*, p.97.

[5] H.A. Doubleday and Lord Howard de Walden (eds.) *Complete Peerage*, vol.9, p.420.

[6] *Ibid*, pp.421–2.

[7] *Ibid*, pp.421–2.

[8] *Ibid*, pp.422–4.

[9] *Ibid*, p.424.

[10] See Chapter IV, p.30.

[11] G.A. Carthew, *History of Launditch* (London, Miller and Leavins, 1877), vol.1, p.249.

[12] I found no link between Piers and the Robert de Nereford, who had been in dispute with regard to the advowson of Apton, in 1223/24 as Blomefield claimed. However, I suspect that Robert was not only a collateral relation but also the one who served as Governor of Dover Castle in 1216.

[13] G.A Carthew, *op. cit.*, p.250.

[14] Francis Blomefield, *An Essay towards a Topographical History of the County of Norfolk* (London, William Miller, 1806), vol.4, p.527 and vol.10, p.99.

[15] Barbara Dodwell recorded the earliest such record in her edition of *Feet of Fines Norfolk 1198–1202* (London, Pipe Roll Society, 1952).

Chapter VI
Later Medieval Times

Events of the fourteenth and fifteenth centuries are now detailed, generally within the successive overall themes of Bergh Apton lordships, its churches and associated ecclesiastical matters, and what is known of the population at large.

Bergh Apton Lordships

In 1304 Denise de Vere, lady of Bergh, was found to be the heir of her grandmother, Denise Butyller (formerly de Munchensy). Denise de Vere died without having left issue in 1313, when her heir was found to be Aymer de Valence, Earl of Pembroke, her half-cousin – that is the only son of her father's half-sister, Joan, by her marriage to William de Valence, Earl of Pembroke.[1]

Aymer de Valence, Earl of Pembroke, married Mary, daughter of Guy de Chatillon, Count of St Pol (Seyn Poul), in 1313/4; he died without issue on 23 June 1324, and was buried in Westminster Abbey. His widow had survived him by over 52 years when she died at Denny Abbey, Cambridgeshire, in March 1377.[2] During her long widowhood, she was to enjoy the Bergh Apton estate and the right of presentation to its living, amongst other estates settled by her husband upon her marriage to him; furthermore, she may also have lived here for a time, and if so presumably occupied a hall or manor-house within the demesne. The Norfolk Lay Subsidy of 1332 records Mary de Seynpoulis (*sic*) at the head of the list of those assessed in Bergh Apton, and the sum of 13s. levied upon her then was by far the largest amount here.[3] In addition, Blomefield not only recorded that Thomas de Rokeles held land belonging to her in Bergh Apton, but also that she presented to the living of Bergh with Apton in 1343, 1353 and 1359 – although this latter right did not require residency by the donor.

Upon the death of Aymer de Valence, Earl of Pembroke, his widow was left with certain privileges as just outlined. However it was his nephew John, 2nd Lord Hastings, son of his sister Isabel by her marriage to John, 1st Lord Hastings, who was found to be heir to the bulk of his estates. The younger John, who was born on 29 September 1286, married Juliane, daughter of Sir Thomas de Leybourne; he died on 20 January 1325, leaving as his heir his son Laurence, born on 20 March 1320.[4]

As a consequence of his being a minor at the death of his father, Laurence, 3rd Lord Hastings was successively placed under the wardship of Hugh le Despencer, Prince Edward (the then future Edward

III), and the Earl of Huntingdon. Laurence was actually granted livery of his estates on 4 February 1339, before attaining his full majority, and on the following 13 October was granted the title of Earl of Pembroke by Edward III. He married Agnes, daughter of Roger de Mortimer, Earl of March, and she was to bear him his son and heir, John, on 29 August 1347.[5]

Laurence, Earl of Pembroke, died on 30 August 1348, so for the second successive time the prospective heir to Bergh Apton inherited as a minor. In this instance the heir, John, Earl of Pembroke, was placed under the wardship of his mother until her death on 25 July 1368. He was granted livery of his estates on the following 12 September, a matter of weeks before he attained his actual majority. It was his second wife, Anne, daughter of Walter, Lord Mauny, who bore him his son and heir, John, on 11 November 1372.[6]

John, Earl of Pembroke, died in Picardy on 16 April 1375, so for the third successive time the prospective heir to Bergh Apton inherited as a minor. This time the heir (again) John, Earl of Pembroke, was placed under the guardianship of his mother and his maternal grandmother, then the Countess of Norfolk. The young John's great-great-great-aunt by marriage enjoyed the Bergh Apton estate, along with the living of Bergh with Apton, and the moiety of Holverston, until her death in 1377. It then passed into the king's hands. Indeed, Richard II presented to this living in 1378. The young Earl of Pembroke married Philippe, daughter of Edmund de Mortimer, Earl of March; she did not bear him an heir, and he died still a minor in December 1389 at Woodstock. As a consequence of his death, his earldom reverted to the Crown.[7]

As for the matter of the succession to the estates, including Bergh Apton, of the late Earl of Pembroke in 1389, they were settled upon the nephew of his paternal grandmother, Sir William Beauchamp, second son of Thomas Beauchamp, Earl of Warwick. Sir William was granted the title of Lord Bergavenny in 1392.[8]

William Lord Bergavenny's wife Joan Fitzalan, sister and co-heir of Thomas, Earl of Arundel, bore him a son, Richard. When William died in 1411, his estates were left in dower to his widow, and as their son – who was created Earl of Worcester in 1420 – died in Joan's lifetime he was not to inherit them. In any case, Joan presented to the living of Bergh with Apton in 1422, 1425 and 1434. When Lady Joan Bergavenny died in 1435, the heir to the estates including Bergh Apton was her granddaughter Lady Elizabeth Beauchamp, only child of her late son by his wife, Isabel Despencer.[9]

Lady Elizabeth Beauchamp brought her inheritance to her husband, Sir Edward Nevill, who was summoned to parliament as Lord Bergavenny in 1450, two years after her death. She had in any case left him a son and heir, George. Edward Lord Bergavenny died in 1476, and George accordingly succeeded to his estates, including Bergh Apton, and his title.[10]

George Lord Bergavenny first married Margaret, daughter of Sir Hugh Fenne, by whom he had his eldest son and heir, George. The latter should have succeeded to the estates – including Bergh Apton – and the title upon his father's death on 20 September 1492, but for some unknown reason these matters were not confirmed until 1497.[11]

Richard de la Rokeley held land in Bergh Apton of the Earl of Pembroke in 1323/4, while his son Thomas de la Rokeleys held the same of the Countess of Pembroke in 1346/7. This Thomas was clearly the one assessed (as Thomas de la Rokel) for 8s.8d., the second highest sum levied in Bergh Apton, in the Lay Subsidy of 1332.[12] In any case, this estate would relate to that granted to Richard in 1295/6.[13]

I found no reference to the Manor of Washingford in the fourteenth and fifteenth centuries, unless one can assume that Robert Wassingforde, assessed to pay the above average sum of 3s. in the Lay Subsidy of 1332 for Bergh Apton, was its lord.

At some time by 1323/4, one-sixteenth of the Munchensy fee – the Manor of Bergh with Apton – was separated from this and held by Henry de Heylesdon. This was in due course to take the name of the Manor of Bergh Berneys (Barneys or Barnes), and was held in socage of the capital manor.[14] This small estate was apparently augmented in 1331/2 when, as Blomefield further recorded, Bartholomew Bateman and Petronilla his wife, and John de Acre and Petronilla his wife, conveyed to John de Berney and Sarah his wife lands in Bergh Apton, Thurton, Seething and Mendham (*sic, recte* Mundham?), part of which Agnes, widow of Henry de Heylesdon held for term of her life. The name Barnes (or Barras) Hill, which still survives in Bergh Apton – historic Bergh – is suggestive of the locality where the aforesaid estate was centred. All the same, the early manor-house or hall of Berneys cannot be identified with the present-day Gravel Pit Farm (Fig.6.1, p.40), known as Barnes Hill Farm in the 1880s (Ordnance Survey), as the overall documentation of the Cooke family, long-time owners of this farm, has discounted this. Agnes Heilesdon was assessed to pay 2s. in the Lay Subsidy of 1332 for Bergh Apton.[15]

John Berney[16] wrote his will on 22 February 1374, and this was proved on the following 8 June. While the testator did not state his place of residence, the text of his will strongly implies that he personally occupied his estate in Bergh. In it he left £1.6s.8d. towards the making of a glazed window in the new chancel at Bergh, to which church he also left his best vestment, a chalice with a towel, and other necessary items for the celebration of Mass in the chapel of St Anne there, where his wife, Sarah, was buried. He expressed a wish to be buried beside her, unless he was permitted by the Bishop to be buried in the chapel of St Anne in Norwich Cathedral where his former wife, Joan, was buried.[17] He left his son, Robert Berney, six cows and a bull at Bergh, but did not make it clear as to whether Robert was to inherit his manor. He also named another son, Thomas, whose mother had been Sarah. He further left an unspecified sum of money to the poor of Bergh.

The next Berney to be identified as the holder of the eponymous manor in Bergh, Robert, may have been a great-grandson of the above testator. Robert Berney died on 10 May 1487, and in his Inquisition Post Mortem dated 26 April 1488 it was declared that he died holding 'lands, etc.,' worth £2.13s.8d. annually in Bergh called 'Berneys Lands'. The heir to this property was named as the deceased's brother, Ralph Berney, at that time a minor aged 17. Ralph certainly enjoyed it once he came of age, as will be detailed in the next chapter.

Parish Church of SS Peter and Paul

The oldest structure in Bergh Apton is the Parish Church of SS Peter and Paul, a Grade II* listed building. The earliest surviving elements of this, until the mid-1550s solely Bergh church, date from the fourteenth century; indeed, they indicate that it was probably entirely rebuilt then.

The Nave
The nave[18] was essentially reconstructed in the fourteenth century with what would have been locally accessed flints, partly rendered and ashlared, with limestone and flint dressings. The chancel collapsed

The present interior of Bergh Apton church, looking towards the chancel that was rebuilt between 1712 and 1715 during Robert Connold's incumbency. He was later buried there. John Berney donated funds to make a glazed window in the earlier chancel, built in 1374.

and was totally rebuilt between 1712 and 1715[19]; John Berney in his will of 1374 (above) stated that it was new then. The two two-light windows with Y-tracery on each side of the nave were products of 1838 rebuilding, but probably set within fourteenth-century openings given that stonework of this apparent date is in their jambs. The south transept was to be rebuilt in 1838, but retains much medieval corework and has a probably contemporary scratch dial (for telling the time) on one of its stone quoins; the north transept was totally rebuilt then. Maybe one of the transepts housed the Chapel of St Anne, mentioned in John Berney's will of 1374.

The West Tower

That notable local landmark, the west tower with its staged diagonal western buttresses, was probably completed towards the end of the fourteenth century, except for the 1838 battlements. It has ashlar and brick details, a two-light west window, and bell openings with stone-chamfered reveals and pointed arches. The bell openings bear signs of having lost their mullions, tracery and hoodmoulds, and instead

A view of Bergh Apton church tower from the north, 1998. Note the outline of the blocked sanctus window in the flintwork of the tower and the roof line from when it was thatched.

contain relatively modern wooden louvres. The eastern face of the tower bears the marks of the original height of the abutting nave, while below these can be seen a blocked Sanctus bell window. With regard to the pitch of the roof of the nave prior to 1838, this clearly indicates that it was covered with thatch.

The South Doorway

The south doorway is of fourteenth-century construction, although it may have been rebuilt in part at a later date. It has corbel heads at the ends of the hoodmould and at the top of the arch; the south porch was to be extensively restored in 1902. The north porch of the fourteenth century was to be brought within the vestry, constructed in 1838.

The Font

The major remodelling of 1838 has left few obvious early features within the church. However, it does possess a fourteenth-century treasure in its fine octagonal stone font. This has four lions and four statuettes set alternatively around its stem, of which two may be woodwoses (green men). At the top of the stem is a frieze of fleurons. Around the bowl are carved the signs for the four Evangelists and four angels, while below it are more angels holding shields.

The Bells

Of the ring of six bells, the sixth is the oldest, dating from the late-fifteenth century and was probably cast by John Baly of Norwich. It bears the legend *Petrus Ad Eterne Ducat Nos Pascua Vite* (May Peter lead us to the pastures of eternal life). According to an inventory of 1552, this – then solely Bergh – church had three full-size bells,[20] respectively weighing six, seven and 8cwt, plus a saunce (or Sanctus) bell of 40lb.[21]

The Joint Living of Bergh and Apton

It should be borne in mind that while testators who chose to endow Apton specifically described its church as such until its abandonment in the mid-sixteenth century, it was certainly viewed by ecclesiastical authorities as early as 1321 as a chapel. In November of that year, judgment was given by John Salmon, Bishop of Norwich, concerning the right to the tithes of the rectory of Bergh with the chapel of Apton appurtenant to the said rectory, in a cause instituted by the Prioress of Carrow and her convent on the one part, and Robert de Redeswell formerly rector of Bergh and William Cross, who succeeded him as party to this cause, on the other.[22]

In addition, the right of presentation to the joint living of Bergh and Apton was augmented by a mediety of the advowson of Holverston in 1323; it was specifically stated as being held at that time by Aymer de Valence, Earl of Pembroke, as belonging to

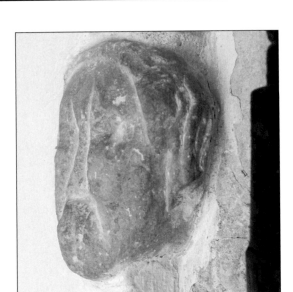

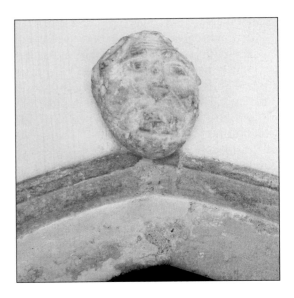

Above left: *A corbel head on the hood mould of the south doorway to the church. This is the one on the left (west).*

Above right: *The centre corbel head on the hood mould.*

Left: *The right-hand (eastern) corbel head. From her own historic research whilst studying for her degree in medieval history, Linda Davy suggests that these faces may relate to those who sponsored the building of the church. It is possible that they were intended to remind those who passed through the door to pray for the sponsors, in order to shorten their time in purgatory.*

The east face of the fourteenth-century font of the church, 2004.
(SEEJAY HARRISON)

An overall view of the south doorway of the church, to put the corbel heads into a general context with each other.

the fees of the Barony of Munchensy, together with his Manor of Bergh Apton. The mediety of the rectory of Holverston was joined to the rectory of Bergh and Apton in 1359; the other mediety was then joined to Rockland St Mary.[23] Curiously, Blomefield had otherwise asserted that the mediety of Holverston was joined to that of Bergh and Apton during the reign of Edward I (1272–1307); the truth of this matter is not one that need trouble us unduly.

Rectors of the joint living of Bergh and Apton in the fourteenth and fifteenth centuries are listed below:

Robert de Redeswell: 1318–1321.
William Cross: 1321–?
William de Merstang: 1328–?
Robert de Winfarthing: 1342–1353.
William de Fratyngton: 1353–1359.
Peter de Thaxted: 1359–1379.
John Curson: 1379–1406.
William Manston: 1406–1409.
Robert Legum: 1409–?
Robert Potter: 1422–1425.
Roger Philpot: 1425–1434.
William Wyrmod: 1434–1439.
John Hall: 1439–?
John Hilles: 1449–1451.

Robert Sterop: 1451–1466.
John Bryan: 1466–?
William Newhouse: 1468–1469.
Stephen Sharpe: 1469–?
Robert Roket: 1471–1513.

Robert Potter resigned in 1425,[24] but was still living in Bergh as a clerk (priest) in 1428. He then failed to answer for a trespass before the Prioress of Carrow, presumably for one upon either the vicarage she enjoyed here or with regard to the tithes with which William de Munchensy had endowed her priory.[25]

Alabaster Saints

In 1965, during the demolition of a derelict cottage debatably of late-medieval or Tudor date, within the grounds of Flintstones – now known as Flint Cottage – Gravel Pit Lane, Bergh Apton (Fig.4.1, p.40), an alabaster figure of St Paul was uncovered within the hearth; a second, similar figure, but too badly weathered to be identified, although very likely of St Peter, was also found. The figure of St Paul is believed to date from the end of the fourteenth century, and, along with its companion piece, may well have been taken from what had been Bergh church at the time of the Reformation in order to save it from the iconoclasts.[26]

An aerial photo of Flint Cottage taken in 1964 which shows a small cottage in a ruinous condition. The white arrow points to the chimney where the statues of St Peter and St Paul were found during the demolition of this part of the property one year later, in 1965. Inset: The statue of St Paul found in the chimney of the cottage in 1965. (NCM)

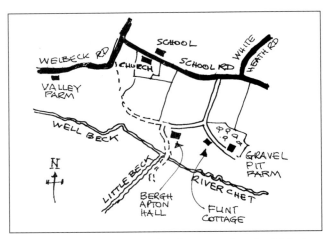

Fig.4.1. Flint Cottage, in the grounds of which two fourteenth-century alabaster figures were discovered in 1965.

The Lollard Heresy

From, or by, 1428 until 1430 Bergh Apton was touched by the then obtaining Lollard heresy. In or just before 1428 when he was burnt at the stake in Norwich, William White, priest, a Lollard and follower of the doctrines of John Wycliffe, taught at a 'school' in Bergh. Of his pupils, a John Skylan, husbandman and son of Walter Skylan of Bergh, was tried before William Alnwick, Bishop of Norwich, and other dignitaries, in 1430. Thanks to John's full confession and his having recanted, his life was spared but he was obliged to face a series of severe penances over the following seven years.[27]

Recorded Crime

In 1305, the king's clerk William Jerberge initiated a hearing with regard to the fact that a William Lawelos of Bergh, together with several other men from (mostly) south-east Norfolk, had broken into his house at Chedgrave and had not only stolen chests stored there which contained records of the justices from certain northern counties, but had also beaten him and his men.[28] Unfortunately, the outcome of this matter is not known.

According to the Norwich Gaol Delivery of 15 March 1316, Philip Fox of Westhall, Suffolk, was taken for the burglary of the home of William Chapeleyn of Bergh, and for stealing his goods and chattels worth £2. He was found guilty and sentenced to be hanged; moreover, it was declared that he had no chattels (possessions) that could be confiscated.[29] Interestingly, William Chapeleyn was also recorded in the 1332 Lay Subsidy for Bergh Apton.[30]

At the Norwich Gaol Delivery of 7 June 1316, Roger, son of Adam Dun of Bergh Apton, was with eight others, taken at Hapton (in Depwade Hundred) for the robbery of goods and chattels worth £10 from Thomas Rikedorn, also of Bergh Apton. Roger was acquitted of this crime.[31]

The Norfolk Lay Subsidy, 1332

The Norfolk Lay Subsidy for 1332[32] listed 52 persons who were assessed to pay a total amount of £5.5s.8d. in Bergh Apton. Those living in Bergh and Apton were not separately distinguished; however, this is the only such list to have survived prior to the reign of Henry VIII.

Mary de Seynpoulis	13s.	Thomas Chapman	4s.
Thomas de la Rokel	8s.8d.	William Estau	3s.6d.
Simon Moysent	4s.6d.	John Kirkehowe	2s.
Richard Kise	1s.6d.	Adam Gerbald	2s.6d.
Roger Philip	1s.	Cecily Ernald	2s.6d.
John Overfen	1s.	William Kyse	1s.6d.
Thomas Muriel	4s.	William Herman	2s.6d.
Adam Gildenewatir	2s.	John Canun	1s.
Henry Gildenewatir	1s.6d.	John de Bergh	1s.
Agnes Heilesdon	2s.	Benedict Atte Chirche	1s.
Henry Baret	1s.	Waryn Waucy	3s.6d.
Ralph Pevarel	1s.6d.	John Stannard	3s.6d.
Geoffrey Jonis	1s.	Robert Kyse	8d.
Robert Hardegray	1s.	Matilda Martin	8d.
Emma Seg	1s.	Nicholas Kyse	8d.
Duce Atte Grene	2s.	Roger Bertelmeu	8d.
William Chapeleyn	2s.	Richard Huyr	8d.
Andrew Custe	2s.	Thomas Boterel	8d.
William Pye	2s.6d.	Andrew Gilbert	8d.
William Gonnild	2s.	Ralph Wyyan	8d.
Nicholas Clerich	2s.	Geoffrey Curyun	8d.
Simon Godwyne	2s.	William Fabre	8d.
Agnes Diker	1s.	Walter Eylmer	8d.
Matilda Atte Forthe	2s.	Mabel Chapman	8d.
Robert Wassingforde	3s.	Benedict Herman	1s.
William Oldman	1s.6d.	Geoffrey Trace	1s.

Fifteenth-Century Lay People

After the Lollard episode of 1428–1430, the names of very few ordinary folk were identified at Bergh Apton until the end of the fifteenth century. Deeds among the Denny-Cooke manuscripts in the Norfolk Record Office refer to a Henry Gildenwater, son and heir of Richard Gildenwater, deceased, in respect of lands in Bergh; also to a Richard Gildenwater, chaplain, one of the grantees of lands and a meadow called Tuckes in Bergh in 1490. Two men with this surname were listed in 1332 (above), and it was still to be found in the sixteenth century. With regard to the deed of 1490, William Belconger was named as a Feoffee of the same property; this surname also occurred in Bergh Apton in the sixteenth century.

John Bussey of Apton died in 1479, having left a will in which he not only made bequests to its church but also named his brother, Edmund.[33] This Edmund, also of Apton, was another grantor of the lands in Bergh in 1490 (above). We will meet one probably identified with Edmund, and other Busseys later, while

An etching of William White, the Lollard priest, at his execution in Norwich in 1428.

Bergh Apton churchyard, 2004, the site of John Skylan's penance of 1430. He was sentenced to a series of penances that demanded thus 'On each vigil of Blessed Mary for a period of seven years he fast on bread and water and on each Friday for three years he abstain from fish and dairy produce. On three consecutive Sundays he has to make a circuit of the cemetery of Bergh Church, at its solemn procession with neck, head and feet bare, clad only in undershirt and breeches in the manner of penitents, with a wax candle weighing one pound, which on the last Sunday he is to offer on the high alter after the gospel at High Mass'. (See 'The Lollard Heresy', p.40)

John Skylan had to perform the same penance immediately outside this church by making a circuit of the market-place at Loddon on three market days. On the last he was required to present the candle at the high altar in Loddon church

John Skylan presented his candle in Loddon church at the high altar, where this more modern altar stands in 2005.

in any case the surname is recalled by Bussey Bridge, which spans the River Chet and links Bergh Apton (historic Bergh) with neighbouring Seething.

William Garbold of Apton wrote his will in 1479, and this was proved in the following year.[34] He had close links with North Burlingham St Andrew, where he asked to be buried; however, he made bequests to Bergh and Apton churches, as well as those of nearby Yelverton, Thurton, Ashby [St Mary] and Kirby [Bedon]. William would appear to have been of the same family as Richard Gerbald, mentioned in the previous chapter. While William did not mention any real estate in his will, a deed enrolled at the Norwich Mayoral Court (for an inexplicable reason) on 9 June 1490 formed a remise and quitclaim* by Henry Kesok and his wife Sibil, daughter of Thomas Garbald, next-of-kin and heirs of William, of lands and tenements that had been his in the the towns and fields of Apton, 'Barowe' and Yelverton, to Henry Heydon, knight, and his Feoffees.[35] The surname under consideration appears to be reflected in the lands called Gorbalds which Robert Athow of what is now (2004) White Willows left his son, Christopher, of Street Farm (now Apton Manor) in his will written in 1711.[36] To this day the field west of White Willows is called Gosbalds.

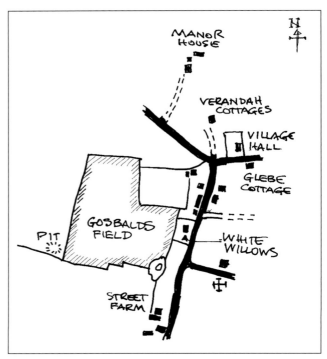

Fig.6.2. The field called Gosbalds. The name is probably a corruption of Gerbald, the surname of its thirteenth-century owners.

References

[1] See H.A. Doubleday and Lord Howard de Walden (eds.) *Complete Peerage*, vol.9. (In *An Essay towards a Topographical History of the County of Norfolk*, vol.10, p.97, Blomefield incorrectly described the latter as lord of Bergh and Apton; he had in any case died in 1296.)

[2] H.A. Doubleday and Lord Howard de Walden (eds.) *Complete Peerage* (London, St Catherine Press, 1945), vol.10.

[3] TNA: E179/149/9 m.75.

[4] H.A. Doubleday and Lord Howard de Walden (eds.) *Complete Peerage*, vol.10.

[5] *Ibid.*

[6] *Ibid.*

[7] *Ibid*; Patent Rolls.

[8] Vicary Gibbs (ed.) *Complete Peerage* (London, St Catherine Press, 1910), vol.1.

[9] Francis Blomefield, *An Essay towards a Topographical History of the County of Norfolk*, vol.10, p.97; Vicary Gibbs, *op. cit.*

[10] Vicary Gibbs, *op. cit.*

[11] *Ibid.*

[12] TNA: E179/149/9 m.75.

[13] TNA: E179/149/9 m.75. I found no unambiguous reference to it after 1346/47.

[14] Francis Blomefield, *op. cit.* p.98.

[15] TNA: E179/149/9 m.75.

[16] NRO: NCC 1374 f.42 Heydon.

[17] At the time he wrote his will he was married to Katherine, daughter of Peter Bedingfield.

[18] With regard to the medieval features outlined, I acknowledge the helpful interpretation of Roy Tricker in his *Guide to the Bramerton Group* (Ashby St Mary, Bramerton Group of Parishes, 1978).

[19] See Chapter XI.

[20] P. Cattermole, *Church Bells of Norfolk Part 1 The Hundred of Clavering* (Aylsham, Golden Ball Press, 1991), pp.2–9.

[21] For Bergh Apton's five seventeenth-century bells, see Chapter VIII.

[22] Bodleian Library MS Ch. Norfolk a.3 no.300.

[23] Francis Blomefield, *op.cit*, pp.99–100; Francis Blomefield (London, William Miller 1805–1810), vol.5, pp.487–488.

[24] C.M. Hood (ed.), *Chorography of Norfolk* (Norwich, Jarrold & Sons Ltd, 1938).

[25] Patent Rolls.

[26] F.W. Cheetham, *Norfolk Archaeology* (Norwich, Norfolk and Norwich Archaeological Society, 1970), vol.35.

[27] N.P. Tanner, *Heresy Trials in the Diocese of Norwich, 1428–31* (London, Royal Historian Society, 1977).

[28] Patent Rolls.

[29] B. Hanawalt, *Crime in East Anglia in the Fourteenth Century*, (Norwich, Norfolk Record Society, 1976).

[30] *Ibid.*

[31] Hanawalt, *op. cit.*

[32] *Ibid.*

[33] Hood, *op. cit.*

[34] NRO: NCC 1479 [Old Style] f.42 Aubry.

[35] NRO: Norwich City Records 1/20 m.26.

[36] NRO: ANF 1715/6 no.158.

*To surrender property and all present and future claims to it.

Chapter VII

Manors in the Sixteenth and Seventeenth Centuries

It is from the early-sixteenth century that the documentation of Bergh Apton, often patchy hitherto, becomes voluminous even though certain sources have not survived. There are no pre-1651 court books for the Manor of Bergh with Apton; and the parish registers that the then rector should have maintained from 1538 are not to be found from prior to 1556.

We have already traced the succession of baronial or aristocratic families who owned the (capital) Manor of Bergh with Apton from the twelfth to the fifteenth centuries. They were absentee landlords with the possible exception of the widowed Mary de Seynpoulis, Countess of Pembroke, who was endowed with this estate and may have occupied it in person for a time in the fourteenth century. For this reason, they would have relied upon a hierarchy of servants, the chief of whom being the steward, to do the following: maintain the manorial demesne or home farm with an associated park; sit at the manor court; keep law and order among those who lived within the jurisdiction of the manor and ensure that its customs were adhered to, particularly in respect of the practice of husbandry and the payment of dues to the lord in cash and in kind.

Lords of the Manor of Bergh Apton in the sixteenth and seventeenth centuries are now detailed. The survival of certain sixteenth-century rentals, together with will evidence, allows information to be given with regard to the farming out of the demesne and other aspects of life within the context of this manor. The commencement of the run of court books in 1651 permits yet even further details to be given. In addition such information as has survived from the approximate period 1500–1700 concerning the Manors of Washingford, a discrete unit from the eleventh century, and the rather later Berneys, hived-off as it were from the capital manor, will be examined. Finally, consideration will be given to the certain other manors having rights in Bergh Apton, but which were centred elsewhere, particularly the one at Hellington.

Lords of the Manor of Bergh Apton

George Lord Bergavenny was the holder of the lordship of Bergh Apton when the sixteenth century opened. Shortly after 1527 his third wife Mary, daughter of Edward Stafford, Duke of Buckingham, bore him his son and heir, Henry. George died in 1535, and the Crown then held Bergh Apton for the duration of his heir's minority.[1]

Henry Lord Bergavenny came of age shortly after

The Abergavenny family's coat of arms.

1548, and was accordingly admitted to his inheritance, including Bergh Apton. He married Frances, daughter of Thomas Manners, Earl of Rutland, who bore him but one child, his daughter Elizabeth. After Henry's death on 10 February 1587, Elizabeth, by then married to Sir Thomas Fane, made claim to her father's entire estate, but the House of Lords did not allow this and the estate, including Bergh Apton, passed to her father's cousin, Edward Nevill.[2]

Edward Nevill, who became the Lord Bergavenny in 1587, was the son of Sir Edward Nevill, beheaded for high treason in 1538. The unfortunate Sir Edward, moreover, was the younger brother of George Lord Bergavenny, who died in 1535. Edward Lord Bergavenny first married Katherine, daughter of Sir John Brome, who bore him his son and heir, Edward, about 1551. The latter inherited upon his father's death on 10 February 1589.[3]

Edward Nevill, who succeeded his father to the title and inheritance in 1589, married Rachel, daughter of John Lennard of Knole, who was to give birth to his elder son and eventual heir, Henry, prior to 1580. Edward Lord Bergavenny died on 1 March 1622.[4]

Henry Nevill, who succeeded to the title of Lord Bergavenny and to the estates including Bergh Apton in 1622, made a second marriage to Catherine, daughter of George Vaux. Catherine bore him two sons who survived to be his successive heirs. Henry Lord Bergavenny died in December 1641 and was initially succeeded by his elder surviving son, John, born about 1614. The latter was to suffer financially at the hands of parliament for his support of the

Royalist cause during and after the Civil War; in the 1650s he was obliged to compound for – that is pay a fine in order to avoid being stripped of – his estates, amongst which the Manor of 'Berghe' was named.[5] John Lord Bergavenny died without issue on 23 October 1662, and was succeeded by his younger brother, George. [6]

George Nevill, who succeeded as Lord Bergavenny in 1662, married Mary, daughter of Thomas Gifford. He died on 2 June 1666, leaving his son George, born 21 April 1665, with a long minority before he could enter into his inheritance, which included Bergh Apton. He eventually married Honora, daughter of John Lord Belasyse, but she left him no heir. George Lord Bergavenny, died on 23 March 1695, whereupon his title and his estates passed to his second cousin once removed, George Nevill.

It is of note that when George Nevill succeeded his distant relation in 1695, his title was variously given as Lord Bergavenny and (the more familiar) Lord Abergavenny; this would also obtain with regard to his immediate heir, while the heirs of the latter were all consistently entitled Lord Abergavenny.

The Bergh Apton Rent Roll, 1517/8

We turn to the documentation for the constitution and nature of the Manor of Bergh Apton. The Bergh Apton rent roll for 1517/8 is held at the Bodleian Library, Oxford.[7] How this document came to be held there is not known; but what is certain is that it is a most fortunate survival. Written in Latin, it is almost completely legible. It describes lands of this manor under three heads: the free tenants, the copyhold tenants, and the farms; and, after making certain general points, these will be dealt with in turn.

Regardless of the category of holding, lands within the jurisdiction of Bergh Apton Manor not merely lay in Bergh and Apton, but in a number of neighbouring parishes and some even further afield. For the free tenants, this included property in Claxton, an unspecified Framingham, Heckingham, Hellington, Holverston, Kirstead, Langley, and Surlingham; for the copyhold tenants, this included property in Ashby [St Mary], Caistor [St Edmund], Carleton [St Peter], Chedgrave, Stoke [Holy Cross], and Thurton; while the farms included property in Carleton [St Peter], Rockland [St Mary], Sisland, and Thurton. (Curiously, maybe, no property was specified as lying in Alpington.) Some of the outlying properties would have related to such as had been owned by Edwin, then his successor Godric, in the eleventh century, although others are likely to have been purchased by, or granted to, lords of Bergh Apton later in the Middle Ages. One can but surmise, given deed evidence for such purchases and grants is mostly non-existent. Furthermore, a number of the entries do not state the parishes where the property concerned was situated; however, it became apparent, thanks to a familiarity with the overall documentation of Bergh Apton, that most of these entries refer to the village. For the most part, further discussion of entries not concerning Bergh Apton itself need not be made. Some of the persons listed in 1517/8 held properties in two of the three categories, and a few in all three.

Free Tenants

The free tenants of the manor paid an annual rent to the lord for their holdings, but were not expected to carry out menial tasks for him. The most significant entry, maybe, is that of Ralph Berney Esq. for his manor and lands in Bergh. It has already been observed that this was once part of Bergh Apton Manor, and was held in socage of it – that is it remained subject to its overall jurisdiction and suzerainty. The living of the rectory of Bergh (Apton is not mentioned) fell into the category of a free tenant in respect of its glebe. Another free tenant was the Prioress of Carrow, in respect of lands 'Rokeles and Surlingham'; from this description it can be assumed that she held lands once apparently part of Bergh Apton Manor which had previously been granted to the de la Rokeles family, while Surlingham lands were clearly outliers.[8] Katherine Bussey held freely a mill called Tuckys and an alder carr at Bergh.

Copyhold Tenants

Before considering the copyhold tenants, it is necessary to give a brief introduction to this form of tenure, one that survived until it was abolished under the provisions of the Law of Property Act, 1922. Until the fourteenth century, most unfree heads of household within a manor enjoyed a holding from the lord in return for performing tasks upon his demesne or home farm, and at certain times pasturing their livestock on the latter in order to manure it. Then, and into the fifteenth century, as lords found it more worthwhile to assure themselves of a regular money income, un-free tenants came to be granted their tenement on this basis. First they would upon taking it up, pay an entry fine, based upon its acreage and the nature of the house and any other buildings it contained. This fine would be paid each time the property changed hands through inheritance or sale, details of the transaction being made by the steward in the rolls of the manor and a copy of this given to the incoming owner as the title, hence copyhold. In addition, to compensate the lord for his loss of their work for him, each copyhold tenant would pay an annual rent, a quitrent, that is one quitting the tenant concerned for his menial duties. As the Bergh Apton rent roll 1517/8 illustrates, apart from paying the annual money for quitrent, some tenants also had to give the lord one or two hens and even, in the case of William Bussey, three geese.

Individual tenements – holdings comprised of a house and land – tended not to remain as unchanging units of property, through sales, partible inheritance, and reversion to the lord. They became split into a number of pieces, and coalesced with either parts or the entirety of other tenements. All this is particularly illustrated in the above-mentioned rent roll. Robert Belconger holding the tenement Custys, while William Moore held an acre of the same tenement; Robert also held the tenement Helemans in Bergh, while William also held the tenement Purwynges in Bergh.

Many of the copyholders in Bergh Apton in 1517/8 held property described as a tenement followed by a personal name – surname, sometimes prefixed by a Christian name. For instance the above William Moore held the tenement Purwynges in Bergh, plus an acre of land of the tenement Custys; moreover, Thomas Curson held the tenement Benedict Harmans and 16 acres, plus seven acres of the tenement Martin Brevers. Such names applied to tenements would have been those of the persons to whom they were first granted as copyhold property. Other than Roger Clerke junr who held the tenement John Clerke, and widow Clerke who held the tenement Roger Clerke, surnames of the copyholders of 1517/8 no longer coincided with the names of the tenements they held then.

Tenement Names
A number of tenement names in 1517/8 hark back to the names of lay subsidy payers in 1332:[9] Benedict Harmans back to Benedict Herman; Custes, back to Andrew Custe; Goodwyn back to Simon Godwyne; Gylberds (and maybe also Gylberds alias Bysys) back to Andrew Gilbert; Benedict Church back to Benedict Atte Chirche; and Traces back to Geoffrey Trace. Furthermore, the tenement Simon Kirkhows of 1517/8 may have an association with the John Kirkehowe of 1332; Kirkhouse, significantly, was the name applied to the present-day Beech Farm as far back as 1595.[10] In any case, two of the tenements of 1517/8 can certainly be identified with present-day property: thus the tenement Grymbalds (Grimballs) to Bergh Apton Manor (-house); and the tenement Thurgodys (Thurgoods) to the row extending from Bettina to Rose Tree Cottage on the west side of Bergh Apton Street. The tenement Benedict (Atte) Church almost certainly lay in the vicinity of Church Farm.

Farms
As for the farms (leasehold property) in 1517/8, these comprised anything from apparently discrete farm units as would be recognised today down to pieces as small as three roods. The lord, through his steward, leased these for a fixed annual rent, mostly money alone, but sometimes together with a set amount of barley, and in one instance merely the latter. The most important farm was that of 'the site of the

Beech Farm, 2004. The original name of the dwelling, Kirkhouse, dates from as far back as 1595.

The barn at Beech Farm which has the date 1698 on its eastern gable. The owner of the farm at the time of writing, farmer Richard Loades, is standing in the foreground.

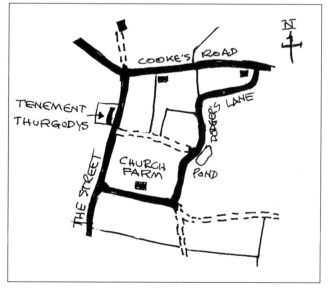

Fig.7.1. The sixteenth-century Tenement Thurgodys (or Thurgoods) on The Street.

The south side of Bergh Apton Hall in the dilapidated state it was in before its restoration by John Averill in the 1980s.

The north (front) façade of Bergh Apton Hall before restoration, 1980.

Manor and the Park and other [unspecified] lands as per the copy [of the lease]' to Katherine Bussey for an annual rent of £5. This entry makes it clear that there had once been a manor-house or hall, which was the capital messuage of the Manor of Bergh Apton, and which had been demolished by 1517/8. Moreover, this site was closely associated with the park, which the amalgam of documentation investigated reveals was generally coextensive with the only part of Bergh Apton – historic Bergh – lying south of the Chet, to the south and south-west of the present-day Bergh Apton Hall. The body of the latter, it must be made clear, exhibits features suggesting that it was built during the reign of Anne (1702–1714); and, while it may have occupied a site close to the medieval manor-house, has not served as such since it was built (nor yet its surviving early-seventeenth-century west wing); interestingly, Bergh Apton Hall was named as Park Farm on both Bryant's Map of 1824–6 and the Ordnance Survey of c.1836. In addition, Katherine also leased an enclosure of 6a.3r. at 'Frums Croft', and 'other divers lands' in Bergh, for a total annual rent of £1.5s.5d.[11]

In Edmund Bussey's will, written in 1504,[12] he left Katherine (his widow) for the term of her life, the tenements, lands, pastures, grazings and appurtenances in Apton, Bergh, Thurton, Ashby, Hellington and Brooke, which he held of the 'lord of the fee', that is the lord of the manor. After her death this property was to go to their eldest son, John, with successive remainders to their sons, Robert and William. Should any of the sons have died in Katherine's lifetime, the property was to be sold after her death by his executors. When Katherine died in 1521 – by which time she had settled in Bergh – she merely declared in her own will[13] that her husband's will was to be performed. As it happened, while no post-1521 reference to this couple's sons was found, a William Bussey (not necessarily their son) paid an annual quitrent in 1517/8 for the copyhold tenement Prathel and Hargreys of 5s., a hen and three geese. The fact that in 1517/8 Katherine held a mill and an alder carr in free tenure has already been mentioned, while it should be added that she also held as copyhold 'divers tenements and lands in Bergh'. It is not known if the freehold and copyhold properties had previously belonged to her husband.

Accounts

In 1540/1, during the time that Henry Nevill, Lord Bergavenny and Lord of Bergh Apton was a minor, and his estates held by Henry VIII, a 'Record of the Court of the Receipt of the Exchequer Concerning Lands in Bergh Apton' was drafted.[14] This document was essentially an account tendered by the reeves of the manor, Stephen Andrews and William Clark, as apparently deputed by the steward, of its profits – £28.18s.8¼d. – for the regnal year concerned. This document includes important information concerning the heart of the manor. Thus (as translated from the Latin original): '£7 [received] for the farm of agistment [grazing] of the Park with the site of the manor there and one pasture, late in the tenure of Robert Maxey'.

Clearly, Robert Maxey had become the farmer of the above property after the death of Katherine Bussey in 1521. There is no reference to him specifically in other documents concerning Bergh Apton; however, there are important pointers to his family's associations here. First, in the Bergh Apton rent roll of 1517/8, a Laurence Maxe had the most extensive holdings – copyhold and farmed – in Bergh Apton after Katherine Bussey, while he was also the free tenant of two pieces of meadow and marsh in Claxton. Next, accounts for the leased-out demesne of the Manor of Bergh Apton, together with other lands and tenements there, calendared in the NRO as Maxes in Bergh Apton, have survived for the regnal years 1543/4 and 1545/6.[15] The contents of these accounts reveal that Robert Maxey must have leased rather more land than just the park and the site of the manor (-house) prior to 1540/1, for some pieces lay in Thurton and Yelverton.

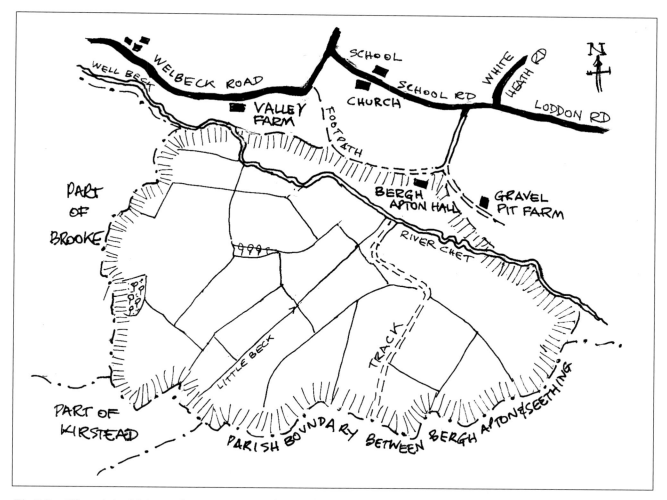

Fig.7.2.   The original Manor demesne was on the southern border of the village, on the River Chet.   It was known at various times as Tenement Maxes and Barrowe Parke before taking its modern name of Bergh Apton Hall.   This would probably have been the location of the 'Hallyarde mill' rented by John Blomvyle in the 1540s.

The accounts of 1543/4 and 1545/6, the contents with regard to the latter year being essentially unchanged in content, indicate that 7s. was paid each year to the collector of the king's taxes.   It is clear from these documents that the Crown had continued to farm the property out, allowing for the additional pieces, since 1540/1.   Henry Nevill, Lord Abergavenny, was not due to become of age and hence enter into his inheritance until at least 1548. They also state that William Bransby was collector of the moneys due from tenants and other sources at Bergh Apton, and that he collected in respect of manors, lands and tenements late of Edward White Esq. and presumably then due to the latter's heir. Edward White had been the elder son of Edmund White of Shotesham St Mary, who died in 1538; Edward and his younger brother, Edmund, were then both under 20 years of age.[16]   Consequently, at some time between 1540/1 and 1543/4, Edward took up the lease of the property with its core being the Bergh Apton demesne, and then died before the latter regnal year.   It may be that his brother and heir, Edmund, did not come of age until after 1545/6; however, there is evidence that the latter died on

3 June 1551, leasing 'a tenement called Maxes in Barrowe and land in Barrowe and Apton'.[17]   This property, in view of evidence already outlined, and that due to be presented, certainly related to the site of the manor and the park at Bergh Apton, although it may no longer have included the extra lands described in the 1543/4 and 1545/6 accounts.   A further detail from Edmund White's will is that he left William Bransby 10s. therein, implying that the latter held a post of some consequence in his employ.

Before taking the story forward, more facts revealed by the accounts of 1543/4 and 1545/6 need to be noted.   John Blomvyle, uncle of the noted Henry Hobart of Hales Hall, Loddon, then farmed the agistment [grazing] of the park at Bergh for £7 annually, plus a surcharge of £1, while he also farmed a mill called Hallyarde – which name suggests that it was close to the hall (or manor-house) site – for 14s. a year, a rabbit warren within the manor for an annual rent of 3s.4d., and finally unspecified premises of the lord for 7s.6d. annually.

In both 1543/4 and 1545/6, the Bergh Apton collector paid John Berney Esq. 7s. in respect of freehold and copyhold land in his manor in Bergh.

The significance of this will be noted when the Manor of Berneys is chronicled later.

As a consequence of the death of Edmund White in 1551, his heir was found to be his sister Anne, aged 19 and married to Henry Doyly by 3 June 1552. By a device called 'ousterlemain', what was effectively the lease of the park (then bearing the name Maxes) at Bergh, together with lands in Bergh and Apton, was granted to Henry in his wife's right on the latter date.[18]

Henry Doyly of Shotesham left his lease of 'Barrowe Parke' to his eldest son, Edmund, for term of his life with remainder to his male heirs in his will, written in 1597 and proved in 1598.[19] Edmund died at Shotesham St Mary in 1612, having in his will left his lease of 'Barrowe Parke' to his son Henry.[20] Henry died on 5 March 1616, apparently intestate. The lease of Bergh Apton Park then passed to his uncle Charles of Trowse Newton, although judging from the genealogy he was not the next heir male in line to inherit it. Be that as it may, it appears that during the latter's lifetime, he acquired the freehold of Bergh Apton Park from Lord Bergavenny. This is known from his will, in which he left the rents arising from his fee simple lands in Bergh, and which when he wrote it in 1618 were in the occupation of Richard Denny, gentleman, of Yelverton, to his executors for ten years after his death for the benefit of his younger son, Thomas, and daughter, Susan. The rents were then to benefit his elder son, Henry, until he attained the age of 22, then he was to have the freehold in person.[21] With the death of Charles Doyly – his will was proved on 6 February 1627 – and the fact that Bergh Apton Park had become a non-seigneurial freehold, its subsequent story will be examined later.

The Manorial Court

With the commencement of the run of surviving Bergh Apton court books in 1651 – paper books had come into general use in substitution for parchment rolls in most manors in the sixteenth century – details of how this capital manor operated 'on the ground', as it were, are manifest. The manorial court generally assembled twice a year, usually in April and October, although when urgent business dictated it would be convened on other occasions.

At the court, all the tenants nominally had to assemble, although a reasonable excuse for non-appearance known as an essoin, presented on one's behalf by a fellow tenant, was acceptable. Tenants who failed to appear without an essoin were mostly fined 3d. The court was usually presided over by the steward of the manor, but in some instances a deputy took his place. The responsibility the successive stewards bore required those appointed to hold this post to possess total integrity and financial acumen, given lords of the Manor of Bergh Apton lived far away until 1869 (saving possibly the Countess of Pembroke for a time in the fourteenth century).

The business of the court was divided into two main heads, that of the Court General (in earlier days known as the Court Baron), and that of the Court Leet.

The Court General

The Court General, comprising the homage (or inquest of office) of ten to 14 chief tenants – all listed by name – dealt with major issues, mostly concerning the transfer of copyhold land. Such conveyances were fully detailed, and a copy given to the incoming tenant as title to the property once he or she had paid the entry fine and made (nominal) fealty to the lord as represented by his steward or deputy. Unfortunately, by the mid-seventeenth century, the descriptions given to what were often a large number of small pieces of land effectively forming the copyhold parts of a discrete farm were anachronistic, that is they no longer related to how such holdings were actually laid out.

The homage at the Bergh Apton Court General of 7 July 1651 (an atypical date) was comprised of the following: Richard Cooke, gentleman; Richard Denny, gentleman; John Cooper alias Cokoe; Gregory Cooke; John Kiddington; Robert Turner; William Chambers; William Meeke; William Turner; William Clarke; Robert Mollett; Robert Feltham; William Fodder.

The Court Leet

The Court Leet was generally responsible for good order being maintained within the jurisdiction of the manor. Its jury was generally comprised of from ten to 16 capital pledges*, each nominally responsible for a group of about ten inhabitants of the manor under the system known as view of frankpledge. It was quite usual for an overlap between members of the homage and the capital pledges. By the mid-seventeenth century, the latter group had little concern with such medieval niceties as maintaining good order in common fields; however, it still appointed two constables to serve annually, often specified as one for Bergh and one for Apton, and a hayward, who would have responsibility for the hedges within the manorial limits for a year from his appointment. The receipt of an annual leet fee of 6s.8d. was one of the lord's perquisites, and with other dues, such as entry fines and those that had to be collected from tenants who absented themselves from court without an excuse, were together placed in the steward's hands for conveyance to the lord's annual audit. Blomefield, incidentally, recorded that Robert Roket, rector from 1471 to 1513, endowed Bergh Apton with 28 acres of land out of which the leet fee of 6s.8d. was to be paid; what became of this source of income has not been revealed by the subsequent documentation.

The jury at the Bergh Apton Court Leet of 23 October 1651 was comprised of the following: William Meeke, John Kiddington, Gregory Cooke, William Chambers, William Turner, William Burrowe, Thomas Wake, John Cooper, Robert Mollett, William Clarke, William Fodder, Richard Cooke.

*Senior representatives, generally heads of household.

The Manor of Washingford

As for the Manor of Washingford, the first we learn of it in the Tudor period was when half of it, together with its mill, lands, pastures, rents, suits and services, were left by William Westgate the elder, of Sisland, to his son and executor, William, in his will written on 1 May 1536.[22] The testator did not mention the other half of this manor in his will, so maybe he did not own it then – indeed, it could already have been in the possession of his son. By the time the latter came to write his will at Sisland on 3 December 1558, he was certainly the possessor of the whole of Washingford. He left this manor in Thurton, Bergh, and elsewhere in Loddon and Clavering Hundreds, to his eldest son William. This latter testator's will was proved on 19 April 1561.[23] With regard to the Westgate family being residents of Sisland, one recalls that Washingford Mill spanned the Chet at a location where it formed the boundary between that parish and historic Bergh. Furthermore, the present-day Washingford Farm(house), rebuilt about 1830, stands in Sisland, against the boundary with Bergh Apton, although its historic farm buildings lie in the latter parish.

The William Westgate who inherited the Manor of Washingford in 1561 was presumably the one who, according to Blomefield, sold it to Francis Wolfe, gentleman, of Thurton. Blomefield added that Washingford Manor was held of Bergh Apton Manor about the reign of Elizabeth for an annual rent of 2s.; however, this was not recorded in the Bergh Apton rent roll of 1517/8. According to C.M. Hood's edition of the *Chorography of Norfolk*[24], in which the Bergh Apton entry is revealed as having been compiled in stages from 1600 to 1604 (and possibly slightly later), Washingford had been held of Bergh Apton for 16s. per annum, but was then held of the Clavering Hundred at an annual rent of 2s. Its lord in c.1604 was the aforesaid Francis Wolfe, concerning whom no further details have been established.

We next learn of Washingford Manor when its owner, Gregory Cooke, yeoman of Bergh Apton and who was buried here on 23 December 1656, bequeathed it to his nephew John Cooke, son of Richard Cooke the elder.[25] The wording of Gregory's will suggests that he lived at what would correspond to the capital messuage of this manor, perhaps identifiable with Washingford Farm:

All that my Mannor of Washingford in Bergh Apton or else where in the said Countie of Norffolc with all the wrightings Evidences Court bookes & Court rolls with all & singular the rights members and appurtenances to the said Mannor belonging or in any wayes apperteyning where I nowe dwele with all the Yardes Gardens Orchards Hemplands And all that the hill [sic, recte mill?] with the crofte to the said Mesuage belonging.

Unfortunately, none of the documents mentioned in Gregory Cooke's will as belonging to the Manor of Washingford has survived.

John Cooke in turn left the Manor of Washingford to his nephew and namesake, son of Richard Cooke of what is now Washingford House, at his death in 1680.[26]

The Manor of Berneys

As for the small Manor of Berneys, this was in the hands of Ralph Berney Esq. at the opening of the sixteenth century. Berneys being held of Bergh Apton Manor, Ralph its lord was listed as a free tenant of the latter in the Bergh Apton rent roll of 1517/8, although the amount of rent he paid was illegible.[27] It is not known when Ralph Berney died, but it was before 1543/4 when John, his son by his second wife, Amy Southwell, had inherited it.

In 1543/4 and 1545/6, William Bransby, collector of the farms that were leased of the Manor of Bergh Apton by the heir of Edward White of Shotesham St Mary, paid 7s. to John Berney Esq. for the additional lease by this heir of the freehold and copyhold land of Berney's manor in Bergh.[28] This implies that John did not occupy the latter in person; indeed, Blomefield confirms that he lived on his estate in Langley.

Inquisition Post Mortem evidence is that John Berney died at Langley on 7 January 1559. It was then stated that Richard, his son and heir, was a minor aged 17. In any case, John had declared in his will, proved 7 May 1560, that his manors (for he also held that of Langley) should effectively pass to Richard once the latter attained his majority, until which time they would be held by his executors.[29] Blomefield noted that Richard Berney sold his eponymous manor to 'Mr Green, a yeoman, whose son Thomas enjoyed it: only 2 copyholders then belonged to it, and the free rents were about 13s per annum.' The evidence is that William Greene of Bergh, yeoman, left his Manor of Berneys to his son Nicholas and his heirs in his will, written 27 February 1604, the day before his burial at Bergh Apton, and proved on the following 19 March.[30] In this will the manor was said to lie in Bergh Apton, Thurton, Mundham and Seething, and was enjoyed with its rents, services, profits, rights, royalties and commodities. The unknown writer whose manuscript was edited as the *Chorography of Norfolk* (ed. C.M. Hood) further noted in respect of 'Barrowe Barney' Manor that Nicholas Green (*sic*), yeoman, was its lord – hence dating this element of his entry for Bergh Apton to after the death of William Greene – and that it had two copyhold tenants, the rest [of the tenants being] free. He further added that it was held in socage of the Manor of Bergh Apton for an annual rent of one pound of pepper plus 3s.4d., and that it held no court.

We next learn of the Manor of Berneys when Nicholas Wrongrey of Carlton [Colville], Suffolk, left it in 1653 to Gregory Cooke of Bergh Apton, the latter to pay 'Mr Stannard' of Bedingham £21 on account of this bequest.[31] Curiously, Gregory Cooke made no mention of his possession of Berneys in his own will, written 9 November 1654.[32]

Deed evidence[33] is that the Manor of Berneys somehow passed to Thomas Beverley, owner of an estate called Beverleys in Bergh Apton. The latter can probably be identified with the Thomas Beverley who died at Poringland in 1670. During his lifetime, he conveyed Berneys and Beverleys to Robert Julians of Bergh Apton, yeoman. The latter left these properties to his eldest son and heir, Thomas, in 1694.[34]

The deed just mentioned is dated 28 September 1711, but might conveniently be considered here as it brings to an end the story of Berneys as has been established at the time of writing. Berneys Manor was described as follows:

All that his Lordshipp or Mannor of Barnes otherwise called the Mannor of Bergh Barnes or howsoever otherwise called with all the rents Fines and services thereunto belonging oweing or payable or which hereafter shall become due owing or payable in right of the said Mannor extending into Bergh Apton Thurton Seething and divers other townes parishes and places in the said County of Norffolk.

The manor was then conveyed by Thomas Julians of Bergh Apton, yeoman, to John Clarke of Beccles, gentleman.

Other Manors

The Manor of Hellington extended into Bergh Apton – essentially historic Apton. This manor, and also that of Claxton, formed part of the divorce settlement of Henry VIII's fourth wife, Anne of Cleves, in 1540, and she held them until her death in 1557.[35] Hellington's run of court books survives from 1636, and includes retrospective information back to 1596. It is from the latter date that the site of the modern-day Holly Cottage in Bergh Apton Street can be chronicled. This property was the only dwelling copyhold of Hellington in Bergh Apton; however, pieces of land that were copyhold of it formed part of the estates of the present-day Bergh Apton Manor (-house), Pond Farm, and Washingford House.

Small pieces of land copyhold of the manors of Banyards, Claxton, Dickleburgh and Manclarkes, Seething, and Thurton, also lay in Bergh Apton.

A 1912 photograph of Holly Cottage (left) when it was used as the Post Office. The bay window of one of the village shops is just visible on the other side of the road.

References
[1] Vicary Gibbs (ed.) *Complete Peerage* (London, St Catherine Press, 1910), vol.1.
[2] *Ibid*, which corrects Blomefield who stated in *An Essay towards a Topographical History of the County of Norfolk*, vol.10, p.98, that his nephew succeeded Henry.
[3] Gibbs (ed.), *op. cit.*
[4] *Ibid.*
[5] R.H. Mason, *History of Norfolk* (London, Wertheimer Lea & Co, 1884), pp.300, 315.
[6] Gibbs (ed.), *op. cit.*
[7] Norfolk Rolls 3.
[8] Neither the anonymous *Chorography of Norfolk* (ed. C.M. Hood) nor Blomefield indicated that any part of the Prioress of Carrow's estate at Surlingham was held of Bergh Apton.
[9] TNA: E179/149/9 m.75.
[10] This retrospective evidence is found in the Bergh Apton court book.
[11] I infer that at least her husband, Edmund Bussey of Apton, had held Katherine Bussey's principal lease previously; he was probably the brother of John Bussey who died at Apton in 1479.
[12] NRO: NCC 1504 f.22 Ryxe.
[13] NRO: NCC 1520 [Old Style] f.29 Alblaster.
[14] ESRO: ABE 39I
[15] NRO: FEL 275 and 277.
[16] NRO:NCC Will 1538 f.292 Attmere.
[17] Fine Roll.
[18] *Ibid.*
[19] TNA: PROB11/91.
[20] NRO: NCC 1612 f.259 Coker.
[21] TNA: PROB11/151.
[22] NRO: NCC 1536 f.64 Hyll.
[23] NRO: NCC 1561 f.385 Bircham.
[24] C.M. Hood (ed.) *Chorography of Norfolk* (Norwich, Jarrold & Sons Ltd, 1938).
[25] TNA: PROB11/269.
[26] NRO: ANF 1681 f.7.
[27] Bodleian Library: Norfolk Rolls 3.
[28] NRO: FEL 275 551x3.
[29] TNA: PROB11/43.
[20] NRO: ANF 1603 [Old Style] f.439 Offwood.
[31] TNA: PROB11/232.
[32] TNA: PROB/11/269.
[33] Norfolk Family History Society Archive.
[34] NRO: ANF 1694 f.149.
[35] Patent Rolls.

Chapter VIII

Sixteenth- and Seventeenth-Century People

We now look at the sources that reveal the identity of Bergh Apton folk in the sixteenth and seventeenth centuries, take a closer look at some of the more prominent families who lived here during this period, and also chronicle the rectors and church matters.

The Bergh Apton parish registers have not survived from prior to 1556. It may be coincidental, but one notes that this was the year following that when Apton church was last recorded as in use (will evidence) and Bergh's church thenceforth served as that of the combined parish. The parish registers from their commencement provide the focal point for information concerning the inhabitants of Bergh Apton, however, this is qualified by the fact that, prior to 1754, marriages where both parties lived in the parish did not have to be celebrated here – although a majority would have been.

Both before and after the start of the parish registers, there exist a number of listings of Bergh Apton folk. Indeed, we have already considered certain names in sources relating to the Manor of Bergh Apton, dating from 1517/8, 1540/1, 1543/4 with 1545/46, and 1651. Otherwise, the lists to be examined were drafted at the behest of central government for taxation purposes or for funding the monarch.

Taxation Records

The Norfolk Subsidy for 1524/5 is a particularly important source in so far as it is the only known listing that distinguishes those living in Bergh from those living in Apton.[1] Thus we find:

Residents of Apton		
Name Assessed for	Amount to be paid	
John Benstleyne	£4 moveables	2s.
Alice Curson	£6 moveables	3s.
John Pedde	£1 wages	4d.
Nicholas Dyaunt	£1 wages	4d.
John Gildenwater	£3 moveables	1s.6d.
Thomas Michells	£2 moveables	1s.
Edmund Chamber	£4 moveables	2s.
Thomas Cates	£2 moveables	1s.
Edmund Heynes	£1 wages	4d.
John Miller	£1 wages	4d.
John Clerke	£1 wages	4d.
John Wellam	£1 wages	4d.
Robert Belconger	£1 wages	4d.
Nicholas Ashwell	£1 wages	4d.
Nicholas Bussey	£1 wages	4d.
John Merton	£1 wages	4d.
Total (to be paid):	13s.10d.	

Residents of Bergh		
Name Assessed for	Amount to be paid	
Richard Wodiard	£16 moveables	8s.
Robert Belconger	£2 moveables	1s.
Roger Turner	£2 moveables	1s.
Roger Clerke	£2 moveables	1s.
William Clerke	£1 wages	4d.
William Turner	£2 moveables	1s.
Robert Sewell	£1 lands	1s.
John Clerke	£2 moveables	1s.
William Duffy	£2 moveables	1s.
Stephen Wigge	£2 moveables	1s.
Nicholas Greene	£2 moveables	1s.
Nicholas Cooke	£5 moveables	2s.6d.
William Holme	£1 wages	4d.
John Mandy	£2 moveables	1s.
Reginald Holme	£2 moveables	1s.
William Cokket	£2 moveables	1s.
William Bransby	£5 moveables	2s.6d.
Total (to be paid):	£1.5s.8d.	

A total of 17 names for Bergh and 16 names for Apton are given above, and from this one might deduce that they had a roughly equal population. On the other hand, the larger proportion of those taxed on their annual wages – the poorest grouping, although not actually paupers, for they would not have been taxed at all – lived in Apton, and this suggests that Bergh was the wealthier of the two communities. Alice Curson is of note as the only woman listed in either Apton or Bergh. She was a widow of Apton, although her dwelling has not been identified.[2]

Subsequent taxation records do not differentiate between Apton and Bergh folk. Those drafted prior to the commencement of the parish registers may be summarised as follows:

Year of Subsidy	No. of Taxpayers	Total
1543/4	30	£1.6s.3¼d.[3]
1545/6	12	£5.8s.[4]
1547/8	12	£3.6s.4d.[5]

Year of Relief (Tax on real estate)	No. of Taxpayers	Total
1549/50	3	£1.14s.[6]
1551/2	9	7s.10d.[7]
1552/3	9	£5.5s.[8]

From the taxation records for Bergh Apton of the sixteenth and seventeenth centuries, post-dating the commencement of the parish registers, we learn that a total of 17 persons paid the Forced Loan of 1597, which amounted to £7.1s.4d. Only seven of their names are completely legible.[9] The subsidy of 1624/5 was paid by ten persons (including 'The Town Land' – see p.55) resulting in a total of £2.16s.[10] In 1662, 17 persons paid a total of £10.6s.[11] as part of the 'Voluntary Present' to King Charles II. The Hearth Tax of Michaelmas 1664 resulted in 39 persons being taxed on a total of 113 hearths. Only four of their names are completely legible.[12]

It seems appropriate to add here that Henry Kedington, the rector in 1603, returned a total of 156 communicants at Bergh Apton.[13] As about 50 per cent of the population about this time in England are likely to have been confirmed, it could be that this would relate to a population of about 300, thus approximating to the 304 enumerated in the census of 1801.

Probate Material

The documents, that give the closest insight into how Bergh Apton folk lived in the sixteenth and seventeenth centuries, and indeed later, are probate records, particularly wills and probate inventories. While not every adult made a will, a sufficiently large number from gentry down to labourers did and their wills illustrated many aspects of their family and domestic lives, their property, their occupations and financial status, and the nature of their Christian belief by evidence of religious and charitable bequests.

Fewer probate inventories than wills have survived. These were drafted on many occasions after the death of individuals owning personal estate valued at £5 or more. In respect of persons who had occupied the larger houses in Bergh Apton, those taking a probate inventory would name each room in turn, listing the artefacts found therein and giving the value of each item. After the listing of a dwelling was completed, the inventory takers would, where relevant, list the contents of farm and other outbuildings, live and dead stock, and also the quantity of crops growing in the fields or harvested and stored. The use of wills and probate inventories will be considered in greater depth in the following two chapters when we look in turn at farming and related activities, and at vernacular architecture.

A third example of probate material, comprising letters of administration in respect of those who died intestate, should be noted, although only limited information is to be found therein – usually that concerning the relationship between such a deceased person and the individual to whom administration of his or her goods and chattels was granted.

Property Deeds

The majority of deeds concerning Bergh Apton property are contained within the extensive Denny-Cooke manuscripts collection in the Norfolk Record Office.

It was not until the nineteenth century that the Dennys and the Cookes' ownership of property here reached its greatest extent. However, deeds concerning the properties which they were to own in due course, together with those they actually owned in the sixteenth and seventeenth centuries, have survived and have been of inestimable use with regard to confirming relationships within families, as well as the more obvious use they have in illustrating the story of properties in the parish from cottages to farms.

It is appropriate at this point to mention the families of Denny and Cooke and other noteworthy families within the context they occupied in Bergh Apton.

The Denny Family

The Denny family owned and occupied the site of the present-day Bergh Apton Manor in historic Apton from between 1552/3 and 1565 until the twentieth century. This house was recorded in manorial records and deeds as the tenement Grimballs from 1517/8 until 1729. In the Bergh Apton rent roll 1517/8, evidence is that Nicholas Pydde then occupied it as copyhold property.[14] However, the Denny family was first recorded in Bergh Apton – specifically Apton – three years earlier when William Denny died leaving a will.[15] William left a wife and also his mother, but unfortunately did not give their Christian names, as well as a daughter, Alice. Maybe his wife and mother can be identified with the two ladies noted in the Bergh Apton rent roll of 1517/8. This source also named another William Denny, who farmed four acres parcel of Sulwong and other lands; a Margaret Denny who held a copyhold tenement late Soppys and other lands; and a Joan Denny, widow, who held a half-acre of the Tenement Gylberds. The precise locations of the properties owned by these three Dennys are not known.

We learn no more concerning Dennys at Bergh Apton until John and his wife, Lettice, settled at the tenement Grimballs (as it seems more appropriate to refer to the house at this time) between the Relief (lay taxation) of 1552/3 and 1565 when this couple first had a child baptised at the Parish Church. When John died in 1593, he had not only left a will but also a probate inventory drafted in respect of his goods, chattels and implements of household. His will is relatively straightforward in so far as in it he left his real estate to his surviving son and heir, Edward. His wife was to continue to occupy the house for life, enjoying the use of the parlour, meat and drink and 'fireing' (i.e. firewood), and furniture including a bed, the biggest chest and a coffer.[16]

John Denny's inventory[17] is a truly revealing document and what it tells us about his farming activities and the structure of his house will respectively be considered later. It clearly reveals that he occupied a house that was adequately appointed

The Denny family coat of arms on a tomb in Bergh Apton churchyard.

with a range of furniture and other artefacts. Items of particular interest in the house include weapons – a bill and a sheaf of arrows – that John would have taken to the annual musters, events which all able-bodied adult males were normally bound to attend. The Bible and two other books reveal that the deceased, and perhaps other members of his family could read; in any case, John is known to have been literate by the fact that he had written his will in person. To this observation it might be added that while the majority of John's contemporaries would have been unable to write their own wills, some literate persons had to use the services of a scribe by dint of illness or incapacity.

Edward Denny, who had been baptised at Bergh Apton church in 1567, died in 1621 at the house he had inherited from his father. Richard, his only son by his wife, Katherine, was baptised at Bergh Apton church in 1598. While Edward was referred to in the corpus of documents examined as a yeoman, Richard took on the appellation of gentleman. When the latter died in 1664, he left his property to his elder surviving son Thomas, who was baptised at Bergh Apton church in 1622.

Thomas Denny married Mary, the daughter of John and Elizabeth Athow of Street Farm (later Apton Manor). His bride was almost 27 years his junior. Thomas died in 1673, leaving his elder son and heir, John, baptised in 1671, a minor. The latter came into his inheritance in 1692, about which time he married Parnell Chicheley, and through which marriage he was also to enjoy an estate centred upon Norton Subcourse. John Denny was the great-great-great-grandfather of Thomas Henry Denny-Cooke, who died at Bergh Apton Manor in 1952.

The Cooke Family

We turn to the Cooke family, long associated with Washingford House in Bergh Apton – historic Apton. The association with Apton, although not necessarily with this property, may be taken back to 1506, when Thomas Cooke of Ashby St Mary left his son, Thomas, land in the former parish. Thomas also had sons called John and Edmund, the first of whom maybe identifiable with the John Cooke who was noted in respect of two pieces of land in the Bergh Apton rent roll 1517/8.[18] At that time John farmed a piece containing seven acres at Hoogate (the modern-day Cooke's Road), while he held as copyhold in his wife's right the Tenement Gracys in Apton. Following an exhaustive study of deed and court book evidence, the latter has been eliminated from any possible identification with an early model of Washingford House.

It was not a John Cooke who was to leave the house known from the continuity of evidence to relate to Washingford House in 1529, but a Nicholas Cooke. The latter was of Bergh when he wrote his will[19] and it was where he asked to be buried; all the same he left a cope* and 2s. to Apton church, just as he had done in respect of Bergh church. It is known from the continuity of evidence that he owned what were to become Gravel Pit and Mere Farms in Bergh (although much of the land associated with the latter lay in Apton), and these he left to Margaret, his wife. As for the property which was to become

The Cooke family coat of arms on a tomb in Bergh Apton churchyard.

*A long cloak, usually ornamented, worn by a priest.

Washingford House, he left it to his son, Richard, upon his attaining the age of 24.

Richard Cooke died in 1558, apparently having left no children by his wife Anne. He described himself as of Apton and Hellington (where he was buried), and left the house and land he had in each village to his wife, she to occupy that in Apton, for the term of her life. Upon her death, the Apton property was to pass to his brother John's eldest son, Richard.[20]

The last-named Richard Cooke must have been born between 1539 and 1558. It was to be during his lifetime that the earliest surviving elements of Washingford House were built. It is not known if he ever married, but he certainly left no surviving children when he died in 1633 – the Bergh Apton parish register record of his burial then described him as an 'old man'. His Apton property then passed to the eldest son of his late brother Gregory of Bergh, yet another Richard.

Richard the son of Gregory Cooke was baptised at Bergh Apton church 1583. He married a Mary, who bore him two sons and a daughter. The elder son, Richard, whose baptismal record was not located, inherited the Washingford House property on his father's death in 1656. By this time, he had already married, his wife was also Mary, and had had the first four of his 14 children. Of these, it was the seventh child, but eldest surviving son, Gregory, baptised in 1657, who was to inherit this property upon his father's death in 1684, the widowed Mary to be accommodated there for the term of her life. Gregory Cooke was also the great-great-great-grandfather of Thomas Henry Denny-Cooke who died in 1952. No marriage was recorded between the Dennys and the Cookes, long-time owner-occupiers of adjacent estates, until that of Richard Denny and Frances Cooke in 1815.

The Meeke Family

Street Farm, in historic Apton, partly dates from the mid-sixteenth century but was extended somewhat 50 or so years later, details of its structural development are given later. Lay subsidy evidence points to this site having been occupied by Thomas Michells prior to 1552, while from then until 1660 the Meeke family occupied it. (Other Michells held the nearby Church Farm in the sixteenth century.) William Meeke, yeoman, the first of his line to own the house, lived here with his wife, Joan, and five children. Marriages within the yeoman and minor gentry families of Bergh Apton were not unnaturally commonplace: William and Joan's daughter Agnes married Nicholas Wrongrey in 1575, who was probably of Hillside Farm which his brother Edmund later owned. Another daughter, Jane, married Gregory Cooke, owner of Gravel Pit and Mere Farms, in 1582. William Meeke died in 1584,

having willed that his wife should be accommodated at his house for the term of her life.[21] Their elder son and heir, John, inherited the property, and he lived there with his wife, Margaret, and their four children.

In 1612, John Meeke conveyed the Street Farm estate to his son William, maybe as a settlement upon the latter's marriage to Elizabeth Mandey, although where this took place has not been established. John and his wife appear to have remained at the house until their respective deaths: she died in 1616, while he outlived her by 23 years, so in apparently having lived to be over 80 he thus enjoyed a long life for this period. William and Elizabeth Meeke's only child, Elizabeth, baptised at Bergh Apton church in 1619, married John Athow, gentleman, in Bergh Apton in 1637. The newly-weds settled at the bride's parents' home, who also appear to have remained there until their deaths, both of which occurred in 1660.

The Athow Family

John Athow was of an armigerous family that can be traced back to his great-great-great-great-grandfather and namesake who died at Brisley, in mid-Norfolk, in 1462. His bride's father, incidentally, had taken to describing himself as gentleman by the time he died, but as in many other instances about this time, he had not been granted arms.

John and Elizabeth Athow had seven children. Two of their daughters provide us with further examples of local marriage alliances. Elizabeth married her third cousin, John Cooke of Washingford House, at Bergh Apton in 1682; Mary married (as her first husband) Thomas Denny of Bergh Apton Manor, but it is not known where and

The Athow coat of arms on Elizabeth Athow's headstone. She was born in 1619 and died in 1708.

when. John Athow served the office of constable for (specifically) Apton in 1663, and was likewise churchwarden in 1668/9 and 1675/6. His brother Henry joined him at his residence in 1675. The latter had been educated at Caius College, Cambridge, and was a licensed schoolmaster. He died at Street Farm in the following year.

The Athow family occupied their house in Bergh Apton Street until 1736, when John and Elizabeth's grandson Christopher moved to Brooke. The last member of the family to own it, the latter's unmarried granddaughter Hannah Athow, died in 1826.

The Tenwinter Family

Of families occupying sites in historic Bergh, the first of these living at what is now Town Farm (the house apparently completely rebuilt after an arsonist burnt it down in the late-eighteenth century) was Thomas Tenwinter who had settled there by 1543/4.[22] He and his wife Jane were successively buried at Bergh Apton in 1559, having left one child, their son Christopher. Christopher Tenwinter left no indication that he had a wife and children in the records of Bergh Apton. In June 1599, one month before his death, he wrote his will as a yeoman of Bergh Apton,[23] in which, after certain bequests to his niece, godchildren, associates, and to the poor, he left a legacy of enduring importance in the story of this parish. To quote from his will:

Town Farm, 1995. The farm was left to the village of Bergh Apton by Christopher Tenwinter when he died in 1599 'in truste to the onely use and behouf of the Town of Bergh Apton aforesaide'. The house and much of the land has been sold over time to benefit the village but some of the lands are still held in the same trust.

Item I gyve and bequeathe unto Henrye Kadington, clerk, Richard Cooke, Edmund Wrongrey, John Meeke, Thomas Turnor, William Turnor, Edwarde Dennye, & Nicholas Mollett, all & singular messuages, landes and tenements and hereditaments as well free as bonde, with all and singular there appurteninge thereunto belonginge, sett lyeinge and beinge in Berghe Apton aforesaid, or elsewhere in the countye of Norffolc. To hold to them… and to their heyres and successors for ever as Feoffes in truste to the onely use and behouf of the Town of Bergh Apton aforesaide. To that intent that the benefitt and profitt comynge, rysinge, and groweinge upon the foresaide… maye by the said Feoffes for the time beinge, or by anye other hereafter to be clerked, named and chosen, or the more part of them soe that present yeare be disposed to the good of the saide Towne for ever. And for performance of my last will and Testament so. Provyded Allwayes, and my mynde and wyll is, that the said Feoffes for the tyme beinge, or the heyres executors or assignes of them or anye of them shall paye or cause to be payd all suche some or somes of moneye in such manner and forme, and to such person or persons, Towne or Townes use or uses, as in this my present last will & testament is mentioned, sett forthe, and declared.

The eight Feoffees appointed by Christopher Tenwinter in 1599 operated as a self-perpetuating board of trustees. As the initial Feoffees died, their respective heirs succeeded them until only four of those originally chosen survived. These four then elected others to bring their number back to eight. This procedure was followed until the Town Farm was sold in 1922; the only exception noted having been in 1680 when five of the Feoffees operating from 1667 were recorded as having died before the survivors elected their successors. Feoffees elected, as opposed to the heirs of deceased Feoffees, usually included the churchwardens and sometimes the rector. They always tended to represent the most important families in Bergh Apton.

White's *Directory of Norfolk* for 1883 noted, 'Since 1660 the rent (from the Town Farm) has been applied in defraying the Churchwardens' and Constables' expenses.' This would appear to have been assumed from the fact that the surviving Feoffees' accounts only date from 1660; however, such defrayments may have obtained from 1599. In any case the Feoffees from the beginning paid an annual dole of £1 to the poor of the parish.

The Doyly Family

During a consideration of the leasing of Bergh Apton Park[24], the point was reached when the freehold of this property, an integral part of the manorial demesne, was acquired from Lord Bergavenny by its hitherto lessee, Charles Doyly of Trowse Newton.

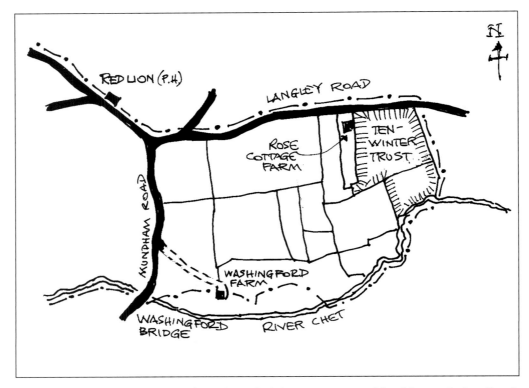

Fig.8.1. The Tenwinter Trust, formed to administer property and land bequeathed to Bergh Apton by Christopher Tenwinter in 1599, still owns this land to the east of Rose Cottage Farm at the time of writing.

In his will the freehold park was to pass to his elder son, Henry, once he attained the age of 22.

Henry Doyly, whose baptismal record has not been located, married Dorothy Day at Scoulton on 6 June 1642. This couple may have settled at Bergh Apton by 12 September 1648, when their unnamed son was buried here. Should they have been living in Bergh Apton then – and the genealogy states the family at this time was both of here and of Brooke, they probably occupied a house associated with the park, maybe an earlier model of the present hall. While the body of this house clearly dates from the reign of Anne (1702–1714), its surviving west wing has features that invite a dating sometime during the reign of Charles I (1625–1649). It is clear from the reference in the Bergh Apton rent roll 1517/8 to the site of the manor[25] that the medieval hall or manor-house, which presumably stood hereabouts, had been demolished by then. The west wing just referred to may have formed the whole or more likely a part of a Doyly house. The house, which they occupied in Brooke, bearing in mind that Bergh Apton Park abutted west against the Brooke parish boundary, has not been identified at the time of writing. However, Henry and Dorothy Doyly's surviving son, William, was baptised at Brooke on 22 January 1652.

Henry Doyly wrote his will as gentleman of Brooke on 9 November 1668; however, he was to be buried as he had requested in Bergh Apton chancel on 7 September 1679. In his will[26] he left his Bergh Apton estate called 'Barrowe Parke' to his son William and his heirs; he did not mention any property he may have owned in Brooke, so his dwelling there was presumably rented, while the lands which he held in Newton Flotman and Flordon were to be sold for the benefit of his daughters. The widowed Dorothy Doyly had died intestate at Brooke by 21 May 1698, when administration of her goods and chattels was granted to her son, William, then described as 'gentleman of Brooke'.[27]

William Bransby

One inhabitant of Bergh, whose dwelling has not been specifically identified but to whom some attention might be paid, is William Bransby, the one we have met in the Lay Subsidy of 1524/5 when he was assessed for the second highest amount of goods there, and also in his role as collector of the farms on behalf of the heir of the lessee of the demesne in 1543/4 and 1545/6. William died in 1555, and in his will[28] asked to be buried in the aisle of Bergh church, which indicates his relatively high social status. Significantly, he left 1s.8d. towards the repairs of Apton church. His extensive property, which he left to his son, Robert, amounted to messuages, lands, tenements, meadows, feedings (grazing grounds), pastures, rents and services in Bergh, Apton, Yelverton and Kirstead.

The Churches of Bergh and Apton

On 30 August 1552, an inventory was made of the goods in Apton and Bergh churches. This was carried out by an order of the Privy Council, ostensibly to collect plate to sell to raise money for the coffers of the young Edward VI, but effectively as part of the process whereby the forces of Protestantism were to remove many trappings of the Church in so far as it had remained Catholic after the death of Henry VIII in 1547. At Apton, items to the value of £11.7s.7d. were to be surrendered, while a chalice and bell weighing 5cwt were to be retained; the churchwardens were named as Richard Cooke, William Spooner and Simon Michells. At Bergh, items to the value of £19.8s.6d. were to be surrendered, while a chalice, an altar cloth, a bell weighing 6cwt and two towels were to be retained; the churchwardens were named as Nicholas Bussey, Roger Turner and Robert Sewell.[29] The respective listings indicate the comparative poverty of Apton church in comparison with that of Bergh. A further point with regard to the 1552 inventory: contrary to what was ordered then with regard to Bergh church, this was to retain its (still existing) tenor bell, then said to weigh 8cwt, in lieu of that weighing 6cwt.

Apton church was apparently still in use in 1555, when William Bransby left 1s.8d. towards its repairs.[30] However, in the following year, when the parish registers of unified Bergh Apton commenced, it is clear that it was Bergh church that had been chosen to serve Apton as well. It may seem to flow against the prevailing tide that Apton church should have been abandoned during the reign of Mary Tudor, that is in the period of the Counter-Reformation. Interestingly, the use of the churchyard at Apton for interments appears to have continued for some time after 1555; in her will dictated and proved in 1559, the widowed Christian Michele of Apton asked to be buried there.[31] No record of this interment appears in the Bergh Apton registers, which may suggest that other post-1555 burials at Apton were not recorded. It might be observed that the site of Apton church was to remain glebe until the Inclosure Award of 1806, while its remains were essentially cleared away in 1834.[32] C.J.W. Messent[33] wrote in 1936 that its foundations were remaining. Some residents inform me that heaps of masonry from this church could still be discerned on its site in the mid-twentieth century. In any case, blocks of ashlar from the church were about the time of its abandonment inserted into the south front of Street Farm, while others were later inserted into the garden wall at Church Farm, and still survive in these two locations.

The Rectors of Bergh Apton

Robert Roket was serving as rector of Bergh Apton when the sixteenth century started. His rectory, and that of his successors until the twentieth century, lay in historic Apton. Richard Bull followed him from 1513 to 1517. The latter's successor, Nicholas Harrison,[34] was buried (presumably in what was still Bergh church) on 19 October 1545 – a sole retrospective entry in the Bergh Apton parish registers, which were not otherwise commenced until 1556.

John Machett, who in serving as rector from 1545 until 1561, experienced the events set in train by the Henrician Reformation, the Counter-Reformation during the reign of Mary, and the Elizabethan Settlement with regard to the Church of England, as they impinged upon Bergh Apton.

John Matchett's successor as rector of Bergh Apton, John Osborne, was not recorded by Blomefield, but is known from the Norwich Diocesan Institution Books. Osborne served as such here from 1562 to 1582;[35] the parish registers recorded the baptisms of five of his children over the period 1563 to 1575, but did not name his wife.

John Osborne's successor was Henry Kedington, he served as rector of Bergh Apton from 1582 until his death in 1606. Interestingly, Henry had been resident in Bergh Apton before the commencement of his incumbency: he married Anne Huke in 1574, and of their eight or nine children, the baptisms of six were recorded in the parish registers, two of them prior to 1582. Henry would appear to have had a somewhat 'Protestant' attitude to his ministry: in the Bishop's Visitation of 1593 he was presented for not wearing a surplice on some Sundays and Holy Days; for not reading the Injunctions every Quarter; and for baptising some children without signing them with the Cross.[36] Beyond this latter record and the parish registers, much is known concerning Henry, his family, his rectory house, his other property, and his farming activities, from his will[37] and probate inventory.[38] What they reveal concerning farming matters and the structure of the rectory house will be respectively examined in the following two chapters.

Henry Kedington's household allowed for the accommodation of several persons; its well-furnished rooms contained from 12 to 15 beds (depending upon how one interprets the probate inventory). As some of his eight or nine children had almost certainly left home by the time of his death, some of this accommodation was surely reserved for servants, both domestic and of husbandry. Of household goods and furniture, Henry left his wife three bedsteads with the bedding, three chests to be chosen by her, all the linen, pewter and brass saving a great brass pot and two kettles, and the contents of the parlour. Those taking the inventory of his goods valued his books at £10, but unfortunately did not list them.

Robert Bate succeeded Henry Kedington as rector in 1606. Little is known concerning him, saving the baptismal record of his son Thomas on 28 February 1613, and the burial record of his daughter Sarah on

Bergh Apton's tower bells rung up and ready to ring. The bell on the bottom right is the oldest in the tower and was made by Richard Brasyer c.1480. It has the Latin inscription Petrus ad eterne ducat nos pascua vita *(May Peter lead us to the pastures of eternal life).*

14 October of the same year. There is some confusion as to the continuity of Bate's incumbency: the glebe terrier dated 6 April 1613 names Thomas Horseman as rector, yet a further terrier of the following October describes Bate as such. Whether Thomas Horseman was one and the same as, or the father and namesake of, the rector from after Thomas Kemp's death in 1627 until 1658 is unclear.

At some time between October 1613 and November 1620, Thomas Kemp became rector of Bergh Apton. He was a member of the armigerous family of Kemp of Gissing; this illustrated by the five escutcheons contained in The Rectory at the time of his death in 1627 according to the probate inventory.[39] This source reveals Kemp's belongings as reflecting those of a gentleman of his day; Henry Kedington in comparison had possessions more in accord with those of a person of yeoman stock. Kedington had no firearms or armour; Kemp had a musket with bandoleers, a sword and handpieces. Kedington's apparel was valued at £4; Kemp's was priced at £30. Kemp's bed and bedding were furthermore far grander than that possessed by Kedington. Kemp's library was valued at £26.13s.4d., and specifically included:

Two Tables containing the Histories of the Foundations and Arms of all the Colleges in both the Universities

Two maps in frames, one of England and the other of Norfolk
Four Tables of the History of Susanna

It was in 1627 that one Robert Hodgkiss of Bergh Apton was presented in the Bishop's Visitation for 'living apart from his wife'.[40] Nothing else was discovered in the records concerning this errant husband.

Thomas Horseman, presumably the Horseman recorded during part of Robert Bate's overall incumbency, or a son and namesake, succeeded Thomas Kemp as rector. He and his wife Mary had eight children, six of whom were baptised at Bergh Apton church between 1627 and 1640. Thomas Horseman died in 1658; but there is evidence that at least some members of his family remained in the village afterwards, though not at The Rectory which they would have vacated shortly after his death. A Mr Horseman – presumably one of Thomas and Mary's two sons, Thomas and Edward, respectively baptised in 1633 and 1634 – paid £1 towards the Voluntary Present to Charles II in 1662.[41] In addition, a Horseman (Christian name and/or status illegible) occupied a house with four hearths in Bergh Apton in 1664.[42] The Revd Horseman's widow was certainly buried at Bergh Apton church on 10 October 1676.

During Thomas Horseman's incumbency, the

second and third oldest of Bergh Apton's ring of six bells were cast and hung; at the time of writing they are the fifth bell, which is dated 1628 and was the work of W[illiam] B[rend], and the third bell, which was cast by John Brend in 1656.[43] It is maybe curious that the latter should have been acquired during the Cromwellian period, when such items were generally regarded as having been frowned upon by the authorities.

Samuel Stead, rector of Bergh Apton from 1658 to 1668, left few traces in the records of the parish. At least it is noteworthy that the surviving churchwardens' accounts were commenced during his incumbency in 1660 (although there was to be a gap in the run of these from 1681 to 1721).

In the year 1660–1661 Richard Denny, churchwarden, accounted for the following:

Three loaves and six and a half pints of wine at Easter: 6s.9d.
Richard Cooke for his charges for going to London [purpose unspecified]: £5.6s.8d.
Edmund Chambers and Edmund Wiseman for Constables' fees: 10s.

In the year 1670–1671, Thomas Denny likewise accounted for:

John Rope paid for carpenter's work at the Town Land: 18s.6d.
William Hewson paid for works done at the Town House: 7s.
Robert Fee for his wages as [Parish] Clerk and for washing the surplices: 6s.6d.

In the year 1680–1681, William Neale and Richard Ward likewise accounted for:

Laid out at the perambulation [beating the parish bounds]: £1.5s.
Given to a sea captain in distress: 1s.
For mending the Town Pump: 1s.

Samuel Stead's successor, Robert Connold, was to be Bergh Apton's longest serving rector, holding this post from 1668 until his death in 1715 – while this present chapter nominally records matters up to the end of the seventeenth century, it will suit the course of the narrative if Connold's entire time is dealt with in the text which immediately follows. He and his wife, Alice, had ten children here over the period 1668 to 1689. His son Samuel, baptised in 1675, assisted his father as curate here for at least the period 1700 to 1702, after which he became rector of Chedgrave. Robert, who outlived his wife by nine years, was responsible for rebuilding Bergh Apton chancel, within which he was to be buried.

During Robert Connold's incumbency, Edward

Tooke of Norwich cast the three latest of Bergh Apton's complement of six bells. These are the second, fourth and first bells, respectively dated 1674, 1677 and 1678.[44] In Connold's time at Bergh Apton, the church acquired a plate cup and paten of 1675, each marked with the Norwich Lion and Castle, the crown, rose and the initials T.H. over a star: these initials were those of Thomas Havers.[45] These two items of plate were sold, together with a paten of 1789, as authorised by a faculty obtained in 1931, to raise money for the bells to be rehung.[46]

The earliest headstone to survive in Bergh Apton churchyard dates from Connold's time here: it commemorates Ralph Ward, who died on 28th February 1686 (Old Style) / 1687 (New Style) aged 54.

Robert Connold's wife died in 1706. As Roy Tricker recorded[47] Connold became 'plagued with gallstones' in 1710; however, this condition was to become but one of his problems. Two years later, he had to report to the Bishop of Norwich that the east wall of the chancel at Bergh Apton had developed an external crack, and that he had had a brick buttress erected to support it. The master builder he had engaged to carry out this work had assured him that it would last for years; this was not to be the case, for the east end of the chancel collapsed, along with part of the roof, shortly afterwards. As Connold further reported to the bishop, the repairs

Robert Connold's ledger stone in the chancel that he restored after a wall collapsed in 1712. Connold died in October 1715 after an incumbency of 47 years and two months. He was Bergh Apton's longest serving rector.

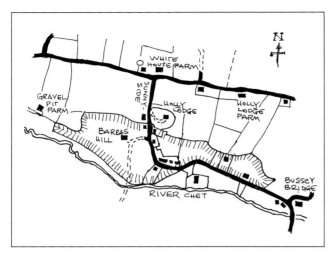

would cost him £200, which he could not afford without the help of some 'pious and well-disposed persons'. The necessary finance was all the same forthcoming, and by Connold's death in 1715 he had completed the rebuilding of the chancel and was indeed buried therein beneath a ledger slab. The chancel was rebuilt in brick, but has since been rendered. Connold's classical-style, round-headed windows remain: two on the north side and one on the south, plus a larger east one; to the east of the south window he set a priest's door.

Fig.8.2.   Common pasture of the village pre-1806 – Barnes Heath, showing later development of buildings.

References

[1] TNA: E179/150/249 m.2.
[2] NRO: NCC 1525 f.73.
[3] TNA: E179/151/32 m.5.
[4] TNA: E179/151/338 m.3.
[5] TNA: E179/151/344 m.3.
[6] TNA: E179/151/363 m.2.
[7] TNA: E179/151/375 m.1.
[8] TNA: E179/152/383 m.1.
[9] TNA: E179/153/510 m.12.
[10] TNA: E179/153/582 m.1.
[11] TNA: E179/154/662 m.1/2.
[12] TNA: E179/367/13 m.1.
[13] Francis Blomefield, *An Essay towards a Topographical History of the County of Norfolk*, vol.10, p.100.
[14] Bodleian Library Norfolk Rolls 3.
[15] NRO: NCC 1514 f.25 Spyrlynge.
[16] NRO: NCC 1593 f.161 Clearke.
[17] NRO: NCC INV 11/17.
[18] Bodleian Library Norfolk Rolls 3.
[19] NRO: NCC 1529 f.27 Attmere.
[20] NRO: NCC 1558 f.48 Woodcocke.
[21] NRO: ANF f.219 Sherwood.
[22] Lay Subsidy evidence.
[23] NRO: NCC 1599 f.149 Pecke.
[24] See chapter VII, p.48.
[25] Bodleian Library Norfolk Rolls 3.
[26] NRO: ANF 1679 f.157.
[27] NRO: ANF Admon. 1696–9 no.205.
[28] NRO: ANF 1555 f.425 Bulloke.
[29] H.B. Walters, *Norfolk Archaeology* (Norwich, Norfolk and Norwich Archaeological Society, 1941), vol. 27.
[30] NRO: ANF 1555 f.425 Bulloke.
[31] NRO: ANF 1559 f.17 Moundeforde.
[32] William White (Limited) (*sic*), *History, Gazetteeer and Directory of Norfolk*, 1st edn (Sheffield, William White Limited (*sic*), 1836), p. 810.
[33] C.J.W. Messent, *Parish Churches of Norwich and Norfolk* (Norwich, H.W. Hunt,1936).
[34] It might be noted that the entry concerned actually gave his surname as Henryson.
[35] NRO: DN/REG/13–14.
[36] NRO: DN/VIS 2/1.
[37] NRO: NCC 1606 f.105 Bowrne.
[38] NRO: NCC INV 21/102.
[39] NRO: NCC INV 33/229.
[40] NRO: DN/VIS 5/3/1.
[41] TNA: E179/154/662 m.1/2.
[42] TNA: E179/367/13 m.1.
[43] P. Cattermole, *Church Bells of Norfolk Part 1 The Hundred of Clavering* (Aylsham, Golden Ball Press, 1991).
[44] *Ibid*.
[45] E.C. Hopper, 'Church Plate in the Deanery of West Brooke,' in *Norfolk Archaeology* (Norwich, Norfolk and Norwich Archaelogy Society, 1910), vol.17.
[46] NRO: PD 497/13/6.
[47] Roy Tricker, *Guide to the Bramerton Group* (Ashby St Mary, Bramerton Group of Parishes, 1978).

Chapter IX

Farming and Other Activities

The nature of farming, that is the way farms were laid out and the kind of husbandry practised, within Bergh Apton from the sixteenth to the eighteenth centuries, is now considered. This will bring us to the eve of that defining point for Bergh Apton (and other nearby parishes), the Inclosure Act of 1801, which resulted in an Award five years later. We will also glance at the evidence for such activities as milling and brick making. Although the photographs pictured here date from the early-twentieth century, they show traditional farming practices which had changed little over the years.

Tenement Grymbalds (Grimballs)

As an initial case study, we may consider the Tenement Grymbalds (Grimballs) of the Bergh Apton rent roll of 1517/8.[1] Apart from the demesne and the glebe, this holding can be chronicled from then not only through to the eighteenth century but on (as a farm) until the late-nineteenth century, though it was known as Bergh Apton Lodge from 1824 and as Bergh Apton Manor from 1869. It is apparent from the overall documentation of Bergh Apton that this farm's development broadly mirrors that of others here; for this reason, fewer details need be given concerning other holdings.

According to the Bergh Apton rent roll of 1517/8, Nicholas Pydde paid an annual quitrent of 5s. and a hen, in respect of the copyhold Tenement Grymbalds – this indicating an average-sized holding. This property

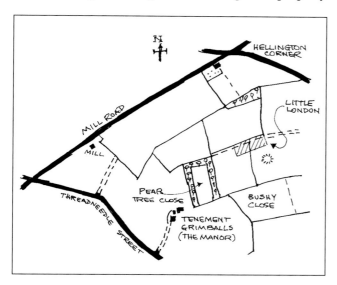

Fig.9.1. Tenement Grimballs, Pear Tree Close, Little London and Bushy Close are all names associated with Bergh Apton Manor since the sixteenth century.

was taken up by John Denny between 1552/3 and 1565, and was to be occupied by members of his family until the mid-twentieth century. Prior to his death, John Denny is on record as having added to his initial holding – the actual extent of which, admittedly, is not known – on three occasions. Firstly, on 5 April 1578, he acquired two acres in Apton from John Snelling of this parish, husbandman, and his wife Beatrix: this piece, which probably lay to the west of Denny's house, had formerly been the property of John Gildenwater then of William, father of John Snelling.[2] The second occasion was on 10 January 1584, when Denny was granted three pieces of land, containing three acres in all, in Apton Field by two husbandmen, Richard Cooke, of (what later became) Washingford House, and Edward (Edmund?) Wrongrey, this was probably part of (what later became) Hillside Farm.[3] This particular transaction is of note, as it would appear to indicate strips or other small pieces in the open field of Apton – lying to the west of (Bergh) Apton Street – being acquired so as to consolidate them in larger closes. John Denny's third acquisition was of two pieces of arable land, each of one acre in Apton, from Robert Malmes, husbandman, on 16 April 1589 – these probably lying to the east of Pear Tree Close (Fig.9.1), the north-eastern area of the present-day Manor property.[4]

Following John Denny's death, the inventory of his goods and chattels drafted on 26 June 1593 provides a detailed insight into the working, stock and produce of his farm.[5] He had a cart, tumbrel (two-wheeled cart), harrows and a plough; and he had wheat, meslin (mixed wheat and rye) and barley in store, presumably from the previous harvest, plus ten acres of winter corn (probably wheat) in the ground. Three rendells (sheaves) of hemp (flax) were also listed. As for his livestock, he had a horse, four head of cattle, six pigs, twelve fowls, four geese and four ducks. His artefacts included those relating to brewing and cheese making and there was even a dairy.

Having inherited his father's property in 1593, Edward Denny continued the policy of extending its limits. First, on 27 May 1594, he purchased three pieces of land with a combined area of 3a.1r. from Richard Cooke of (what later became) Washingford House – these pieces apparently lying to the east of Denny's house.[6] Next, on 6 April 1598 he acquired unspecified land, which apparently lay in the same general area as just mentioned, from John Peede, yeoman of North Walsham, who had inherited it from his father and namesake, yeoman, late of Apton.[7] Thirdly, he purchased a 14-acre close of pasture in three pieces, together with a barn, on 1 April 1601 from Nicholas

Dannocke, gentleman, of Yelverton. This close lay to the west of the then (pre-1853) course of The Street, opposite Verandah Cottages.[8]

There were no known additions to the Denny farm following the purchase of 1601 until at least 1729. Some of the farm as it existed over that period was copyhold of the Manor of Bergh with Apton, some of that of Hellington, and the rest freehold. From 1622 until 1766, the copyholds of Bergh Apton were listed consistently as a messuage (the Tenement Grimballs), a cottage (now Verandah Cottages), and 18a.1r.0p. in Apton; from 1664 on until 1859 the copyholds of Hellington were listed consistently as 14 acres in Apton and ten acres in Hellington. All this

The Wall family, 1910. Leonard and Anna Maria raised eight children at Lenwallen, a small cottage off The Loke on Threadneedle Street. Raymond (left) was the youngest and the one to continue the family tradition of market gardening on land adjacent to the family home. Lily went on to raise four children in Bergh Apton and was living at Lenwallen when she died in 1998 at the age of 93. Reggie (far right) went on to have two children but died aged 26 in a motorcycle accident on Threadneedle Street in 1926. Nine years earlier one of his older brothers, Clifford, had died in the fighting around Ypres in the First World War.

data comes from the relevant court books and rentals.

On 23 January 1729, Freeman Denny, his wife Thomasine and his mother Parnell mortgaged their estate for £700 with William Norris, gentleman of the Inner Temple, London. The property concerned was then described in detail:[9] it extended to 50a.2r.0p. in Apton (some of which was interspersed with strips of glebe) in 12 pieces, 38 acres in three pieces in Hellington, and three acres in two pieces in Yelverton. From the description of these, it was possible to plot 93.5 per cent of this farm's extent, which is all but two pieces totalling six acres in Apton. This description of the farm together with a similar record of Street Farm (now Apton Manor) in 1704,[10] indicate that listings of copyhold land in court books of the eighteenth century (and apparently as such from the mid-seventeenth century) no longer related to how the farms concerned were actually constituted. Such descriptions were merely perpetuated by successive stewards to indicate the overall acreage of copyholds, upon which were based the entry fines and quitrents due to the lords of the manors concerned. The independent yeomen and minor gentry farmers of Bergh Apton had of their own volition concluded that their holdings were far better managed when wholly (or all but wholly) comprised of hedged fields.

As for the continued survival of strips in sometime open fields in Bergh Apton, this mostly concerned the conservatively held glebe – the territorial endowment of the rectory of this parish. While a few pieces of this were in the form of closes, much of it remained in strip form until the Parliamentary Inclosure of 1806. Exceptionally, in 1773, Richard Denny, owner-occupier of the Tenement Grimballs (Fig.9.1, p.61) and Hannah Athow of Beccles, owner of Street Farm, came to an agreement with the Bishop of Norwich whereby they they swapped land with the then Bergh Apton rector, Nevill Walter, so as to extinguish glebe lying within their estates.[11] Perhaps due to an oversight, one half-acre strip of glebe in the Dennys' Bushy Close (Fig.9.1, p.61) was not to be extinguished until 1865. In 1773, the Revd Walter gave Denny, in all, four strips of glebe amounting to three acres in exchange for three acres of Reed's Pightle (Fig.13.1, p.109). The latter piece did not form a part of the Denny property in 1729, and it was not possible to determine from whom it was subsequently acquired.

The inventory drafted as a consequence of the death of Richard Denny in 1774[12] details a far more extensive farm than that enjoyed by his great-great-great-grandfather in 1593. The premises by 1774 had come to include stables, barns and outhouses, while the dairy (as in 1593) was an integral part of the house. The farm itself was worked with a wide range of implements. A total of 74 acres of land were described as in tillage: wheat, barley, oats, peas, clover and none-such (a plant used for fodder) were being grown, while there were also varying amounts of wheat, barley, oats

Above: *An aerial photo of Pond Farm on Dodgers Lane in 1960, then in the occupation of Jack Ellis.*

Left: *Aubrey Parfitt with his horse on Church Farm, c.1950.*

Below: *Kenny Seely ploughing with Blossom and Smokey at a drawing match c.1959 at Alpington or Yelverton.*

Aubrey Parfitt (left) *who farmed at Church Farm (see photo on p.63). Parfitt is 'stooking' or 'shocking' sheaves of wheat to dry the grain before stacking, as was the practice in the years before grain dryers. The house and barn can be seen in the background. Straw stacks like those in the stack yard near the house were once a familiar sight but are now but a distant memory.*

George 'Squire' Freestone (right) *farmed at Valley Farm in the Chet Valley. The man on the left is Horace 'Dough' Farrer.*

Left: *Walter Cain at the stables of Whitehouse Farm in 1919.*

Far left: *Gily Littlewood of Threadneedle Street with David the pig at Town Farm, 1948. The produce boxes behind Gily bear the name Tyler Bros (South Repps) Ltd.*

Break for harvest tea at Church Farm, c.1935. Dodger Wright (second from left) *is the man who gave his name to Dodgers Lane. The man carrying a shotgun under his arm* (third from left) *was probably shooting the rabbits that emerged as the corn was cut. Mrs Jonathan Westrup is standing on the reaper and binder with tea for her husband's workers.*

Left: *Arthur Smith* (right) *and Neville Jermy hoeing sugar beet at Washingford House farm in the 1980s. Arthur Smith worked on this farm for 38 years having started out at Valley Farm as a boy. Neville Jermy spent most of his working life at Washingford House farm and still lives in the village.*

Above: *A stand for milk churns (seen here outside Holly Lodge Farm barn) was once a familiar sight at every farm that had dairy cattle. This one was last used in the 1980s when Michael Loynes was the tenant farmer.*

Left: *Harvest at Washingford House farm, late 1950s. Left to right:* Tom Baldwin, George Roe, Neville Jermy (on the load), *Reg Isbell* (driving).

Threshing at Washingford House farm, late 1950s. These were the days of straw stacks, threshing machines and hessian sacks – long before the coming of the combine harvester! Kenny Seely is driving the tractor with George Roe and George Long picking up.

Verandah Cottages as they were during the early part of the First World War. These cottages are virtually unchanged at the time of writing. The ladies are Annie Alexander (left), whose husband Robert was a traction-engine driver, and her daughter Eva. Robert must have worked on Washingford House farm, for which this was a tied cottage. The family left this cottage in 1915, shortly before Annie's son Walter was killed in the war, and moved to Brooke. They returned to Sunnyside in Bergh Apton a few years later and lived there for many years.

and peas in store. The livestock included 15 horses, 33½ (*sic*) head of cattle, 66 sheep, and 14 pigs, together with fowls and bees. Within the house, cream and cheese were prepared and beer and cider brewed; while the presence of spinning-wheels suggests that wool from the sheep was spun on the premises.

The Richard Denny who inherited the farm currently under consideration was to extend it on a number of occasions. In 1778, he acquired from Christopher Upton, cordwainer, of Ashby St Mary, 4a.3r.0p. including a house and barn in Little London, east of Pear Tree Close (Fig.9.1, p.61) and abutting onto Apton Heath.[13] In 1779, he purchased (what later became) Royston House – then a house with associated smithy – from Michael Beverley, gentleman of Tibenham. In 1787, he acquired a field of 13a.2r.0p. (subsequently known as Denny's Piece; Fig.4.2, p.28), abutting onto the boundary with Thurton to the east, from Elizabeth Gardiner, widow of Aldeby. Finally, he bought a smallholding with a house and barn, lying immediately east of the property purchased from Christopher Upton, from Robert Page, carpenter, of Brooke, in 1790 – at which time it was in the occupation of John Burcham.[14]

It is a happy accident that two probate inventories have survived to illustrate farming at what is now Bergh Apton Manor as described above. For some similar-sized farms, no such documents have survived, and details of the husbandry that obtained there had to be derived from other sources. With regard to the historic Street Farm, its owner William Meeke left his wife a dairy cow and five heifers in his will written in 1583.[15]

The Bergh Apton Glebe

We have already touched upon the matter of the Bergh Apton glebe.[16] The glebe was an endowment enjoyed by successive rectors: in 1613 it was comprised of 51 pieces extending to 48a.3r.16p.[17] Bergh Apton rectors could not only enjoy the produce of their glebe, for until 1841 they were entitled to the great tithes of the parish derived from virtually all the lay-owned land.

Beyond their glebe and the entitlement to tithes, some Bergh Apton rectors had further interests in husbandry. Such a rector was Henry Kedington, who died in 1606; his will and probate inventory reveal many details concerning his farming. He could not bequeath his glebe, for this automatically passed to his successor as incumbent, but he was able to leave two farms in Bergh Apton which were to be successively held by his widow, his son John, then the latter's son and namesake, until 1664. The first farm

Blackcurrant pickers of the 1920s whose names are not recorded in any village archive.

A tea break for Sam Debbage's fruit pickers, 1960. Left to right: Betty Dye, Nellie Jermy, Ivy Reeve, Dorothy Debbage, Marjorie Carpenter, Joan Dye and Maud Drane.

An aerial photo of Crossways Farm, Church Meadow Lane, c.1980. The orchard and neatly planted rows of vegetables have since gone. This holding was farmed by Sam and Dorothy Debbage who lived in this bungalow which is flanked by new houses in 2005.

Extensive market gardens like those run by Charlie Carver were famous as far away as the Midlands and employed many Bergh Apton people. Charlie is seen here in 1930 with one of his daughters in the background and with pickers, left to right: Fred Mallet, Sam Debbage (Charlie's foreman), ?, Charlie Carver and Fred Pitchers.

concerned was described as having been purchased by the testator from Thomas Michell – this is the core of the present-day Church Farm. Kedington's second farm cannot be related to an existing one on the available evidence, he merely having noted that it had been 'John Boultes and Faith his wifes'.[18] Judging from his probate inventory,[19] Kedington's farming activities were typical of those obtaining in the Norfolk wood–pasture zone of his day: he grew wheat, barley and meslin, peas, vetches (plants of the pea family used for fodder) and hemp (flax). His livestock consisted of horses and sheep, beef and dairy cattle including a bull, geese and hens. He owned a plough, carts and harrows. From his barley he produced malt, with which he brewed his own beer. His family made butter and cheese from his dairy cows. He had in store small amounts of hemp and wool, albeit no artefacts relating to spinning and weaving were listed in 1606.

The glebe terriers from 1613 to 1716 describe two barns by the Parsonage (Rectory) at Bergh Apton, after which only one was noted. The inference from the terriers over the period 1725 to 1777 is that the other barn had been converted to serve as a coach-house and stable block; the terrier of 1784 confirms that this was so. The terriers record brewing and dairying activities at The Rectory to 1747 and 1827 respectively.[20]

Glebe was in essence a conservative kind of holding: other than the exchanges with Richard Denny and Hannah Athow of 1773 referred to earlier, that of Bergh Apton remained otherwise unchanged until the Inclosure Award of 1806. The exchanges of 1773 brought about a reduction in the number of pieces of glebe to 34, with a total area of 49a.0r.25p. The glebe terriers of 1791, 1794 and 1801 reveal that the then rector, Nevill Walter, retained nine pieces extending to 29a.0r.22p. for his own use, leasing the remaining 25 with a total area of 20a.0r.3p. to the landowners and tenants within whose farms these pieces were interspersed.

Pastoral Farming

Examples given above indicate farms in Bergh Apton with the typical mixed husbandry of the wood–pasture zone. More exclusively pastoral farming was found in the park within that part of historic Bergh south of the River Chet. A number of field names incorporating the word 'Meadow', admittedly recorded on maps of the first half of the nineteenth century, suggest that the sometime park remained a centre for grazing throughout the period under consideration, as well as beyond.

Woodland

Woodland has been a valuable possession throughout the ages: Katherine Bussey held freely an alder carr at Bergh, according to the Bergh Apton rent roll of 1517/8.[21] The manorial collector, William Bransby, received 9s.4d. for the sale of 50 faggots of underwood in 1543/4.[22] Timber and faggots in the possession of Christopher Tenwinter at the time of his death in 1599, according to the probate inventory,[23] may well have derived from his plantation, subsequently known as the Town Grove (see map, p.21). The Town Farm Feoffees management of this, as recorded in their accounts from 1660, refer to its exploitation for timber, especially oak, which was sold to farmers and tradesmen in the village.

Rabbit Warrens

The possession of a rabbit warren was a perquisite of a capital manor, and the one in Bergh Apton near to the park was leased by John Blomevyle for an annual rent of 3s.4d., according to the accounts of 1543/4 and 1545/6.[24]

Dovecotes

David Farrow, c.1908. Farrow lived in Lodge Cottage on Threadneedle Street and was the coachman to the Denny-Cooke family at the manor-house.

Another perquisite of the manor was a dovecote, such as survives in the grounds of nearby Kirstead Hall. Bergh Apton's dovecote was in or near to the park, and was let to Thomas Garrarde, according to the last accounts cited. The existence of another dovecote, which unusually for the day may not have had a seigneurial origin, is inferred from the name Dovehouse Close, which abutted onto land acquired by Edward Denny from Nicholas Dannocke in 1601.[25] This Close had come to form part of the Dennys' estate by 1729.[26]

Sixteenth-Century Mills

It is unclear if certain references to mills in Bergh Apton in the sixteenth century related to water-mills or windmills. Katherine Bussey freely held a mill called Tuckys, according to the Bergh Apton rent roll 1517/8. According to the accounts of 1543/4 and 1545/6, John Blomevyle leased a mill called Hallyarde (Fig.7.2, p.47). We can be more certain that the mill at Washingford, referred to in the will of William Westgate in 1536, was indeed a water-mill.[27] Rather later, a memorandum in the parish registers dated 1 October 1702, would appear to relate to the windmill of Samuel Dicks, miller; 11 of the principal inhabitants then agreed that he could build a dwelling-house, presumably on Apton Heath by his mill (no.26 on map, p.21), in return for paying the parish officers an annual acknowledgment of 6d. Faden's *Map of Norfolk*, surveyed between 1790 and 1794, shows a windmill upon the latter site – though named Yelverton Heath by this cartographer.

Brick Making

One site in Bergh Apton has a name that denotes its past use for brick making. The 23 acres of Kiln Grove, then known as Kiln Close in Appleton Furlong, were under cultivation in both 1661 and 1704;[28] moreover, the Meeke family owned this part of the former Street Farm land in the sixteenth century. Significantly, the Norwich Chamberlains' Accounts contain the following references:[29]

> In the year from Michaelmas 1585, tile and brick was brought from Bergh Apton, Meek specifically being paid £1.8s. for 2,000 bricks for use at Pockthorpe Gates. John Meek was later specified as providing a further 5,000 bricks from his kiln for use at St Benedict's Gates and Walls.
>
> In the year from Michaelmas 1590, Meke of Bergh (sic) was paid £14.14s. for 21,000 bricks for use in the rebuilding of Whitefriars Bridge.

Fuller's Earth

The record of the Privy Council proceedings for 19 November 1624 provides a fascinating anecdote with which to bring this chapter to an end:

> Whereas one, Richard Cooke of [what later became Washingford House] Apton, and Edmund Meeke of Yelverton, in the county of Norfolk, have of late digged certaine earth which is found to be good fullers earth, whereof the Lords and others, the commissioners of trade, were informed and therupon they did addresse theire letters to the Reverend Father in God, the Lord Bishopp of Norwich, in inhibite them from transporting any of the same beyond the seas untill they should receive further direccion; now forasmuch as upon heareing of the said

The quintessential ploughing scene. Monty Seeley on Washingford House farm's Loddon Dyke, close by the Norwich Road, in 1985.

Frank Cushing judging a drawing match in 1959. Also pictured are: Arthur Saunders, Kenny Seely, and David Seely, with the ploughing team Blossom and Smokey in the background.

> cause this day at the Councell Table it appeared that the said Cooke and Meeke had most contemptiously carried themselves not onely in transporting and selling the said earth in greate quantities to marchauntes to be transported (contrarie to the inhibicion given unto them by virtue of an order of this table) but alsoe in their miscarriage and misbehaviour toward the said Lord Bishopp, it is therfore ordered that neither the said Richard Cooke, Edmund Meeke, Thomas Meeke nor Katherin Meeke nor any other by theire allowance or with theire privitie shall hereafter transporte or sell to any marchauntes to be transported any of the said earth, but shall sell the same onely to the fullers and other such traders to be used and imployed meerely within the kingdome, and not otherwise, and to that end the said Richard Cooke shall enter into bond with suertie [surety] for the performance thereof. And it is further ordered that the said Richard Cooke and Edmund Meeke shall in all humblenes submit themselves to the said Lord Bishopp for theire said peremtorie [imperious] and grosse misdemeanour and carriage towardes his Lordshipp; of all which the justices of the peace of that

county and other, the magistrates and officers whom it may concerne, are hereby to take notice and in case any informacion be given and the truth therof made appeare unto them or any of them against any persons mencioned in this order, or any others, offenders in like kinde, that they cause ererie such person to enter into bond to answer theire contemptes (at a day prefixed) before this Board.

With regard to the above case, fuller's earth that was used in the preparation of certain cloth was a particularly zealously guarded national commodity. It is admittedly unclear from the above proceedings if Cooke and Meeke had extracted it from a site in Bergh Apton, however, it is likely that the Meekes named were related to the brick makers of the sometime Street Farm.

Gilly Littlewood ploughing with a David Brown 'Cropmaster' tractor at Town Farm in the 1940s.

Bob Debbage (driving) and his father Sam working a tractor hoe on land they farmed on White Heath Road in the late 1960s. They rented the land from Mr Gooch who lived at Orchard House, where George and Audrey Harvey live in 2005.

References

[1] Bodleian Library Norfolk Rolls 3.
[2] NRO: Denny-Cooke MS 3.
[3] NRO: Denny-Cooke MS 4.
[4] NRO: Denny-Cooke MS 5.
[5] NRO: NCC INV 11/17.
[6] NRO: Denny-Cooke MS 6.
[7] NRO: Denny-Cooke MS 7.
[8] NRO: Denny-Cooke MS 12.
[9] NRO: Denny-Cooke MS 14.
[10] NRO: Denny-Cooke MS 33.
[11] NRO: Denny-Cooke MS 17.
[12] NRO: Denny-Cooke MS 123.
[13] NRO: Denny-Cooke MS 25.
[14] NRO: Denny-Cooke MS 29.
[15] NRO: ANF f.219 Sherwood.
[16] Full descriptions of this glebe known as the Glebe Terriers survive back to 1631; however some earlier indication of the Glebe Terriers' nature and extent was noted in the anonymous *Chorography of Norfolk* between 1600 and 1604 (ed. C.M. Hood).
[17] NRO: DN/TER 15.
[18] NRO: NCC f.105 Bowrne.
[19] NRO: NCC INV21/102.
[20] NRO: DN/TER 15.
[21] Bodleian Library Norfolk Rolls 3.
[22] NRO: FEL 275.
[23] NRO: NCC INV 16/196.
[24] NRO: FEL 275 and 277.
[25] NRO: Denny-Cooke MS 12.
[26] NRO: Denny-Cooke MS 14.
[27] NRO: NCC 1536 f.64 Hyll.
[28] NRO: Denny-Cooke MS 33; Bergh Apton Court Book.
[29] NRO: Norwich City Records 18a; NRO: NLA 43876 Gilbert.

Chapter X

Vernacular Architecture

The pioneering landscape historian, W.G. Hoskins, presented the thesis that there was a great rebuilding of the housing stock of all but the poorest social class throughout England – save within the four northernmost counties – within the approximate period 1570–1640. Hoskins opined that this wave of rebuilding was commenced by the wealthier yeomen, and very soon adopted by the smaller farmers known as husbandmen.[1] Bergh Apton has a fine stock of housing broadly dating in whole or in part from the time Hoskins termed the 'Great Rebuilding'. We may take a closer look at some examples of such property, both within the actual context of their structure and, moreover, in the light of how contemporary documents revealed their layout in late-Tudor and early-Stuart times.

Vernacular architecture is understood to mean buildings essentially constructed from materials obtained locally, by craftsmen using traditional methods. It excludes property planned by an architect, or at least strongly influenced by the prevailing fashions executed by this profession. The earliest example in Bergh Apton is Bergh Apton Hall, which (other than its earlier west wing) bears the stamp of having been built during the reign of Anne (1702–1714).

Two houses in Bergh Apton have parts of their surviving structure predating the 'Great Rebuilding': Hillside Farm[2] and Street Farm, now called Apton Manor.

Hillside Farm

The oldest section of Hillside Farm dates from the mid-sixteenth century, while evidence of its fine timber framing, fully exposed throughout its interior, suggests that it was further extended in the late-sixteenth and again in the early-seventeenth centuries to provide an excellent example of a Norfolk 'long' farmhouse. While its brick façade was rendered and refenestrated about the late-Georgian period, its massive external eastern stack, clearly dating from the sixteenth century, provides debatably the finest example of such a feature in the parish. Hillside Farm, moreover, retains a thatched roof, unlike most yeoman farmhouses in the parish, which were once so covered, but are now tiled.

Street Farm

As for Street Farm, William Meeke settled here in 1552, and it would appear that he was soon afterwards to reconstruct his house. Elements of its east gable and the lower courses of the south front, eastward of the tower porch, would appear to date from about the 1550s. Specifically, there are patches of flint work in these areas and also, in the lower-eastern section of the south front, blocks of ashlar. There can be little doubt that this ashlar was taken from Apton church which stood 250yds away, and which, having ceased to be used for services after 1555, would (as in so many similar cases) have been systematically robbed of elements of its masonry, long before the bulk of its remains were cleared away in 1834. Given surviving examples of farmhouses proved to date from the mid-sixteenth century in Norfolk, it is likely that the Street Farm as built (or rebuilt) then was a two-cell house, extending from the east gable by the roadside west to roughly where the surviving main stack was to be built in the early-seventeenth century.

Hillside Farm, 1999. This is the home of farmer Martin Holl and his wife Carrie. The chimney-stack mentioned in the text is clearly shown.

This aerial view of the original Street Farm clearly shows the old farmhouse and its buildings as well as the new farmhouse beyond it that was completed in 1974 for Derek and Jill Harvey who tenanted the farm. The address of the house was changed to Apton Manor in the time of Miss Ann Colman's occupation in 1980s to avoid postal address confusion with the Harvey's house. The long low central farm building was the home of Harvey's Farm Shop for more than 25 years until it closed on 31 July 2004.

Street Farm[3] was rebuilt as a typical Norfolk 'long' farmhouse in the early-seventeenth century. This rebuilt house certainly retained elements of the earlier one; indeed, a further pointer to the greater age of at least parts of the east gable is that the early-seventeenth-century stack is internal and was built against a wall which was already in existence.

Let us consider the house as rebuilt in the early-seventeenth century in detail. It is largely built of two-inch bricks, laid for the most part in English bond; its principal timbers include the stopped and chamfered bridging joists/tie-beams in the ground- and first-floor rooms, and the trusses in the attic. It is likely that its (now) pantile roof was originally thatched.

The house was divided into three cells: from east to west, parlour, hall and kitchen. The parlour and parlour chamber above it were warmed by hearths set into the stack then built within the body of the house against the east gable. The ground-floor hearth is graced by a painted bressumer and a panel of guilloche design on plaster above it; in addition, painted lines to its chamfers and soffit distinguish the bridging joist closest to the hearth. There are no grounds for believing that this paintwork is not contemporary with the features so decorated.

The Main Stack

The main stack at Street Farm rises between the hall and kitchen (early names), and it carried four flues so as to heat both these rooms and the respective chambers over them. The fireplaces on the eastern side of this stack would have been blocked when the hall staircase was inserted in the early-nineteenth century. In the rebuilding of two centuries earlier, a stair

would appear to have been set against the north side of the main stack – there are also indications that at this time another rose by the north side of the eastern stack. To the south of the main stack, one might have expected to find evidence of a baffle entry typical of this period; however, the façade bears no signs that there was ever an entrance at this point, so one can only assume that it was situated where the porch doorway is now.

The Tower Porch

Street Farm having been home to a large and even extended family of Athows in the later-seventeenth century, it should come as no surprise that such established gentry sought to upgrade this house. Indeed, over the approximate period 1670–1700, three particular extensions affording additional status to the house were built. Of these, it is likely that the tower porch was constructed first. Christopher Barringer has pointed out certain similarities of detail between this porch and those dressing Grumbold's Bridge at Clare College, Cambridge, and dated 1638–1640. Indeed, having observed that the Street Farm porch is likely to mark the position of the early-seventeenth-century front entrance, there is more than an outside chance that the existing porch is a rebuilt version of an earlier one – such as may have had to be rebuilt, as its footings were unstable.

The Turret

Two other status symbols were added to the north side of the house. The easternmost of these is likely to have been the turret, which is earlier and may well share the same dating as the tower porch. This turret would have been built with the principal purpose of housing a stairwell, this rendering one or perhaps both of the hitherto existing stairs superfluous.

The North-West Wing

The other status feature, and the most extensive one, is the north-west wing, for which a date approaching 1700 is suggested. This was contrived with rooms with higher ceilings than those in the main range of the house, and even its attic (which is aligned north-south) stands proud of the main one. This wing is heated with hearths warming the ground-floor room, and the chamber above. The latter is attained by a stair at its south-eastern corner, the small landing just beyond its door having rail work with carpentry clearly dating from c.1700. The north-west wing rises above a cellar, this entered by a doorway, again of contemporary dating.

Bergh Apton Manor

Most people who pass the essentially late-Georgian Bergh Apton Manor, set in its tree-studded park, would not suspect that beneath this fine property lie

The west front of Bergh Apton Manor, May 2003. The photograph shows the new south-facing conservatory and the summer-house (the roof just visible above the hedge) that were completed by Kip and Alison Bertram in 2003.

the likely footings of a house dating from the late-sixteenth century, then known as the Tenement Grimballs, and somewhat more tangible remains of its successor of the early-eighteenth century. Here, John Denny and his wife, Lettice, settled at some time after the Relief (Lay Subsidy) of 1552/3, but certainly by 1565 when their first-known child was baptised at Bergh Apton church. Following John Denny's death in 1593, a probate inventory was drawn up of all his belongings.[4] The rooms of his house then were named as follows, permitting an attempt to be made to indicate its likely form: parlour; hall; buttery (meaning kitchen in this instance, given its contents); parlour chamber; hall chamber; backhouse (service accommodation at the rear of the house); dairy; backhouse chamber.

The parlour, hall and buttery , would have formed the three-cell axis of a typical Norfolk 'long' farmhouse. Unusually, it was the buttery that was not chambered over, rather than the hall, which might have been expected at this time – should it have been a late-medieval, open hall, predating the 'Great Rebuilding'. The backhouse with its chamber above probably abutted onto the rear wall of either the parlour or the hall; the dairy may have abutted onto the house, although it could have formed a detached unit. It is somewhat surprising that the parlour did not contain a hearth – the presence of one in any room having been indicated by associated artefacts – although it was normal at this time for it to have been used as a master bedroom, as witness the posted bed therein, rather than in the chamber over it. The presence of artefacts denoting a hearth was only noted in respect of the buttery and the backhouse.

Washingford House

A quarter-mile south-east of Bergh Apton Manor, the casual visitor to the village cannot avoid the sight of the two tall axial stacks of Washingford House, and might well consider them both to date from about 1600; indeed, this would be true in respect of the

eastern stack, the western one being a nineteenth-century replacement of the original. This site, as gathered from the documentary evidence, had been occupied as early as 1529 when its owner Nicholas Cooke, who lived elsewhere, left it to his son Richard. Of the wider c.1600 house, there are few actual survivals other than the stack just remarked upon; however, from this feature and other clues, we can build-up a picture of the dwelling that occupied this site about the end of the reign of Elizabeth I.

It would appear that the house was largely rebuilt in brick, the brickwork of the lower courses of the façade (south front) appearing contemporary with that of the octagonal shafts of the eastern stack. The bricks most likely came from the kiln of the Meeke family of Street Farm. The rebuilt Washingford House extended to three sections analogous to those of the present-day main range, which forms a typical

This is Washingford House as a ruin in the 1950s, before it was bought by Michael Harris of Holverston Hall. He, and his son Christopher in his turn, returned the house to its former glory before Christopher sold it in 1997 to Nigel and Paris Back who have continued the development of the house to suit modern life.

Washingford House in 1987, 30 years after its restoration. This dwelling was home to Christopher and Ann Harris until they moved into a fine barn to the west of this house that they converted into a home in 1997/8.

South Norfolk 'long' yeoman farmhouse. Unfortunately, no probate inventory has survived to list the rooms of this house, together with their contents; however, it would appear that from west to east the ground floor had a service end, a hall section and a parlour. The principal entrance was by a door in the north wall, providing what is known as a baffle-entry by the chimney-stack dividing the hall and parlour sections of the house. A passage to the north side of the hall was removed during alterations in 1963 in order to prevent draughts. The nature of the space to the south side of the chimney indicates the site of the staircase, which afforded access to the upper rooms. These were directly seated over the lower rooms; the superior nature of the hearth warming the eastern bedroom indicates that this, the parlour chamber, according to the normal rule in houses of this design, was the master bedroom.

While Washingford House as rebuilt c.1600 was brick-skinned, it was otherwise timber-framed. The bressumer over the hearth in the erstwhile hall section, now the study, is an original feature, albeit this particular hearth bears signs of two subsequent phases of reconstruction. Another contemporary timber, in the form of a tie-beam, spans the ceiling at the opposite end of this room, albeit reset at its present height when this ceiling was lowered in 1861. That the house had originally been thatched is indicated by the bases of the chimney shafts, albeit a daguerrotype, apparently taken shortly before the alterations of 1861, shows that the house had acquired a pantiled roof by then.

Town Farm

A house for which a probate inventory of 1599 exists to give some indication of its layout then, but which no longer stands thanks to a late-eighteenth-century arsonist, is Town Farm.[5] This inventory indicates that the house was then a small one, retaining its late-medieval open hall. The rooms actually noted were hall, then parlour and back-house which each had a chamber above. Of the artefacts listed, the only piece of hearth furniture was a single 'dogge iron', which implies that its deceased owner, Christopher Tenwinter, did not have a closed-in hearth. A house of this nature is likely to have been timber-framed throughout, that is it would not have had a brick skin, and also thatched. Judging from his will,[6] Tenwinter was not short of money, so it is possible that he had not improved the house – which he had in any case inherited from his father – by closing-in its hearth and ceiling over the hall out of mere conservatism.

Once in the hands of the Feoffees to whom Tenwinter had bequeathed his property, it is likely that Town Farm would have been improved along the lines that he might have effected but chose not to do. Given other documented work in Bergh Apton,

as well as that indicated by architectural evidence, this rebuilding is likely to have been completed by 1640 – indeed, had it been carried out after 1660, it would have been documented in the churchwardens' accounts (which incidentally included those of the Feoffees). At least it is known that the house remained thatched after this time, given a number of payments recorded in these accounts for repairing it.

Other Notable Houses

Bergh Apton has a number of other houses that display to a greater or lesser degree features of vernacular architecture. Those for which at least a mention must be given in this respect are as follows: Bussey Bridge Farm, which displays some good early-seventeenth-century timber-framing within its ground floor. Sadly, its first floor was gutted by fire on 1 April 1965. Gravel Pit Farm again dates back to the early-seventeenth century, maybe a little earlier, part of its rear elevation still possessing the original bricks laid in English bond with diapering; Whitehouse and Holly Lodge Farms, are both basically of seventeenth-century construction, but much modernised. Beech Farm is also of the seventeenth century, and has a fine, late-seventeenth century brick and thatched barn – this intriguingly dated 1681 on its western gable and 1697 on its eastern one.

Top: *Holly Lodge Barn cart shed on Loddon Road before it was converted into a house in 2000.*

Above: *Holly Lodge Barn before conversion, showing the barn owl hole in the eastern gable that has been retained in the new house. Despite being named Holly Lodge, this building was a separate farm holding to Holly Lodge Farm, but part of the same estate.*

Bussey Bridge Farm Cottages, 2002. The records of many of the men who worked for Bussey Bridge Farm and lived at these cottages are held in the village archive.

The Rectory

It now remains for us to examine that remarkable case study, the historic Rectory, known at the time of writing as Bergh Apton Stud. The anonymous *Chorographer of Norfolk* (ed. C.M. Hood), whom we know from internal evidence wrote his account of Bergh Apton over the period from 1600 to or shortly after 1604, stated: 'To Barrow [Rectory] belong very convenient dwelling houses with necessarie outhouses...' Yet, for the earliest full revelation of the nature of this house, reference must be made to Henry Kedington's probate inventory of 1606,[7] followed in succession by the glebe terrier of 1613 and Thomas Horseman's probate inventory of 1627.[8]

The composition of The Rectory in the years 1606, 1613 and 1627

1606	1613	1627
Kitchen	Kitchen	Kitchen
Hall	Hall	Hall
Parlour	Parlour	Parlour
Parlour chamber	Bedchamber	Parlour chamber
Buttery	Buttery	Buttery
Study	Planchered room over the buttery	Study
Chamber by the study	Planchered room over the lower bedchamber	Little chamber
Chamber over the parlour	House contrived for baking, brewing and malting	Buttery chamber
Backhouse		Hall chamber, with inner closet
Backhouse chamber		Dairy
Christopher's chamber		Servants' chamber
		Malthouse
		Backhouse.
		Chamber over backhouse

Formerly The Rectory, now Keith Freeman's Bergh Apton Stud, renowned for breeding Thoroughbred horses. The photograph of the south façade shows this fine building at its best in the 1970s.

While the above lists differ somewhat – they were, after all, compiled by different individuals or sets of individuals – a close analysis shows that the house was effectively changed over the period 1613 to 1627 by its hall being ceiled over, and by a second stack being added in association with this ceiling operation. With regard to the differences in the successive descriptions, the compilers set their own patterns; they did not follow any given set of rules as to how to describe a property, saving outhouses and farm buildings, should there have been any, tended to be featured last. The families living at The Rectory in the three years concerned naturally differed in their compositions and possessions; the residents adapted or ordered the house to suit themselves. Rooms could be sub-divided – parts of a single room having markedly differing functions – to the extent that those whose sought to describe the layout of the house, especially in 1627, in so doing seemed to endow it with a complexity it did not actually have.

In accordance with the principles of the 'Great Rebuilding' of W.G. Hoskins[9], that late-medieval component of The Rectory, its open hall, was ceiled-over to suit the demands of its early-Stuart occupants for increased comfort, and growing material possessions. It may be gathered from the 1606 inventory that The Rectory was in the form of a U-shaped house, this probably extending from north to south about the site of the northern half of the present day house. The northern or service end was traditionally closest to the yards and stable; a stack with a hearth to either side rose between the kitchen and the open hall in the centre of the house; at the south end was the parlour. Only the end sections of the house were chambered over, and these upper storeys were probably jettied outwards. Outhouses extended from the northern end of the house, almost certainly from the eastern rather than the western wall. Similarly, a study projected from the southern end. This description still obtained in 1613, but by 1627 the hall section had been ceiled-over and a second stack inserted. By this time the hall had a hearth, with a further hearth set into the same stack in the room over the parlour – parlour chamber, or what we would call the master bedroom, at the southern end of the house.[10]

References
[1] W.G. Hoskins, Making of the English Landscape, (London, Hodder and Stoughton, 1955).
[2] I acknowledge access to notes made by members of the Brooke Buildings Recording Group when they analysed its structure in 1984.
[3] I acknowledge with gratitude the fact that many of the points set out below concerning the structural development of Street Farm were made by Christopher Barringer MA FRGS, with whom I visited this house in 1989.
[4] NRO: NCC INV 11/17.
[5] NRO: NCC INV 16/196.
[6] NRO: NCC 1599 f.149 Pecke.
[7] NRO: NCC INV 21/102.
[8] NRO: NCC INV 33/229.
[9] Hoskins, *op. cit.*
[10] With regard to this analysis of The Rectory, I owe much to discussions with the late Alan Carter MA FSA.

Chapter XI

The Eighteenth Century

The identities of successive lords of the Manor of Bergh Apton in the eighteenth century are now noted; all of them were absentee landlords. We then turn to the Cooke family, prominent landowners here, of which certain members were also successive lords of the small Manor of Washingford.

We look at other families of importance in the secular life of Bergh Apton during the eighteenth century, and then turn to the succession of rectors of the parish. 'Gentrification' is a theme that concerned certain lay and clergy families during this time, and is taken into account. Finally, we observe a number of events that touched upon the lives of more ordinary folk.

Lords of the Manor of Bergh Apton

George Nevill, Lord Bergavenny (Abergavenny) was the lord of the Manor of Bergh Apton when the eighteenth century opened. Exceptionally, during his time as lord, it was not he who presented to the living of Bergh Apton (as a consequence of its being vacant in 1717, following the death of Robert Connold two years beforehand), but Ashe Windham Esq. of Felbrigg. Lord Bergavenny died on 11 March 1721, having left two sons and a daughter by his wife, Anne, daughter of Nehemiah Walker. His elder son, George Nevill, inherited the title and the estates, and again reverted to the name Abergavenny). He died from smallpox on 15 November 1723, having left no issue by his wife, Elizabeth, daughter of Colonel Edward Thornicroft.[1]

The next heir to the title, and the estates was Edward Nevill, younger son of George Nevill, Lord Bergavenny and his wife, Anne. From this time onwards the name Abergavenny is consistently used. He also died from smallpox, on 9 October 1724, and left no issue by his wife, Katherine, daughter of Lieutenant-General William Tatton. As a consequence, the title and estates passed to the first cousin of the deceased brothers, William Nevill, son of their late father's younger brother, Edward.[2]

The new Lord Abergavenny of 1724, lord of the Manor of Bergh Apton, married his predecessor's widow, Katherine. Their son and heir, George, was born on 24 June 1727. The latter succeeded to the title upon the death of his father on 21 September 1744, and to the latter's estates once he became of age; moreover, he was raised in the peerage when he was created Viscount Nevill and Earl of Abergavenny on 17 May 1784. At his death on 9 September 1785, he left as his heir his son, Henry, whom he had by his wife Henrietta, widow of the Hon. Richard Temple and daughter of Thomas Pelham. Henry Nevill, Earl of Abergavenny, is noted for having restored the ancestral home, Eridge in Sussex; of him and his son and heir, John, born on Christmas Day 1789 more in the next chapter.[3]

Lords of the Manor of Washingford

The lord of the Manor of Washingford when the eighteenth century dawned was John Cooke, son of Gregory of (what later became) Washingford House. John lived with his wife, Elizabeth (née Athow), at one or other of the Bergh Apton properties he had inherited along with the manor in 1680; however, it has not been established whether he occupied (what became) Gravel Pit Farm, or Mere Farm (where the early house was demolished in the twentieth century).

John Cooke died intestate in 1736. The heir to his property, and to the lordship of Washingford, was his son, John, who had been born in 1686. The latter dictated his will as gentleman of Bergh Apton on 18 September 1739, leaving his property in Bergh Apton

The coat of arms of the Cooke family on the ledger stone of Frances Cooke in the nave of the Parish Church.

and Thurton, including the Manor of Washingford, to his mother, Elizabeth, and her assigns for the term of her widowhood, although charged with the payment of his debts and legacies. The testator died early in 1740, and it was on 15 February of that year that the executor, Christopher Athow of Brooke, renounced the execution of his will. The latter's sister Elizabeth Cooke, mother of the deceased, also renounced as next of kin, but asked for the execution to be granted to her son's cousin, Thomas. The latter accepted this responsibility, and was sworn to perform it on the same day.[4]

According to the calendar of the Denny-Cooke manuscripts in the Norfolk Record Office, Samuel Rix of Denton, cheese factor (one likely to have been the chief creditor of the deceased John Cooke), Elizabeth Cooke of Bergh Apton (widow, mother of the deceased), and Thomas Cooke, gentleman, of Bergh Apton (his cousin), together conveyed his lands in Bergh Apton and Thurton to Robert Stone of Bedingham, gentleman, on 10 March 1740. Given the latter wrote his own will a week later, without mentioning any property in Bergh Apton and Thurton, and that he had died by 28 April 1740 when his will[5] was proved it would appear that he had in the week between taking up the aforesaid estate and writing his will reconveyed it to Thomas Cooke alone. Elizabeth Cooke, widow, died in 1746.

Thomas Cooke of what might validly be referred to as Washingford House from 1740, for he then became lord of Washingford Manor, had been born about 1697, given his age at death. He had in fact inherited Washingford House at the death of his father, Gregory, in 1705, until he came of age it was held in trust for him by his uncle, Charles Cooke.[6]

Thomas Cooke and his wife Ann had two children at Washingford House: Frances and Thomas were respectively baptised at Bergh Apton church on 10 December 1746 and 12 September 1750. Ann was buried there on 13 May 1766, her husband likewise on 1 October 1771. Thomas Cooke had written his will on 25 September 1767, by which time his son and namesake was the only other surviving male member of this family. Bearing in mind this situation, he divided his estate as follows: (what later became) Gravel Pit Farm, with a nearby cottage, to his daughter, Frances; the Manor of Washingford, the Washingford House estate, Mere Farm (as it was to become), lands in Hellington and Thurton, and his goods, chattels and personal estate to his son, Thomas.[7]

Thomas Cooke, who came into his father's estate in 1771, likewise occupied Washingford House in person. He married Elizabeth, daughter of Robert Grimer, gentleman, of and at Seething on 2 January 1792, and by whom he had two children who survived infancy: Frances, baptised at Bergh Apton on 29 September 1793; and Thomas, born there on 16 April 1796.

The Gentrification of Washingford House

In the previous chapter Washingford House was considered as an example of vernacular architecture, although other than in respect of its eastern stack, it now displays few obvious manifestations of sixteenth and seventeenth-century work. The reason for this is in part due to 'gentrification' of the house in the early-eighteenth century, a process shortly to be described, and in part due to a further rebuild in 1861. It is apparent on stylistic grounds that considerable alterations took place at Washingford House in the early-eighteenth century; moreover, it is unlikely that this work would have been carried out prior to about 1718, for it was only then that Thomas Cooke came of age and fully entered into his inheritance here. Stylistically, it is unlikely that the work was done after 1740, hence at least a few years prior to the owner's marriage to Ann Sherwood of Bergh Apton on 19 June 1745 at St John Maddermarket, Norwich.

The rebuilding of Washingford House more than doubled its accommodation. In outline, the new extensions appeared simple enough: parallel, two-storey wings projecting from the rear of the house. In effect, the interconnections required in the marrying of the old and new parts were considerable; indeed, this may have been why the bulk of its original brick structure, other than the stacks, had to be replaced. The east wing was constructed to form a hall, this having a wide external doorway superseding the baffle entry of the seventeenth century, and resulting in that feature becoming an internal door. To the rear of the hall was a further room, while again within the hall a stair rose. The west wing contained (as it does in 2004) the kitchen, secondary stair, and ancillary accommodation. The new first-floor accommodation essentially comprised a stairwell and two bedrooms within each wing.

Further to the alterations to Washingford House as just described, and in accordance with the prevailing architectural spirit, its main range, hitherto thatched given the nature of the axial stacks, was pantiled to match the two new wings, and it was refenestrated with sashes – of which the ones then inserted still survive in the west window of the south-western bedroom. Also contemporary are the false blocked-window recesses on the north face of each bay. Interestingly, the features just discussed partly accord with those at The Rectory when it was 'gentrified' between 1719 and 1725, to be considered later.

The Manor of Washingford

Court books for the Manor of Washingford have survived back to 1750. Unlike the Manor of Bergh Apton, the capital manor, the lordship of Washingford had no attendant authority within the parish, such as the appointment of constables and haywards.

Consequently, at least from 1750, its records indicate that it only held a Court Baron, and that solely when there was a need to record deaths of its copyhold tenants, and the transfer of copyhold land. John Van Kamp, gentleman, was the steward of Washingford, at least for the period 1750–1799. Otherwise, its courts were normally only attended by two tenants, assembled as the homage: Thomas Hase and Catherine Fenn thus attended on 27 July 1750, and Gardiner Utting and John Barber on 13 May 1799.

Bergh Apton Manor

A quarter-mile to the north-west of Washingford House, what is now Bergh Apton Manor was the home of the Denny family. The eighteenth century opened with this house being owned and occupied by John Denny, his wife Parnell, and their children – they had ten between 1693 and about 1706, of whom three died in infancy. John had inherited a house that one would assume was unchanged in essence since that built in the sixteenth century. Given what can be gathered of it from a probate inventory drafted in 1774, it would appear (from the evidence of known analogies) that the three-cell house as described in 1593 was subjected to rather more 'gentrification' as was the case with Washingford House and The Rectory in the early-eighteenth century, and may even have experienced a near complete rebuild then. On the other hand, the analysis of the early-eighteenth-century house, as detailed below, can in respect of its three main sections accommodate the likelihood that they were analogous to the three of that of the sixteenth century. The suspicion is that the

rebuild was carried out in the lifetime of John Denny, who was to be buried at Bergh Apton on 22 December 1723. Should the house have had such an extensive rebuild later than this, it is unlikely that the need would have arisen for a further more or less complete programme of rebuilding between 1825 and 1839. It should be noted now that John Denny's heir in 1723 was his then eldest surviving son, Freeman, who died without issue in 1745. He was succeeded by his younger brother, Richard. It was the latter who died as owner of the house under consideration in 1774, and in respect of whose estate the probate inventory was drafted.

The rooms of Bergh Apton Manor as detailed in the probate inventory of 1774

Bakehouse	Kitchen Chamber
Dairy	Menservants' Chamber
Scullery	Iron Garret
Kitchen	Parlour Chamber
Small Beer Cellar	Small Chamber
Mild Beer Cellar	Hall Chamber
Old Beer Cellar	Pantry Chamber
Hall	Maidservants' Chamber
Parlour	Corn Chamber
Pantry	Staircase
Bakehouse Chamber	

It is known from later map evidence (1801–1825) that this house lay on a west to east axis, while in 1774 its main ground-floor rooms were parlour, hall and kitchen, with the ancillary/service accommodation of pantry, scullery and bakehouse undoubtedly to the

The west façade of Bergh Apton Manor with a carriage outside the front door in the early 1900s. The room on the left was the music room, no longer there (see p.73); it used to house an organ.

rear (north side), probably under an outshut or catslide roof. A three-cell cellar lay beneath the house. The first floor had three principal rooms, the chambers over the parlour, hall and kitchen; and it would appear that the bakehouse, small, maidservants' and pantry chambers fitted beneath the outshut or catslide roof over the ground-floor ancillary/service accommodation. Three rooms lay within the attic space: one only described as a garret – the iron garret – plus the menservants' and corn chambers. The site of the staircase within the house cannot be suggested with too much confidence; it is unlikely to have risen by a stack, for it was large enough (that is with landings) to house two clocks, two chairs, a trunk and four pictures. The heated rooms, those with fireplaces, in 1774 were the three main rooms on the ground floor, but only the parlour and hall chambers above. The latter fact leads to the conclusion that the hall and parlour flues lay back to back, forming a large axial stack, while a simple stack rose from the kitchen – probably against the wall dividing that room from the hall. The house was well furnished. The hall included amongst other things a bureau, three tables, two armchairs and seven small chairs; the parlour's contents included two tables, three armchairs and six small chairs, all of mahogany, a small pier glass, 14 pictures and a 'bath stove'. We learn that the bed and bedstead in the parlour chamber had green hangings, while in the hall chamber the hangings were blue, and in the pantry chamber they were yellow.

The only surviving son of Richard and his wife Ann, (née Bernard), and heir to the Denny estate in 1774, was also named Richard. He was baptised at Bergh Apton church on 16 August 1754. The younger Richard married Mary, daughter of Roger Kerrison, at Kirstead, her birthplace, in 1783. The first two of this couple's children died in infancy; the others, born at Bergh Apton, were as follows: Mary Ann, born 30 December 1787; Richard, born 21 December 1789; and Elizabeth Mary, born 29 May 1792.

Richard Denny served as churchwarden at Bergh Apton church from 1775 until 1793. He was to be buried here on 17 February 1794, and his monumental inscription was the first of the family here to bear arms, although his forebears back to his great-great-grandfather had adopted the appellation of gentleman. A proven link has yet to be established between the armigerous Dennys of Great Yarmouth, Raveningham and Toft Monks, and the Bergh Apton family. He was not only survived by his mother, who died at Bergh Apton in 1796, but also by his wife who was to remain a widow for 52 years. Notwithstanding the survival of his wife and mother, in his will he appointed his executors Matthias Kerrison of Bungay, merchant, and Alderman John Buckle of Norwich, guardians of his children – of whom his son, Richard, was to inherit the Bergh Apton estate upon his coming-of-age.[8]

Street Farm/Apton Manor

As for Street Farm, later called Apton Manor, the Athow family remained in residence until 1736. The occupation of this house with its farm remains unclear from then until 1776, from which time it was tenanted. No 'gentrification' of the house would appear to have occurred here in the eighteenth century, although it has to be borne in mind that it had been extended on more than one occasion in the previous century.

Bergh Apton Park/Bergh Apton Hall

William Doyly, gentleman of Brooke and owner of Bergh Apton Park, was buried at Bergh Apton on 17 December 1710. He died intestate, and ten days after his burial administration of his goods and chattels was granted to his widow, Anne.[9] William had left as his heir his son, Thomas, baptised at Brooke on 28 March 1705, and hence a minor. The body of Bergh Apton Hall, the dwelling associated with the park, bears stylistic indications of having been built, apparently with at least the considerable influence of an architect, during the reign of Anne (1702–1714).[10]

Bergh Apton Hall is a red-brick house, having a steeply pitched, hipped and pantile roof. Two chimney-stacks are placed symmetrically on the ridgeline. The house is comprised of two storeys plus an attic. Its north façade is of seven bays with

The coat of arms of the Kett family on a tomb in the churchyard.

the dividing pilasters having moulded brick capitals. It has a central doorway, over which the first-floor window is square-headed with rusticated quoins and a flat-keyed rubbed brick arch. Internally, there is a good contemporary staircase. We should not regard this house as an example of mere 'gentrification' of the previous one on the site; it was clearly constructed as a discrete dwelling. What is now its west wing – 'long room' – that was initially retained for ancillary accommodation serves to remind us of a part (or maybe even the whole) of what had been a house here dating from the second quarter of the seventeenth century.

It is not known when and where the widowed Anne Doyly died. Her son Thomas married Martha, daughter and heir of Thomas French of Hempnall, in 1740, although where this marriage took place has yet to be identified. This couple had three sons at Bergh Apton: Thomas, William and Henry, respectively baptised in 1744, 1746 and 1747. In 1829, J. Chambers noted that this family moved from Bergh Apton to Hempnall when William was aged four, hence about 1750.[11] The accounts for the Manor of Bergh Apton from 1753 and the rental of 1766 both confirm the date given by J. Chambers for Thomas Doyly's departure, and indicate that he sold his Bergh Apton estate to William Fellowes Esq. of Shotesham St Mary and Lincoln's Inn, London. In any case, for some reason, this sale took place in 1749, whereupon Fellowes let the property for a further year to its vendor for £120;[12] maybe the latter decided he needed further time to prepare his intended home at Hempnall for his family's arrival.

William Fellowes, who founded the Norfolk and Norwich Hospital in 1771, died in 1775 having left the Bergh Apton Hall estate to his son and heir, Robert.[13] Shortly afterwards Robert sold it to Thomas Kett, (one admitted to those parts of it which were copyhold of Bergh Apton in 1777). Kett, a banker, and his descendants were to own this property until it was sold by Lord Canterbury in 1919. The hall itself was successively occupied by the following tenants: Thomas Bound, gentleman, from 1751 until his death in 1760; his widow Sarah until her death in 1775; and their son Edward until his death on 6 January 1801.

Arson at Town Farm

John Riches, who became the Town Farm tenant in 1783, was to witness dramatic events here. The Feoffees' accounts dated 31 October 1796 record:

Expenses of the several Witnesses to Thetford on the Prosecution of Martha Dawson for setting Fire to the Town Farm Barn &c, for the Indictment, Swearing Witnesses &c £14.6s.10½d.

This statement initially appears straightforward, yet in the light of having investigated it, matters of substance that it might have illuminated remain unclear. First, it would appear to record a suit brought to the Assizes (held in Lent) at Thetford. Yet, a search of the records of these from 1794 to 1797 uncovered no account of this case. As arson was then a capital offence, it may be that the case was dropped as the evidence against the accused was not considered watertight: while these times are often (and frequently rightly) viewed as the 'bad old days', most juries would not have found against such accused persons and hence have them sent to the gallows unless their guilt were indisputable.

We also have to ask what precisely was burnt at the Town Farm, and when did this fire occur. The lack of a comma between 'Farm' and 'Barn' in the above quotation might suggest that the barn and not the farmhouse was set alight – the '&c' following 'Barn' presumably related to other farm buildings.[14] However, there are grounds for supposing that the farmhouse was at least badly damaged, for the accounts which recorded the fire also noted the rebuilding of the house as well as the barn over a period of two years from Easter 1795. While the expenses concerning the prosecution of Martha Dawson were not entered until 31 October 1796, one can only assume that the Feoffees had their own reasons for delaying such a payment.

Bergh Apton's First Public House

A house which no longer exists, but which stood from the eighteenth century (if not earlier) until at least 1914 must not be overlooked in the story of Bergh Apton. This was the first-known public house in the village, to which reference is primarily made in deeds in the Denny-Cooke manuscripts. Situated some 200yds west of Bergh Apton Manor, on the

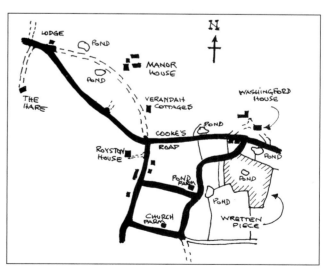

Fig.11.1. The site of The Hare and Royston House. The latter was its successor as a licensed premises for a short time in the late-eighteenth century before becoming a dwelling. Also shown is the changed route of Bergh Apton's principal street after Mr Denny's works of 1853 (see p.91).

edge of the pre-Inclosure Apton Heath, this had been known as the Adam and Eve over an unspecified period prior to 1767. By the 3 July of that year it had come to be called The Hare and was owned by Dr John Beevor of Norwich. Subsequently, it passed into the ownership of Edward Upton, gentleman, of Bergh Apton, who died on 7 May 1795. By then, the sign of The Hare had been transferred from this site to the building known in 2004 as Royston House; the Alehouse Recognizance for 1794 recorded the occupier of this as Thomas Boyce,[15] while deed evidence is that it was then owned by Richard Denny, who in fact died in that year, having left the bulk of his estate in trust to his son and namesake, then a minor. Boyce actually occupied Royston House from 1791 to 1824, according to the overseers' accounts; however, the sign of The Hare is unlikely to have hung here as late as 1803, as Boyce's dwelling was not described as a public house then in the *State of the Claims*, published at the behest of the Inclosure commissioners.

Eighteenth-Century Rectors

As for rectors of Bergh Apton in the eighteenth century, with the end of Robert Connold's long incumbency in 1715, there ensued an unsettled time for the parishioners. When a terrier was prepared on 26 June 1716, there was no rector; the spiritual care of the parish was entrusted to a priest-in-charge, Richard Newman, while a sequestrator, John Kerridge, took care of the glebe. Thomas Dunch was presented to the living in 1717, only to relinquish it two years later. In 1719, Richard French became rector of Bergh Apton.

The Rectory

French was a member of the gentry, and certainly wealthy – given the extent and nature of the work he was to carry out at The Rectory, rebuilding it to serve as a home of refinement. He did not entirely appreciate the value of the house as it stood when he commenced his incumbency. He demolished what is believed to have been the southern parlour section, and downgraded the rest of the building to serve exclusively as service accommodation. Terriers from 1725 to 1827 describe the surviving part of what one can construe as the late-medieval house at various lengths, but it seems to have stood as most fully described in those from 1791 as follows:

An older building adjoining thereto with chambers over the same being 28' x 27' with a tiled roof and mud walls used as a kitchen, washhouse and pantry.

I suspect that the term 'mud walls' is more likely to relate to wattle and daub construction than to clay lump. The terrier of 1725 recorded what French had 'new built' as 'consisting of sundry lower and upper rooms'; however, it was left to the terrier of 1729 to be more informative about the newly erected section: 'Mansion house consisting of a hall, parlour, kitchen, buttery, with planchered rooms over'.[16] At the time of writing, this house is called the Bergh Apton Stud.

The section of the house rebuilt by French essentially survives and, indeed, is its oldest surviving part. It is of solid classical design, somewhat novel for a period when houses were still being built with baroque features. The structure is brick with a pantiled roof; colour washed and partly rendered walls. A portico porch juts out from the centre of the west wall – which wall bears symmetrically placed sashes, each with nine lights. The west window on the ground floor at the southern end of the house is blocked, this more likely an architectural conceit than a device to avoid window tax. Much of the glass in these windows is original.

The upper window third from the south (not counting that over the portico) deserves special mention. Here, scratched with a diamond from the outside (and hence reading mirror-fashion internally), is the legend:

A Lovely Girl M. Hutchinson Dec 31 1752/3
[L]ove, Honour & Friendship A French

While this might suggest that Hutchinson was the lady, in actuality the opposite was the case. Hutchinson was the author of this inscription, presumably scratched during a clandestine climb as the last hours (or minutes) of 1752 ticked away. 'A French' was Anne, the rector's youngest daughter, then aged 23. It has been established that she was not to marry her impudent yet daring visitor. *The Norwich Mercury* of 25 March 1797 noted: 'Died a few days since, at Tivetshall aet. 68, Mrs Baxster, youngest daughter of the late Revd Richard French of Bergh Apton'. Unfortunately, this unusual memento of a long-ago courtship has been sullied: lower down the pane upon which Hutchinson scratched his message, an insensitive, twentieth-century hand, perhaps that of an evacuee child of the Second World War, has etched an aeroplane and two dogs' heads!

The west wall of the c.1720 work is now the only one to stand as built: the north wall then abutted onto the older section of the house and now abuts onto a later extension; the south wall bears an early-nineteenth-century bay and in any case was then extended eastwards; the east wall is now an interior one.

Within the c.1720 section, were four ground-floor rooms: hall, parlour, kitchen and buttery – the latter described as a pantry in the terrier of 1740, and apparently merged with the kitchen by that of 1747. Over these, the upper floor had 'good planchered' rooms. Other features ordered by Richard French include the stairwell, lit by octagonally set lights of plain glass, centred by a red glass 'eye', and the brass door furniture.

The memorial stone to Richard French who died on 8 November 1764 and to Jane, his second wife, who died on 13 January 1800. Richard French was the next longest serving rector of this parish with 45 years service – just short of Robert Connold's remarkable record.

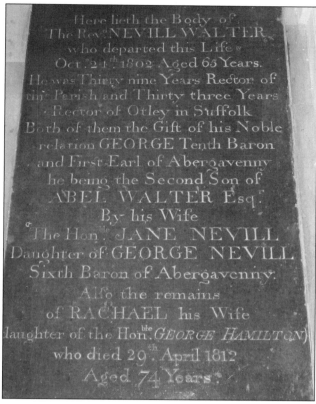

Revd Nevill Walter was rector of Bergh Apton from 1765 to 1802. This is his gravestone, under the altar, that records the gift of George 10th Baron and 1st Earl Abergavenny who was patron of the living. Nevill Walter's incumbency of this parish was concurrent with that in another, Otley in Suffolk.

Stable accommodation at a rectory was only to be expected, indeed it was first recorded here in 1606. As if to reflect the gentry status of Richard French, it comes as no surprise that two stables were listed in the terrier of 1740, while a coach-house had been built by 1747. Terriers from 1784 state that the stables and coach-house had been fashioned from the second barn, which French, not a farming rector, would have found superfluous to his requirements.

Richard French was buried at Bergh Apton on 8 November 1764. There was a short interval before his successor, Nevill Walter, was presented to this living in 1765. He was the son of Jane Nevill, daughter of Lord George Bergavenny, who died in 1721, by her marriage to John Abel Walter. Jane, only child of Nevill Walter and his wife Rachel, married the Revd Robert Churchman Kellett, rector of Illington and Newton Flotman, in 1794. Towards the end of Nevill Walter's incumbency, he took to employing officiating ministers or curates. This signified that Bergh Apton's parson had become even more of a gentleman of leisure than his contemporary, the diarist of Weston Longville. Nevill Walter died in 1802 at the age of 65.

Nevill Walter presented Bergh Apton church with a paten, made by John Kidder in 1789;[17] however, this was to be sold, together with a cup and paten of 1675, as authorised by a faculty of 1931, in order to raise money for the bells to be rehung.[18]

Bergh Apton Parish Registers

Occasionally, the Bergh Apton parish registers included information beyond the basic records of baptisms, marriages and burials. Thus we read:

Marie & Sarah twins impos[e]d uppon Robert Hacon by a cheat of the Towne of Woodton procureing him to marry an ill woman big with child by an inhabitant of the s[ai]d Towne, & by a litle summ of money to free themselv[e]s from so ill a woman, & so great a charge; the children were baptised Novemb[e]r the 23[rd] [1701].

Churchwardens' Accounts

After a break of 40 years, the run of Bergh Apton churchwardens' accounts resumed at Easter 1721. Here follows a selection of entries from these, giving a flavour of eighteenth-century life in the parish:[19]

In the year 1721–2 amongst other things, Christopher Athow, churchwarden, accounted for:

Two barrels [of beer] when the bells were hung: 5s.
For pipes and tobacco at that time: 1s.
To Simon Reyner for cutting the church bushes: 2s.

In the year 1730–31, Christopher Athow and John Cooke likewise accounted for:

Gave to fifteen of the slaves redeemed out of slavery: 5s.
Gave to three more of them: 1s.6d.

For fencing the churchyard: 8s.
For mending the church door: 1s.6d.
Paid to William Collins for mending the barn and stable [at the Town Farm]: 10s.

In the year 1740–1, Thomas Doyly likewise accounted for:

To my journey to Norwich at the Bishop's Visitation: 2s.d.
To nine poor sufferers by sea: 1s.6d.
Paid for stubbing and clearing the churchyard of bushes: 2s.

In the year 1750–1, Richard Denny likewise accounted for:

Paid six travellers allowed to pass: 1s.
Bought three locks for the church gate: 9d.
Paid Mr French Rector for making out a bill for the Register of Births Weddings and Burials for two years until Lady [Day] 1750: 5s.

In the year 1760–1, Samuel Caley and Richard Denny likewise accounted for:

Paid Isaac Dann for seven days work and a half in drawing [dredging] one side of the Beck between Barrow Common and Rush Fenn belonging to Brooke Hall at 1s.4d a day: 10s.
For making a new [glebe] terrier: £1.1s.
A journey to the Bishop's Visitation: 2s.
Paid fees there: 9s.
The carpenter's bill for work done at the Town Farm: £2.19s.8d.

In the year 1770–1, Richard Denny and Edward Bound likewise accounted for:

Paid for three locks for the church chest: 2s.6d.
Paid Mr Walter for a book of homilies and a hood: £1.8s.
For washing the surplice three times: 7s.6d.

For fencing against the churchyard: 1s.

In the year 1780–1, Richard Denny and Mr [Edward] Bound likewise accounted for:

Constable[s'] bill and levy money: £4.3s.4d.
Mr Caley's bill for malt: £1.8s.6d.
Land Tax [for the Town] Farm: £3.16s.
[For killing] 37 dozen sparrows: 6s.2d.

Overseers' Accounts

A less informative source compared with the church-wardens' accounts, but still useful, the Bergh Apton overseers' accounts survive from 1779. In the year 1795/96, Mrs Mary Denny, overseer of the poor (which position was then rarely held by a woman), accounted for the following, amongst other items of expenditure:

To the [Heckingham] House [of Industry] with Bircham's wife and child: 1s 6d.
Sent to the [Norfolk and Norwich] Hospital Widow Fish with a fractured arm: 1s 6d.
Making rates and entering accounts: 5s.

The Town House

The same Mary Denny was the widow of Richard Denny who died in 1794. It was her husband who had built 'the town-house on the common', given the context in which it was mentioned in the *State of the Claims*, printed in 1803 in association with the Inclosure commissioners' proceedings. The precise spot where this Town House was erected is unclear. It would have been used to house certain pauper inhabitants of Bergh Apton, and maybe putting them to useful tasks, instead of sending them to the Loddon and Clavering House of Industry, established at Heckingham in 1762. Matthias Kerrison guardian of Richard Denny, son of the aforesaid Richard and Mary, and a minor in 1803, held this property on his behalf.

References
[1] Vicary Gibbs (ed.) *Complete Peerage* (London, St Catherine Press, 1910), vol.1.
[2] *Ibid.*
[3] *Ibid.*
[4] NRO: ANF 1738/9 O.W.182.
[5] NRO: NCC 1740 f.65 Goats.
[6] Evidence of Bergh Apton Court Books; NRO: NRA 43876 Gilbert.
[7] NRO: ANF 1771 f.113.
[8] NRO: ANF 1794 f.164.
[9] NRO: ANF Admon. 1710–4 no.61.
[10] Proof is lacking, but I strongly suspect that this work was under way about the time that William died; more-over, once it was completed, his widow and son – plus a daughter, Dorothy, whose existence is known from the genealogy, although her baptismal record has not been located – moved here from Brooke.
[11] John Chambers, *General History of the County of Norfolk* (Norwich, John Stacy, 1829), vol.1, p.82.
[12] NRO: FEL382.
[13] NRO: FEL778.
[14] Encountering a lack of precision in the use of punctuation marks in the late-eighteenth century is not unexpected.
[15] NRO: C/Sch/1/16.
[16] NRO: DN/TER 15.
[17] E.C. Hopper, 'Church Plate in the Deanery of West Brooke,' in *Norfolk Archaeology* (Norwich, Norfolk and Norwich Archaelogical Society, 1910), vol.7.
[18] NRO: PD 497/13/6.
[19] NRO: PD497/25.

Chapter XII
The Nineteenth Century

During the course of the nineteenth century, Bergh Apton changed in rather more ways than it had done in any single century since the time it was first chronicled. Generalisations can at the worst appear fatuous; yet, it would probably be true to say that in certain respects between 1801 and 1900, it acquired features of palpable modernity, such as compact farm units, a school, a Post Office, a parish council, and regular horse-drawn transport facilities. Indeed, there are so many themes, which cannot be ignored over this period, that in some ways it is hard to choose how best to present them. The enduring institution of Bergh Apton's church with its rectors, the Manors with their lords and the 'gentrification' of their homes, will be dealt with initially. A member of the Denny family did not acquire the Manor of Bergh Apton until 1869, but it suits the course of the narrative to consider the Denny family throughout the nineteenth century within this context. Then follows the story of Inclosure, and its many far-reaching consequences, and that of Tithe Apportionment; each particularly and inevitably linked with farming, land ownership and occupation. We will then look at population statistics, housing, and further 'gentrification'. Provisions for the social needs of the inhabitants will be outlined, especially education, the postal service, shop keeping, and transport, while the significance of Bergh Apton Parish Council will be assessed.

Rectors of Bergh Apton

The nineteenth century opened with Nevill Walter serving as rector of Bergh Apton. He died on 24 October 1802 at the age of 65; and, until his successor was presented to the living towards the end of 1803, an officiating minister by the name of Ralph Hopper served the spiritual needs of the parishioners. In any case Augustus Beevor, rector from then until his death in 1818, generally delegated his responsibilities to a curate throughout his incumbency.

Rectors of Bergh Apton during the first half of the nineteenth century submitted details concerning their parishioners to the Archdeacon of Norfolk, as witness the Visitation Books. Nevill Walter reported in 1801 that 'many common people attend the Anabaptist Meeting at Claxton and other places'.[1]

The Hon. John Nevill's submission in 1820 was that 'thirty poor Methodists [from Bergh Apton] assemble at Claxton'.[2] In 1838, the Hon. John Thomas Pelham noted that his parish included 'one Roman Catholic and twenty-four dissenting families, diminishing of late'; yet 14 years later he felt obliged to report that

This illustration from 1824, drawn by John Berney Ladbrooke, is the earliest known image of Bergh Apton church, and shows the chancel built in Connold's time, including his priest's door.

Claxton chapel was the place of worship attended by dissenting parishioners of Bergh Apton. It was some three miles north of Bergh Apton and would have involved them in a long walk there and back, probably several times each Sunday. The house is now the home of Richard White and the base for Claxton Opera.

there were 'a considerable number of dissenters'.[3]

Two members of the Nevill family were Beevor's immediate successors. The Hon. John Nevill was rector from 1818, but from August 1827 consistently used the services of an officiating minister. He served simultaneously as the rector of Otley in Suffolk. John Nevill, born on Christmas Day 1789, was the son of George Nevill, Earl of Abergavenny, and in due course he inherited his father's lordship of Bergh Apton. John Nevill's first cousin, Henry Walpole Nevill, became rector of Bergh Apton in his place in 1831, and also used an officiating minister throughout his incumbency, which lasted until his death on 3 March 1837; he too was simultaneously rector of Otley.

Gentrification of The Rectory

This is a convenient place to look at the first nineteenth-century example of 'gentrification' with regard to houses in the village to be considered in this chapter. According to the terriers made between 1827 and 1834 The Rectory and its surrounds were contrived so as to take on the shape and appearance such as obtains for the most part today – this property known at the time of writing as Bergh Apton Stud. During this period the remaining part of what we might term the late-medieval house was demolished.[4]
Another building was demolished at that time and was described in terriers from 1791 to 1827 as:

An outhouse on a brickwork pinning, studded and boarded, externally 21'x 20', with a tiled roof, comprising a dairy and a chaise house with a chamber over the same.

The building just described would relate to the north-eastern wing of the house as it has been conceived to exist from the descriptions over the period 1606–1627. The 1834 terrier gives a detailed picture of the part of the house rebuilt by Richard French about the early 1720s, three new additions, and the still surviving outhouses.
I take these sections in turn, quoting from the terrier then adding relevant comments. First:

Brick built mansion house externally 38'x 27' with a tiled roof having a passage with a staircase therein and two rooms on the ground floor with chambers over them.

The above relates to the block rebuilt by Richard French. It infers that it had been altered between 1827 and 1834, for it has come to contain but two ground-floor rooms – the present-day hall and drawing room. Round-headed arcading in these rooms suggests a late-Georgian date, as does the fireplace in the hall. Its extension eastwards at least in this part of the house also occasioned extensive alterations to the décor – see the third section to be considered, below. In addition, a curved, single-storey brick bay was set into the south wall of French's block.
The second section of the 1834 terrier continues:

Also an addition thereto built externally 39'x 34' of brick and tiled in lieu of an old building taken down which was formerly used as a kitchen, washhouse and pantry, this new building being used as a kitchen, backhouse and servants' hall having chambers over the same and garrets.

This last extract closely corresponds with the appearance of this part of the house, as it exists today.
The third section of the 1834 terrier states:

Since 1827 an addition attatched to mansion house, 20'x 17' used as a dining-room with a sleeping room over, it also has a room 19'x 13' used as a study.

The above corresponds to Richard French's work of a century beforehand. However, the 1834 terrier neglected to state that this 'addition' was given a bow front similar to that added to the south front at this time, save that it is of two storeys.
The fourth section of the 1834 terrier reads:

And there has been erected [since 1827] a detatched building 44'x 17' used as a coach-house having a chamber over the same used as a laundry. All which additions are brick built and tiled and have been raised in [place] of the building described [in 1827] as a dairy and chaise-house with a chamber over the same [taken down since 1827].

The Hon. John Thomas Pelham
The Hon. John Thomas Pelham served as rector of Bergh Apton from 1837 to 1852. He had been born on 21 June 1811, the second son of the second Earl of Chichester. Whilst at Bergh Apton, he frequently delegated his spiritual responsibilities to an officiating minister or curate; indeed, he was absent from here when the census was taken on 6 June 1841, The Rectory then having been left in the occupation of six servants and a 'teacher'.[5] In 1847, Pelham was honoured by having been appointed chaplain to Queen Victoria – which post would clearly have required not-infrequent absences from Bergh Apton. All the same, in the census of 30 March 1851, he was indeed occupying The Rectory, together with his wife, Henrietta, their three children, two visitors and five servants.[6]
John Thomas Pelham's incumbency of Bergh Apton was particularly marked by the major works

John Thomas Pelham (1812–1894) who was Bishop of Norwich from 1857 until his death. This fine illustration of young Pelham hangs in the vestry of the Parish Church and probably dates from his time as rector of Bergh Apton (1838–1852). He and his wife are buried beside each other in the churchyard at Bergh Apton.

carried out at the church in 1838, as authorised by a faculty.[7] With the work partly subsidised by the sale of the lead from the roof, which was replaced with (cheaper) slate, and with further financial assistance from the Incorporated Society for Repairing Churches and Chapels, John Brown, the diocesan surveyor lowered the nave roof, remodelled the chancel and south transept, completely rebuilt the north transept, gave the transepts and nave 'Gothick' windows, rebuilt and extended the north porch to serve as a vestry, replaced the inner doors, and furnished the tower with its distinctive, brick and flint chequered battlements, brick corner finials and roll-top copings. The height of the tower consequent to these alterations became 65ft. Brown gave the chancel painted principal rafters, purloins and small collars, retimbered the crossing, and fitted each transept with a gallery. However these galleries were to be removed in 1881. The ceilings of the nave and transepts were so painted and grained in 1838 so as to give the appearance of wood, but they are actually formed of plaster. This ligniform work is considered by some to be unique. He was also responsible for the surviving west gallery, which has a solid balustrade with coloured, traceried panels. At the same time, Lady Amelia Pelham, sister

of the rector, presented the clock, which continues to grace the tower. The face of this clock is 9ft across diagonally, while its mechanism is driven by a weight of 3cwt. From Pelham's time, Bergh Apton church possesses a plated cup and paten dated 1849.[8]

John Thomas Pelham, who was Bishop of Norwich from 1857 to 1893, was buried at Bergh Apton on 5 May 1894.

> **Church Attendance Records**
> On Sunday 30 March 1851, a Religious Census was taken, of which the following attendance records were submitted by John Thomas Pelham in respect of Bergh Apton church:[9]
>   At morning service: 88 worshippers, plus 75 attending Sunday school.
>   At afternoon service: 145 worshippers, plus 57 attending Sunday school.

Wyndham Carlyon Madden

From 1852 until his death in May 1864, Wyndham Carlyon Madden was rector of Bergh Apton. He frequently used an officiating minister or curate to care for his parishioners' spiritual needs; indeed, he was away from The Rectory when the census was taken on 7 April 1861. He had left his home in the care of his unmarried sister, Sophia Macleod Madden. With her were his five daughters, a grand-daughter, a niece, a visitor, a governess, and five servants.[10] During Wyndham Carlyon Madden's incumbency, Bergh Apton church acquired a plate flagon dated bearing the date 'Xmas (*sic*) 1858'.[11]

William Ford Thursby

William Ford Thursby was Madden's successor as rector of Bergh Apton, enjoying this living until his own death in 1893. During his time here, he bore the cost of reseating the chancel in 1865 – these seats have since been removed – while the church as a whole was restored and reseated in 1881. This latter work included the removal of the galleries of 1838 in the transepts.[12] Other than this structural work at the church in 1881, Thursby 'and his friends', according to directory evidence, paid for an oak pulpit and reading desk, while he also had the south transept window reglazed by Ward and Hughes in 1885.

The churchyard was extended by one rood in 1880, this land having been given by Lord Canterbury of Brooke House.[13]

On 28 July 1873 the net income from the living of this parish was stated to be £581.16s.11d.; while on the following 5 September, William, 5th Earl of Abergavenny and his trustees conveyed:

All that Advowson, Patronage and Perpetual Right of Presentation to The Rectory and Parish Church of Bergh Apton [to the Revd William Thursby of Ormerod House, Burnley, Lancashire, for the sum of £5,000], subject to the incumbency of the [latter's son the] Rev. William Ford Thursby... who is now in his 42nd year.[14]

Madden's second wife Charlotte (née Leeke) from a daguerreotype from c.1865, in the possession of John Madden.

Wyndam Carlyon Madden, rector from 1852 to 1864, portrayed in an oil painting in the possession of his descendant John Madden.

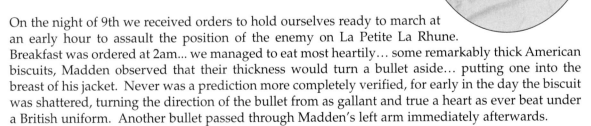

Right: Madden as a young Army officer in the 1820s. In 1852 he was presented to the living of Bergh Apton by Lord Abergavenny, his wife's uncle. He was instituted by the Bishop of Norwich on 27 December 1852 and inducted by Revd Richard Cooke Denny on 30 December. Madden was born on 31 August 1793 in the Madras Presidency, educated at Westminster School and joined the 43rd Regiment of Foot when only 14 years old. He served throughout the Peninsular War, then entered Queen's College Cambridge in 1820 and was ordained priest in 1823. An account of his wounding in the Battle of the Nivelle is recorded in the Historical Records of 43rd Regiment, *published in 1868:*

On the night of 9th we received orders to hold ourselves ready to march at an early hour to assault the position of the enemy on La Petite La Rhune. Breakfast was ordered at 2am… we managed to eat most heartily… some remarkably thick American biscuits, Madden observed that their thickness would turn a bullet aside… putting one into the breast of his jacket. Never was a prediction more completely verified, for early in the day the biscuit was shattered, turning the direction of the bullet from as gallant and true a heart as ever beat under a British uniform. Another bullet passed through Madden's left arm immediately afterwards.

Prior to this Madden had been wounded in his right shoulder at Badajos, an engagement in which his brother William had been killed. His family in Canada still has the musket ball with which he had been wounded. Later in the campaign his half-brother Colonel Henry Ridewood was killed and, later still, so was his brother Edward. Hugh Wilkinson who is Madden's descendant wrote in 2002: 'I am sure these bitter blows and his attempts to understand how God would allow them to happen, influenced him in deciding to take Holy Orders.' Madden preached a moving sermon, of which the text still exists, at the presentation of new Colours to his old regiment on 22 March 1847. He is buried in Bergh Apton churchyard along with three of his children who died in infancy and his niece Henrietta, the daughter and only child of his half-brother Henry Ridewood.

Revd William Ford Thursby, rector of Bergh Apton from 1864 to 1893.

this sum was to be distributed annually at their discretion in coal amongst the poor of the parish.

Thomas Fraser Lloyd

Thomas Fraser Lloyd had served as William Ford Thursby's curate since 1884, and upon the death of his employer was presented to the living of Bergh Apton in his stead. He was the first incumbent here for about a century that did not delegate his spiritual duties – which 'personal ministry' policy was followed by all of his successors. His incumbency was further marked by the insertion of the north window, portraying the Good Shepherd, by Ward and Hughes in 1896, dedicated to the memory of William Ford Thursby by his widow. Lloyd left Bergh Apton to become rector of Bramerton in 1897.

Harvey William Gustavus Thursby

In place of Thomas Fraser Lloyd, Harvey William Gustavus Thursby became rector of Bergh Apton. He was the nephew of William Ford Thursby, and was to serve as the incumbent here until 1920. With regard to the Parish Church itself, at the end of the nineteenth century the roof was being repaired in 1898, mural decorations were added to the chancel in 1899, all at the expense of Miss Fanny Charlotte Thursby, the rector's sister. Norman and Beard of Norwich placed a new organ in the gallery in 1900 at a cost of £400.

The purchaser was actually a first cousin of the 5th Earl's maternal grandmother, Honor (née Thursby) Leeke, and hence was the Earl's first cousin twice removed.[15]

William Ford Thursby generally employed a curate to carry out his spiritual duties at Bergh Apton. Interestingly, the census of 3 April 1881 revealed that his then curate, George E.C. Stiles, who lived at The Hollies, Bergh Apton, had been born in New South Wales, Australia, about 1836.[16] During Thursby's time at The Rectory, he extended the kitchen north of the dining-room outwards in the form of a two-storey, wooden bay; moreover a conservatory was constructed outwards from the east wall of the dining-room, although the evidence of the Ordnance Survey reveals that this was demolished by 1961.

In the census taken on 2 April 1871, and in that held on 3 April 1881, William Ford Thursby and his wife Fanny were absent from The Rectory, and it was respectively occupied by five, then by four servants.[17] In the census of 5 April 1891, Thursby was indeed in residence here, and was enumerated with his wife and six servants.[18] He died on 8 May 1893, having left in his will £600 in trust with the rector and churchwardens. The income arising from

Revd Harvey W.G. Thursby, rector of Bergh Apton from 1897 to 1920.

The interior of the church in 1922. This postcard shows the decorative fleurs-de-lys painted in the chancel in 1899, the costs of which were met by Miss Fanny Charlotte Thursby, sister of Harvey W.G. Thursby. They were over-painted only in the 1950s. Also clearly visible are the flags that bedecked the chancel at that time as a permanent feature clearly recalled in 1999 by the late Herbert Boggis.

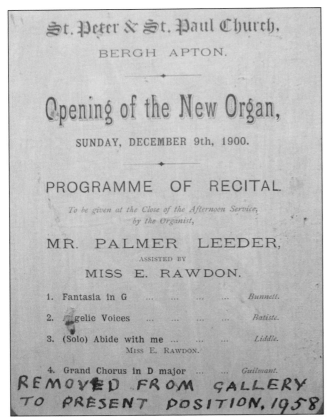

The printed programme, glued to the inside of the organ case, is of a recital given by organist Palmer Leeder and his pupil Miss Rawden to mark the commissioning of a new Norman & Beard organ donated by public subscription in 1900. On completion of a major overhaul in the last year of the twentieth century, the instrument returned to service exactly 100 years to the day of its first perform-ance. That evening Richard Bower (who carried out the restoration) gave a recital that included some of the pieces performed in 1900.

The organist Palmer Leeder (left) and his descendant John Garrett, portrayed in a small locket worn by John's wife Sally.

Palmer Leeder, the parish organist, gave a concert to celebrate its installation on 9 December that year. Additionally in 1899, William Ford Thursby's widow presented a silver-gilt jewelled chalice and paten, and a silver-mounted glass flagon in his memory. Hart, Peard & Co. of Birmingham had made this set in 1874.[19]

The Manor of Bergh Apton

Henry Nevill, 2nd Earl of Abergavenny was the lord of the Manor of Bergh Apton when the nineteenth century opened. He died on 27 March 1843, and was succeeded by his son John as 3rd Earl.[20] As we have seen, the latter, as Revd the Hon. John Nevill, had served as rector of Bergh Apton from 1818 to 1831. However, John, 3rd Earl Abergavenny, was not to enjoy the lordship of Bergh Apton for long, as he died on 12 April 1845.

His heir as 4th Earl was his brother William, who had been born on 28 June 1792. William had married Caroline, daughter of Ralph Leeke and his wife Honor, the latter the only daughter of Walter Harvey Thursby.[21] William Nevill, Earl of Abergavenny, died on 17 August 1868. His son and heir, also William, who had been born on 16 September 1826, conse-quently succeeded to the title as 5th Earl and at the same time became lord of the Manor of Bergh Apton.[22] Having acquired this lordship amongst his estates, he shortly afterwards resolved to sell it, and accordingly had it valued by Mr Rolla Rouse. Rouse considered it to be worth £1,069.9s.9d., that is excepting the Mill House which was then on lease, with about 30 – [free and copyhold] – tenants. He advised a reserve of £950, and did not think it would fetch more than £1,050.[23]

Annotations on a copy in the East Sussex Record Office of the Particulars and Conditions of Sale of the

[Earl of Abergavenny's] Norfolk Estate, auctioned by Mr Phillips at the Royal Hotel, Norwich, in 44 lots on 5 August 1869, reveal that the Manor of Bergh with Apton, Lot 42 in the sale, was purchased by the Revd Richard Cooke Denny for £1,320; moreover, that the conveyance of this manor to him was dated 11 November 1869. The latter was the owner-occupier of what then became known as Bergh Apton Manor: it would suit the course of this narrative if we next consider the story of this house and its Denny owners from the beginning of the nineteenth century.

The Denny Family

At the turn of the nineteenth century Richard Denny, a minor under the guardianship of his late father's executors,[24] was heir to the estate based upon what would become Bergh Apton Manor. He became of age and able to act in accordance with his own wishes on 21 December 1810. As if it were a comment on the troubled times, as well as upon Richard Denny's standing in the locality, he was commissioned as a lieutenant in the Loddon troop of Yeomanry Cavalry on 6 June 1812 (see opposite). Later, between 1836 and 1845,[25] he was appointed a Justice of the Peace.

Richard Denny married Frances, only daughter of Thomas Cooke of Washingford House, at Bergh Apton on 25 July 1815. This couple were to have seven children, of whom the eldest was Richard Cooke (Cooke being his second Christian name). He was born on 24 August 1816, and in due course purchased the lordship of Bergh Apton as detailed above.

Between the years 1825, when the Estate Plan map was drawn and 1839 when the Tithe Map was drawn the evidence shows that Richard Denny had his Bergh Apton home rebuilt, essentially creating the house, which stands today. Indeed, it was named Bergh Apton Lodge on Bryant's Map of Norfolk, surveyed between 1824 and 1826.[26] Directory evidence confirms that this property was known by that name until 1869, when Richard Cooke Denny acquired the lordship of Bergh Apton and it could properly be renamed the manor. In accordance with the then prevailing architectural taste, Denny's property was rebuilt in gault clay bricks with a hipped slate roof, and given an entrance portico with two Doric columns. All the same, while this house gives the appearance of an entirely fresh build, triangulation of the 1825 plan and the 1905 Ordnance Survey has revealed that it was rebuilt upon the larger extent of the previous footings: specifically, from the entire length of the façade (south front) back to a line up to and including the (western) entrance portico and marked internally by the drop in part of the ground floor level. The only section of masonry above ground level which was apparently retained from the earlier house is the red brick wall to a height of about 7ft rising from a low plinth of the same material, this

The Loddon troop of Yeomanry Cavalry was part of an earlier form of the modern Territorial Army. This badge was unearthed in a Bergh Apton garden indicating, perhaps, that a previous occupant had been a somewhat careless member of the unit.

forming a section of the external eastern side of the house from its south-east corner back to the south-west corner of the north-east wing. In addition, it would appear that the cellars of the earlier house were retained with little if any alteration.

The consequences of the Bergh Apton Inclosure Award of 1806 had enabled Richard Denny to give his home a parkland surround; this process was brought to its conclusion by his having obtained an Order in 1853, one which permitted him to have the highway from Bergh Apton to Alpington running by his house diverted up to 100yds further to the south-west (Fig.11.1, p.81). Denny was obliged to finance this work, and the new road had to be approved by his fellow magistrates before the old one was abandoned. As Denny already owned the land between the old and new courses of this road, he was thus able to extend his park south-westwards – such as graces this village to the present day.

Richard Denny died at Bergh Apton Manor on 10 October 1856, having left his son Richard Cooke the estates he had inherited from his own father.[27] He left his daughter Harriet certain property, which he had acquired subsequently, such as Church Farm, which he had purchased in 1833. Richard Cooke Denny studied at Trinity College, Cambridge, and subsequently took Holy Orders – although the only living he was to hold was that of Hellington from 1879 to 1882. He first married Julia Steward, by whom he had a daughter who was to predecease him. Julia Denny died in 1849, and her husband later married Jane Deeker Harrison. Richard Denny had five sons and four daughters by his second wife. Of these children, it should be noted that the eldest son, Richard Harrison, was born on 23 June 1859, and the second son, Thomas Henry, was born on 8 March 1863.

According to the census of 7 March 1861, Bergh Apton Lodge was 'under repair and building'.[28] Given a comparison between the outline of the house on the Tithe Map of 1839 and that on post-1861 examples, the only building work likely to have been carried out in 1861 was the remodelling of the northwest (service) wing; which section of the house was in any case to be demolished in 1961.

The Manor of Washingford

As we have seen, Richard Cooke Denny purchased the lordship of Bergh Apton in 1869 and 11 years later, his uncle, Thomas Cooke of Washingford House, conveyed to him the lordship of Washingford.[29] We can now consider the story of this latter manor since the start of the nineteenth century.

Thomas Cooke of Washingford House had inherited this estate together with the Manor of Washingford from his father in 1771. He died there in 1814, having bequeathed all his property in Bergh Apton, Hellington and Thurton to his son and namesake, saving that his widow should enjoy Washingford House with three acres of garden and pleasure ground for the rest of her life. He did not leave his daughter Frances anything, maybe as she had already been given a settlement in advance of her marriage to Richard Denny, which took place as we have seen in 1815.[30]

Thomas Cooke, lord of the Manor of Washingford from 1814, left Bergh Apton between 1837 and 1841, during which period he married a Hannah from Norwich, her maiden name has not been established. In the early years of their married life, this couple lived successively at Reepham and Swannington. Thomas's mother died at Washingford House in 1843, and he and his wife subsequently shared their time between here and Prospect House at Swannington.

Thomas and Hannah Cooke had a childless marriage; nevertheless, they decided to 'gentrify' Washingford House in 1861, and work was being carried out at the time of the census.[31] Luckily, a daguerreotype was taken shortly beforehand, which showed the front of the house. The subsequent rebuilding involved converting the main range from one of two and a half storeys to contain three. The ridge level was not raised, the extra span and headroom required afforded by building-up the outside walls and lowering the existing ceilings. What would appear to have been red pantiles on the photograph just mentioned were replaced by black-glazed ones.

Washingford House in a daguerreotype image taken in about 1861 that shows the original house before work was done to enlarge it and improve the south aspect.

Washingford House before 1914. The picture shows just how dramatic and extensive were the changes made to the original house. A third storey has been added under a completely different roof structure, but the basic characteristics of the east face of the building are virtually unchanged.

From the time his wife died in 1876, Thomas Cooke spent the rest of his days exclusively at Washingford House. He conveyed the lordship of Washingford to his nephew, Richard Cooke Denny, in 1880; moreover, following his death on 29 July 1882, Denny inherited his Washingford House estate – this also including Mere and Gravel Pit, then respectively known as Sumps and Barnes Hill, farms which Thomas[32] had inherited from his aunt, Frances Cooke, in 1826.[33] From, or by 1890, tenants occupied Washingford House until 1954.

Richard Cooke Denny, lord of the Manors of Bergh Apton and Washingford, died at Bergh Apton Manor on 2 October 1890. In his will,[34] he left his

Washingford House estate and the Manor of Washingford to his second son, Thomas Henry, on the condition that he adopt the surname of Cooke – which he did by Deed Poll on 13 December 1890, albeit in the form of Denny-Cooke. As for the Bergh Apton Manor estate, and the lordship of Bergh Apton, the beneficiaries were Thomas Henry and his elder brother, Richard Harrison Denny, as trustees, upon the understanding that their mother, Jane Deeker Denny, should occupy the manor for term of her life. She died there in 1913.

Richard Harrison Denny had married Isobel Mary Beatrice, daughter of George Henry Christie, of and at Framingham Pigot in 1889; this couple initially resided at Framingham Cottage on the Christie estate. Thomas Henry Denny-Cooke married Beatrice Jessie, daughter of the Revd J.C. Martyn of Long Melford, in 1896; this couple resided at Richmond, Surrey, until 1914.

The Inclosure of Bergh Apton

We turn to the Parliamentary Inclosure of Bergh Apton that was entitled as 'An Act for dividing, allotting, and inclosing the commons and waste grounds, in the parishes of Bergh-Apton (*sic*), Thurton, Yelverton, Alpington, and Holveston, in the county of Norfolk'.[35] This parish was not treated in isolation, but with its neighbouring parishes. While certain landowners living in Bergh Apton had estates extending into some of the other parishes subject to the same Act, and vice versa, for the most part matters set out in the following paragraphs will relate exclusively to Bergh Apton.

Parliamentary Inclosure in the late-eighteenth and early-nineteenth centuries has to be viewed against the need for the country to be more self-sufficient at a time of rapidly rising population, and the disruption of trade which was a concomitant of the years of conflict with Revolutionary and Napoleonic France and its allies. Hence, a drive towards the more efficient exploitation of agricultural land was probably the most significant tool that could be brought into play to aid this self-sufficiency, though one which did not benefit everyone, at least in the short term, as we shall see in respect of Bergh Apton.

As for the procedures attendant upon the Inclosure Act in respect of Bergh Apton (and associated parishes), three commissioners were sworn-in to administer these: which, apart from dividing up the commons and wastes, included making new rights of way, closing certain existing ones, and sanctioning swaps of land between landowners with the minimum of 'red tape' in order to give them more compact holdings. The general rule was that each landowner was awarded a piece or pieces of the commons and wastes proportionate in area to the extent of the property they already owned. The awards made were expressed to be freehold and

copyhold according to the proportion so held by each landowner on the eve of Inclosure. The awards of copyhold the commissioners related to the individual manors concerned. Further allowances were made in respect of the lords of the manors to compensate them for the rights they would lose on the enclosed commons and wastes, for the surveyors of the highways to have access to gravel for road maintenance purposes, and for the trustees of the poor to compensate those for whom they bore responsibility for their loss of rights, particularly in respect of grazing stock and gathering fuel.

A primary duty of the Inclosure commissioners was to appoint a surveyor to map the parishes, as they existed, indicating their precise bounds, the names of the landowners and the extent of their estates with their individual components, roads, paths, and other natural and man-made features. Internal evidence dates what one might call this pre-Inclosure Map of Bergh Apton (etc) to about 1803 – this, together with associated papers made by the surveyor, are held in the Norfolk Record Office.

Shortly before the surveyor finalised his pre-Inclosure Map, persons owning land in Bergh Apton (and associated parishes) were asked to submit details in writing of what they claimed to hold and under what tenure, and their interests in the commons and wastelands due to be divided and allotted, to the commissioners. The Revd Walter Nevill, who died on 24 October 1802, was a signatory (both in respect of his glebe, and also as one of the Feoffees of the Town Farm estate), which gives some indication of the time the claims were submitted. There were effectively 29 persons declaring ownership of real estate wholly or partly lying in Bergh Apton. The commissioners had these declarations (together with those relating to the other relevant parishes) printed as a *State of the Claims*, bearing the date 20 January 1803, and therein ordered that objections by interested persons to any of the claims made by others should be made to them by the end of that month, with duplicate copies of these submitted to the commissioners themselves by their next meeting. This was to be held at the public inn called the Angel in St Peter Mancroft parish in Norwich, on the following 3 February, at which the commissioners would adjudge the claims in the light of objections.

No record appears to have survived concerning the commissioners' actual decisions. The appointed surveyor then compiled the pre-Inclosure map with regard to his manuscript listing of owners of Bergh Apton property. Internal evidence indicates that the latter document was drafted prior to Lady Day 1804. In it, 32 landowners were named, together with the extent of their holdings. This number excludes the Earl of Abergavenny, whose Manor of Bergh Apton entitled him to rights in respect of land, although he did not actually hold land here as freehold, leasehold or copyhold. A few small proprietors had not bothered to submit their claims. This did not compromise their rights within the mechanisms of Inclosure, but it inevitably increased the number of landowners over those appearing in the *State of the Claims*. In addition, the surveyor noted that the surveyors of the highways and the trustees of the poor were entitled to a respective share of the lands to be enclosed.

Of the 32 landowners just referred to, it is of interest to note the following statistics:

No. of landowners	Area of land held
10	less than 1 acre
5	1–10 acres
12	10–100 acres
5	over 100 acres

As for the land that was to be inclosed, the largest block was Apton Heath (Fig.2.1, p.14), which also extended into the parishes of Alpington, Yelverton and Holverston. (Apton Heath further extended into Hellington, a parish that was to be subject to a later Inclosure Award.) Within the Bergh Apton element of this heath, there were in any case two small pieces of long-enclosed land, upon one of which stood a windmill. The commissioners ordered the laying

down of new roads over Apton Heath, supplanting the unfenced tracks that had hitherto traversed it.

A second major block to be enclosed was White Heath (Fig.1.2, p.13), shared between Bergh Apton and Thurton. Here again, the commissioners had new lines of highway laid down.

The third block to be inclosed was Barnes Heath (Fig.8.2, p.60), situated in the south of the parish, in part bounded by the Chet against the boundary with Seething, and which also included a locality known as Whipscrew Hill. This heath also contained two small pieces of long-enclosed land. The commissioners defined the course of the road now known as Sunnyside as it ran through, then against, this erstwhile common land.

Four other pieces of hitherto common land were to be enclosed: against the boundary with Thurton, one small piece lay to the south-east and another to the south-west of Thurton churchyard. The third piece lay to the south-east of Hillside Farm, between Welbeck Road and the Chet (Well Beck), which here forms the boundary with Brooke parish. From opposite the yard of Hillside Farm the fourth piece concerned, for the most part a narrow strip, lay to the south side of Welbeck Road as far west as Wellbeck Bridge, this broadening as it extended north of this road to either side of its junction with Lower Kiln

Welbeck Cottage with its well in the foreground, c.1960.

Lane. Where this last piece bordered the River Chet (Well Beck), it paralleled the common land in Brooke parish, which was to be the subject of a later Inclosure Award. The roads running through or by these last four pieces of common in Bergh Apton were also ordered by the commissioners to be properly demarcated.

The final and most significant duty of the commissioners was to make their Award, which appeared in 1806, in respect of which all those benefiting had to pay a proportionate sum towards the total cost of the enclosure proceedings. Those receiving awards of former common were ordered to hedge and ditch these where they bounded the highways, or lands of other proprietors. To accompany the Award, and reflect its provisions, a further map was surveyed.

It would have taken but a few years for the hedges separating the new enclosures and lining the new roads to mature, so these were ordered by the commissioners to be formed with quicksets. Once these flourished, and the sometime commons cropped, maintained as pasture, planted with trees, developed as parkland, or built upon, and with the small pieces awarded to the surveyors of the highways excavated for gravel, the face of Bergh Apton was irrevocably changed. This change was also manifest in certain places where strips of open-field land had been swept away at the behest of the commissioners, with swaps between the landowners concerned allowing these pieces to be merged into, or brought within, hedged enclosures. The localities within the parish where the majority of such strips had survived up to Inclosure were Cook Stow Field and the field south of White Heath; also, more generally, where the glebe had been held in this form.

The Rural Poor

Not long before the publication of the Bergh Apton Inclosure Award, the *Norwich Mercury* for 28 December 1805 reported that a meeting of the Brooke Association for Prosecuting Horse stealers, Etc., had been held at the King's Head there some 17 days earlier. Members of this association lived as far away as Hempnall; closer to Brooke, Bergh Apton members were listed as T. Tompson Esq., the Revd A. Beevor, and Messrs S. Clarke, J. Harvey and T. Cooke. This association offered a reward of £10 for anyone providing information that led to the successful prosecution of a horse thief.

We may view the existence of the above association as a reaction to increased lawlessness in the countryside. Some of this would be a concomitant of the stress occasioned by high prices for foodstuffs and other necessities of life, which fell particularly hard upon the rural poor, during the years of the nation's conflict with Napoleonic France. Such stress would become all the more felt once the traditional

access to grazing and fuel collecting on commons was terminated by the decisions of the Inclosure commissioners. It is true that they had allocated 22 acres in Bergh Apton for the benefit of the poor through their trustees; however, this land was let to a farmer or farmers in the parish with the income so derived used to purchase coal, which was maybe only small comfort to the pauper inhabitants. All the same, the commissioners' decisions were to lead to the increased ability of farmers as a body to produce the food needed by a rapidly rising population, and also freed former common land to house the same. The population of Bergh Apton rose from 304 in 1801 to 604 in 1851, then, after an inexplicable dip to 544 in 1861, to attain its all-time peak of 621 in 1871.

The Post-Inclosure Period

In the post-Inclosure period, we may take Samuel Clarke, one who had been the tenant at the then Street Farm from 1792, and who remained as such until 1823, as an example of an improving farmer. He had somehow become acquainted with the radical politician, writer and agriculturalist, William Cobbett, who first mentioned Clarke in respect of his turnips on 8 November 1821. During the following month, Cobbett stayed with Clarke at Bergh Apton, and from there travelled with his host to a number of locations in Norfolk and Suffolk. Cobbett particularly admired Clarke's swedes, of which he had 30 acres in rows.[36] Rather later in the nineteenth century, William Ford Thursby, rector from 1864 until his death in 1893, was an enthusiastic farmer of his own glebe, as witness the terriers which reveal that he kept cows and pigs. In addition, he purchased Valley Farm in 1891 for the sum of £900.[37]

Other landowners in the post-Inclosure period had taken to gentrifying their property beyond examples already considered – The Rectory, Bergh Apton Manor

Street Farm (later renamed Apton Manor) where the writer and political activist William Cobbett stayed with Samuel and Lucy Clarke in the 1820s. This was the time that he toured agricultural England gathering information that enabled him to publish his Rural Rides *that railed against the conditions of the farm workers of those times.*

A lithograph of Bergh Apton Cottage (later renamed Bergh Apton House) in the 1879 sale catalogue of the Brooke Estate. It was built as a dower house to Brooke House and was sold in 1946 to the Beauchamp family of Langley. Since 1958 it was the home of the late and much-respected surgeon John Stephens and his wife, Barbara, who continues to live there in 2005.

The south aspect of Holly Lodge, the principal home of the Canterbury family during their ownership of the Brooke Estate from the 1870s to 1946.

A view of the churchyard, 2003. Some interesting characters are buried here, such as Brettingham Scurll, manservant to the diarist Parson Woodforde of Weston Longville, and Christopher Barlee, 'a local prize fighter of great celebrity' (Walter Wicks, Inns and Taverns of Old Norwich, 1925) of the 1830s. Sadly the exact location of both graves is unknown.

and Washingford House. Bergh Apton Cottage, known as such as long ago as 22 May 1819 (according to an advertisement in the *Norwich Mercury*), renamed Bergh Apton House in recent years, had then recently been the subject of an extensive rebuild as a 'cottage orné' (a small picturesque house in a rural setting) by its owner and hitherto occupier, Charles Tompson, who offered it for letting with its grounds of 34 acres. Thomas Smallpiece Clarke, eldest son of Samuel of Street Farm, built Holly Lodge on a virgin site in the then favoured white brick about the same time, given architectural and map evidence.

A resident of Bergh Apton from 1818 (Norwich Poll Book evidence) until his death here on 15 April 1842 was Brettingham Scurll, one who had been a servant of the diarist of Weston Longville, 'Parson' James Woodforde, from 1783 until the latter's death in 1803. Scurll had come to own an estate in Norwich and a double-dweller cottage in Hardley, but as he did not possess a house or land of his own in Bergh Apton it is unclear why he chose to settle here.[38] He described himself as a yeoman when he wrote his will on 3 December 1840,[39] and of independent means when he was enumerated as the lone occupant of a dwelling on the common – meaning the former Apton Heath – in the census of 6 June 1841.[40]

The Tithe Apportionment Schedules

In 1839, a Tithe Map was surveyed for Bergh Apton; this was prepared to complement the Tithe Apportionment Schedules that were issued in 1841.[41] Tithes had hitherto been paid in kind here, save when compounded for a cash settlement with the incumbent for the time being – the only example discovered of this arrangement in Bergh Apton was with Nevill Walter back in 1784, as revealed by the Norfolk Archdeaconry Visitation Book.[42] The Tithe Commutation Award of 1841 rendered tithes thenceforth payable in the form of an annual rent charge, calculated on the basis of the prevailing price of corn in the district.

A particular feature of Bergh Apton Tithe Apportionment Schedules is that they name every plot of land in the parish, each plot given a specific number so that it can be identified on the associated Tithe Map. The names of fields and other pieces of land in some cases merely relate to their approximate size, such as 'Seven Acres'; others reflect a particular characteristic or characteristics, such as 'Coney Furze', which one would suspect contained furze bushes and was frequented by rabbits. Burnt House Close and Burnt House Yard, to either side of Loddon Road, suggest sites associated with a property then long-since destroyed by fire. Enclosures with name elements such as 'Sandy' and 'Blacklands' clearly indicate the nature of their soil. 'Hempland Close' (Fig.2.2, p.15) hearkens back to a time when flax was a common crop; likewise 'Wretten Piece' (Fig.11.1, p.81), in which a pit for retting hemp (steeping in water to extract the fibre) would have been situated. This commentary could be taken much further; but, suffice it to say that the most remarkable survival as a field name, not merely in 1839/1841, but through to the present day, is 'Gosbalds', which, as noted[43] relates to a personal name first encountered in a land transaction of 1202.

Of the 40 landowners listed in the schedules of 1841, including the 'corporate' surveyors of the highways and trustees of the poor, it is of interest to note the following statistics:

No. of landowners	Area of land held
10	less than 1 acre
16	1–10 acres
7	10–100 acres
7	over 100 acres

The Tithe Apportionment Schedules further reveal that the parish, which was said to extend to 1,960 acres, was comprised of the following categories of land: 1,536 acres of arable (more than 78 per cent); 347 acres of meadow and pasture (less than 18 per cent); 56 acres of wood (less than 3 per cent); and 21 acres of roads (a little more than 1 per cent).

The growth in the number of small landowners between the eve of Inclosure and 1841 can be explained by the partible (dividable) inheritance of tiny units of property, and by the erection of cottages on former common land such as those at Hellington Corner. A few former common-edge cottages such as those at Little London, which were not given road access in the Award of 1806, had been abandoned by 1841.

The Census of 1841

The 1841 census was the first in which every person was named and, when appropriate, had his or her occupation (or in some instances lack of one) described. It is thus of interest to note the following facts concerning Bergh Apton in 1841.[44]

Of the total population of 564, 544 declared they had been born in Norfolk, 19 were born outside the county, and one did not give such information. These folk occupied 120 houses; also in the parish one house was unoccupied, and another was then being built. Details of the 222 inhabitants for whom occupations (or lack thereof) were declared may be listed, in descending order of numbers, as follows:

Agricultural Labourers: 95
Servants: 36 of whom 27 were female and 9 were male
[Of] Independent [Means]: 28
Farmers: 22
Cordwainers: 7
Dressmakers: 6
Tailors: 4 including an apprentice
Blacksmiths: 3 including father and son James and
  Thomas Waterson
Carpenters: 3

The yard of the blacksmith's shop in Mill Road (a private house at the time of writing), photographed in the early 1930s. Left to right: a very young Arthur Smith, Mr Baker of Stoke Holy Cross and Arthur's grandfather, Arthur William Smith (with his hand on the horse's flank). The yard here was also used as a space for boys of the village to practise boxing. The rector of Yelverton in 1914 was an Oxford blue for both cricket and boxing and would teach local boys to box. It is reported that when the gloves (which the boys were allowed to take away for practice) became very bloody they would harden and boys ended up with bloody noses, skinned faces and puffy eyes.

George and Liza Keeler of Threadneedle Street, 1910. Liza's skirt is the work of one of the excellent dressmakers who lived on the street that bears their trade name. George was a carpenter on the Beauchamp estate of Langley and a noted pub fiddler in his spare time. Billy Keeler (left) became a market gardener in the village and died in 2002, aged 99. Alice moved away to London but youngest son Ted (seated) was publican at the Bergh Apton (Hellington) Bell. Ted also worked at some point for his younger brother Percy (far right) who ran sand and gravel pits in Bergh Apton, Brooke and Howe. The eldest son, Ernest, joined the Army and then the police force.

Gardeners: 3

Gamekeepers: 2 the father and son Samuel and Stephen Aldus

Wheelwrights: 2 of whom one James the son of Peter Freston, blacksmith

Attorney's Clerk: 1

Cattle Dealer: 1

Clerk [in Holy Orders]: 1 – not the rector, absent when the census was taken, but the [Hon.] Revd Somerville Hay of Bergh Apton Cottage

Machinist: 1

Miller: 1 George Goff of the Windmill and Mill House

Police Officer: 1 Thomas Dawson of Hellington Corner

Registrar: 1 John Dawson of Hellington Corner

Shopkeeper: 1 Harriet, daughter of Samuel Harvey, cordwainer

Schoolmistress: 1 Mary Ann, wife of Peter Hubbard, gardener

Teacher [apparently meaning governess]: 1 Ann Ingram, living at The Rectory

[Occupation Illegible: 1]

The Census of 1851

The census of 1851 was the first to give precise (or relatively precise) birthplaces for each person enumerated. Bergh Apton's then population of 604 lived in 124 houses; there were also seven unoccupied houses.[45]

Birthplaces of Bergh Apton population, as listed in 1851 census:

Bergh Apton: 260

Elsewhere in Norfolk: 313

Suffolk: 15

Middlesex (including London): 6

Hampshire: 2

Warwickshire: 2

Ireland: 2

Cheshire: 1

Devonshire: 1

Sussex: 1

East Indies (British Subject): 1

Population of Bergh Apton, according to censuses of 1861–1891.

1861 census:[46] population 544, living in 129 houses; there were also 4 unoccupied houses.

1871 census:[47] population 621, living in 123 houses; there were also 9 unoccupied houses and one under construction.

1881 census:[48] population 464, living in 113 houses; there were also 18 unoccupied houses.

1891 census:[51] population 465, living in 111 houses, of which 43 had less than five rooms; there were also 11 unoccupied houses.

It seems appropriate to mention at this point that the sharp fall in the population of Bergh Apton since 1871 is likely to have been a consequence of the severe agricultural depression which set in midway through this intercensal period, occasioning a flight of farm labourers to Norwich and other urban centres in search of work in industrial concerns, and even to coal mines and other mineral workings in the North of England; some were even driven to emigrate, particularly to North America.[49] All the same, within the wider context of husbandry, favoured by the proximity of Norwich, market gardening (as revealed by directories) became a noted occupation in Bergh Apton in the mid-nineteenth century, followed later in Victoria's reign by fruit growing – the village became particularly noted for the quality of its cherries. It should also be noted that Bergh Apton's windmill was last recorded in use in 1872,[50] it had been demolished by 1881, according to the Ordnance Survey.

Education

An examination of the Bergh Apton Marriage Registers for the early-nineteenth century reveals that many of the parishioners then were unable to sign their names. Such illiteracy was becoming a source of concern to authorities at both a national and a local level. Rectors of Bergh Apton were called upon to report educational facilities within their parishes to the Archdeacon of Norfolk, as shown in the Visitation Books. In 1820, the Hon. John Nevill reported that while he had no school, 'there is a house licensed this year' to serve as one.[52] Between 1820 and 1831, evidence for the existence of a school at Bergh Apton is scanty; however, White's *Directory of Norfolk*, 1836, revealed that the parish had a National (i.e. Church of England sponsored) School which had been instituted by the 'late Rector', that is John Nevill who relinquished the living here in 1831. In 1838, the Hon. John Thomas Pelham reported to the Archdeacon that he supported both a day school and a Sunday school, and that no child in the parish was uneducated. The former was attended by an average of 40 children, who each paid 1s. every quarter for the privilege; 100 children attended the latter.[53] The site of Bergh Apton's national school prior to 1839 is not known.

The school at Bergh Apton, which was in use until 1981, was built upon a site of one rood taken out of the Town Farm land, opposite the church, which was conveyed by the Feoffees to the rector and churchwardens on 1 January 1839. It was to be for the purpose of educating:

the poor children of… Berghapton [sic] in the principles of the Christian Religion according to the Doctrines and Disciplines of the United Church of England and Ireland.[54]

In 1845 the Hon. John Thomas Pelham informed the Archdeacon:

the Day School was attended by seventy-five pupils; in addition, his Sunday School attracted eighty-five children, while (significantly) an Evening School held during the winter half of the year was attended by thirty-five adults.[55]

The Bergh Apton School managers' minute book survives for the period 1865–1899.[56] Some excerpts from this follow:

At the meeting held at The Rectory on 14 December 1865, the Master asked for a rise. However, not being satisfied with the offer of an annual salary of £50, one-third of the grant received from the Government, the Night School pence, plus the occupation of the School House rent-free, he handed in his resignation.

Mr William Plumpton took charge of the School on 1 April 1869; he was to pass the examination at the government-supervised training school, Peterborough, at Christmas 1873.

On 15 June 1875, the report of the Government Inspector was minuted:

The children work honestly and quietly, and have acquitted themselves very well. The result is very creditable to the Master. The supply of books is insufficient.

On 8 October 1878, the minutes state:

The Managers of the School having heard certain reports respecting Mrs Potter, Sewing-Mistress, are of [the] opinion that she is not a fit person to be retained in that post.

On 6 November 1890, it was declared that as the average number of children had exceeded 60, it was necessary to appoint as assistant teacher and sewing mistress Mrs Walker, wife of the master. On 8 May 1891, this couple accepted in total a salary of £105, with rent-free occupation of the School House. This offer did not appear to please them in the long term, for in the following October their respective posts were taken over by Mr H. Flint and his daughter, the former at a salary of £90 and the latter at one of £16 – their accommodation again rent-free. It was this autumn that the payment of 'school pence' was abolished under the provisions of the Elementary Education Act, 1891.

Bergh Apton School Logbook

Further details of Bergh Apton School in the nineteenth century are to be found in the logbook dating from 1883 to 1901.[57] Some excerpts from this follow:

[The week] 15 to 19 January 1883
Mr Henry Nursey complained about some of the school-

Bergh Apton School, c.1898. The teacher on the far right is Miss Anna Nettie Horrocks who taught for a quarter of a century and who was still remembered with a measure of awe and fear in the 1990s by some of those whose education was completed under her. The teacher on the left is Miss Baldry, the infant teacher. The photo includes the following pupils: Jimmy Annis (third row, second from left); Rosa Alexander (second row, fourth from left); Robert Annis (second row, 13th from left); Billy Alexander (front row, first on left).

Glebe Cottage, 1980s. This was once the village Reading Room, and was used as a changing room by footballers and cricketers who played on the field opposite that belonged to Thomas Henry Denny-Cooke. The Reading Room was also used for the meetings of the 37th Norwich Scout troop, started in 1930 and led by Dick Fairhead.

boys throwing stones at his ducks. Cautioned all the boys about throwing stones.

16 February 1884
Wilson Clare absent all the week, saw him this morning picking stones in a field at Yelverton. On Monday a stag hunt in the parish. The meet was opposite the School at 11.30a.m. Quite useless going on with lessons. Let the children into playground to look.

12 February 1886
St Valentine's Day falling on the Sunday, the Revd Thursby ordered the School to go on Monday for their Valentines round the village.

30 April 1886
Julia Fox absent last week helping her mother to pick stones. Mary Ann Fox no boots.

9 January 1888
Caned W.L. Martin for pulling Lucy Vann's hair in School.

9 July 1889
The children are being photographed this morning.

27 November 1890
Snow 2 feet deep School closed.

24 April 1891
Herbert Goodwin being ill with diphtheria, the whole family are excluded for the present.

20 April 1894
Cautioned all Sunnyside girls, especially Kiddles and Blighs, about quarrelling, and being saucy to people going to and from School.

5 May 1896
H.M. Inspector's Report: 'There is a very nice tone

throughout the School, and the work is neat, accurate and intelligent. The girls' porch should be altered so as to admit more light, and a few more pictures are required for the infants.'

25 May 1898
School reopened this morning after a fortnight's holiday, the extra week was required for putting down new floor in School, cleaning well and altering the drainage of premises.

The Reading Room

Glebe Cottage housed the parochial lending library and reading room that gave access to reading books for Bergh Apton residents who, in some instances, could not afford their own. Unfortunately, the stock does not appear to have been attractive, even given the tastes of early-Victorian readers: the Archdeacon was informed in 1845 – the earliest known mention of this facility – that the books were 'not in much request'.[58] All the same, it is pleasant to record that the Bergh Apton reading room survived until well into the twentieth century, it last having being recorded in 1933.[59]

Churchwardens' Accounts

Parish records reveal other aspects of village life in the first half of the nineteenth century. Among the disbursements of Robert Batchelder, churchwarden, in 1810/1, we find:[60]

For fencing in the Churchyard: 1s.6d.
To several boys for catching thirty-nine and a half dozen sparrows: 9s.10½d.
Repairing the style too [sic] Church: 2s.6d.

While in the year 1820/1, the churchwarden, Edward Hylton, recorded:

Paid the Ringers 15s. [twice] and 10s. [once].
Paid for [an] iron chest: £3.3s.
Expenses at [the] Confirmation [at] Bungay: 5s.
Paid a woman to dress the feathers for [a] pulpit cushion, etc.: 1s.6d.

Overseers' Accounts

As for the overseers' accounts, during the year from Easter 1823, J. Dawson, overseer, recorded:[61]

Daniel Weddup for his apprentice taken [at] Michaelmas 1821 (last instalment): £3.
Richard Denny, Esq., for his apprentice taken [at] Michaelmas 1823 (first instalment): £3.

[The above payments relate to an arrangement whereby farmers were paid out of the poor rates for taking on village youths as apprentices.]

Providing for a deaf and dumb woman who came wandering into the parish: 3s.
54 weeks pay for the [presumably illegitimate] child of Sarah Goodrum @ 1s. a week: £2.14s.

Ten years later, the same source reveals that J. Dawson was again serving as overseer of the poor. Amongst other disbursements, he then accounted for:

List of Lunatics (clerk's fee): 4s. [An overseer's duties included the submission of a list of parochial 'lunatics' to the Justices of the Peace.]
Journey to the [Union] House to report the servant of Mr H.W. Nevill [the rector] who was delivered of a [presumably illegitimate] child: 2s.6d.
Journey to Loddon with Richard Chettleburgh to be examined for settlement [that is to determine if he had a right to live in Bergh Apton]: 2s.6d.

Provisions for the Poor

Poor rates in Bergh Apton were relatively low, partly due to the income arising from the Town Farm. This fact was particularly marked upon in 'An Account of the Livings of the Earl of Abergavenny… in May 1818…'.[62] Other provisions for the poor were noted in the rector's report to the Archdeacon in 1852, when he mentioned a clothing club, a shoe club, and coal funds;[63] the coal funds, given directory evidence, were at least in part derived from the income from the land allotted to the trustees of the poor in 1806.

The Bergh Apton Friendly Society

A self-help scheme for artisans and husbandmen flourished for at least the 1877–1889 period. This is evidenced in the survival of the Subscription and Accounts Book of the Bergh Apton Friendly Society.[64] Strictly speaking, this might have been known as the Bergh Apton and District Friendly Society, for of the 121 members listed in 1877, only 33 were Bergh Apton residents while the rest lived in 13 parishes to the north, east and south. Its members subscribed 1s.6d. every four weeks, and were in turn entitled to claim sickness benefit and funeral expenses.

Property

Some small property owners were able to alleviate their relatively poor circumstances in the mid-nineteenth century by selling their cottages: the Denny-Cooke MSS in the Norfolk Record Office reveal that James Starling sold what is now Endene to Richard Denny in 1847, while the latter purchased the cottage which once stood at the corner of The Street and Dodger's Lane from Isaac Browne – one who then became Denny's tenant there at an annual rent of £6. Richard Cooke Denny purchased Holly Cottage from Freeman Carr, husbandman, in 1869.

Larger units of property came onto the market through the death of a previous owner: Hannah Athow's trustees sold Street Farm to its former tenant, Samuel Clarke senr, in 1827; while a year later they sold her Hillside Farm property to the Revd John Holmes of Brooke Hall.[65] Other properties of consequence changed ownership through inheritance: Bergh Apton Hall and Holly Lodge Farm were left by George Samuel Kett of Brooke House to his nephew and executor, Henry Kett Tompson.[66] The latter was not to enjoy this property for long, as he died at Brooke House (having recently changed his surname to Kett-Tompson) on 18 November 1872, having bequeathed it together with Bergh Apton Cottage (which later became Bergh Apton House), Bussey Bridge Farm and Holly Lodge to his brother-in-law and executor, John Henry Thomas Manners-Sutton, 3rd Viscount Canterbury.[67]

Transport

Bergh Apton was far from being an isolated parish; many villagers in, say, the nineteenth century would have thought nothing of walking to Norwich (7 miles) or Loddon (5 miles) and back in the course of a day. Directory evidence is that what would have been a horse-drawn carrier's service linked Bergh Apton with the city in 1842. Jonathan Wright was specifically named as providing such a facility in 1846. In 1854, Freestone's service left the Queen's Head, St Giles Street, Norwich, for Bergh Apton on Saturdays, while two years later the departure point had become the Star and Crown in Timberhill. In 1858, Joseph Greengrass passed Bergh Apton en route from Norwich to Loddon; the *Post Office Directory* does not make it clear if he travelled through the village, or if this service had to be accessed at Hellington Corner.

Postal Services

As for postal services, the inauguration of the Penny Post in 1840 made this communication a widely attractive proposition. Directory evidence is that letters for Bergh Apton were received via Brooke in 1846. Eight years later, mails were sent off from Norwich for Bergh Apton at 7a.m., and vice versa at 6.20p.m; furthermore, a foot post was provided between Bergh Apton and Thurton. Bergh Apton's own Post Office was first recorded in the eponymous directory of 1858.

Trades

The list of occupations (on pp.97, 99) in Bergh Apton in the census of 1841, is most revealing; while such a listing can be supplemented by directory evidence – indeed, had there been space in these pages, by similar summaries of subsequent nineteenth century

Annie McPherson, the postmistress, and her daughter, Elizabeth Jessie, photographed in 1910.

This is the east side of the Hellington Bell when Fred Preston was landlord. The cottages in the background, still there at the time of writing, are on the other side of the main road. The man standing at the head of the pony is thought to be William Holman, otherwise known in the Preston family as 'Uncle Willy'. The children are probably George Preston and either Sarah Kate or Frances Preston, children of the landlord. We don't know the significance of the distemper brush hanging on the wall!

Billy Loyd delivering meat for Ward's the butcher's in Loddon, 1925. The business is still trading in 2005. Butchers were renowned for their use of fast ponies and light carts to ensure that their produce was delivered to their customers absolutely fresh.

The new Hellington Bell, 1930s. The pub was licensed to sell only beers, ales and stouts and owned by Stewart & Patterson. It was built in the 1890s by brothers Lenny and Maurice Redgrave who demolished the rear part of an original building of 1836 but incorporated the front into the new pub. The Prestons were the first landlords, followed by the Blithes, Doughtys and Keelers. This photograph dates from the time of the Prestons' occupation, with their customers outside. The pub was sold by Steward and Patteson on 27 December 1956 with a covenant that it would not be reopened as a pub.

The Red Lion, c.1900. The pub was in Thurton, at the eastern end of Lion Lane, but was known locally as the 'B'rapton Lion'.

censuses. It should be observed that the earliest directory to record Bergh Apton in detail, that of William White in 1836, indicated the presence here of the following tradesmen: two grocers, two tailors, a blacksmith, a gardener, a miller and a victualler. The latter was John Dawson, who sold beer at the Trowel and Hammer at Hellington Corner – which site had been a part of Apton Heath, inclosed in 1806 – and who was to describe himself as a registrar in the 1841 census. This provides the first record of a public house in the parish since the demise of The Hare between 1794 and 1803.[68] The Trowel and Hammer was to be renamed the Bell by 1881.[69] Whilst on the topic of public houses, it should be stressed that the Red Lion, incorrectly listed under the heading of Bergh Apton in some directories, actually lay in Thurton parish; all the same it was the most conveniently situated pub for the inhabitants of the south-eastern part of Bergh Apton – while residents of Beech Farm and nearby cottages would have found the George and Dragon at Thurton their nearest inn.

Bergh Apton Parish Council

Within the parish of Bergh Apton, parish officials – those essentially associated with the church, such as the churchwardens, and those with lay responsibili-

ties, such as the overseers of the poor – continued to exercise their functions throughout the nineteenth century. Following in the steps of the first democratically elected Norfolk County Council in 1889, legislation provided for the establishment of elected Parish Councils in 1894.[70] As a consequence of this, a parish meeting was held at Bergh Apton School on 4 December 1894, chaired by the rector. It was then that the first persons to serve as parish councillors were elected, not by means of a secret ballot but by a show of hands: they were W. Bracey, J. Everett, E.A. Leeder, J. Lord, D. Lovewell, C. Mayhew, M.A. Redgrave and S.J. Strowger.[71] Interestingly, this initial membership was comprised of four agricultural labourers, two farmers, a blacksmith and a builder. At the first meeting of the Parish Council, ten days later the rector, T.F. Lloyd, was unanimously elected chairman. However, the totality of evidence for Bergh Apton points to villagers of every class living together with rather more ease and harmony than in many other Norfolk parishes, particularly during a period of agricultural recession, thanks to a considerable degree to its benevolent squirearchy and dedicated clergy.

Among the responsibilities that Bergh Apton Parish Council had from its inception were the care of parish property, the maintenance and repair of footpaths, the protection of boundaries, and

The rector and choir of Bergh Apton, c.1900. Left to right, back row: ?, ?, Joe Read, Palmer Leeder, ?, ?, ?; middle row: Lenny Wall, ?, William Loyd, ?, Revd Harvey W.G. Thursby, ?, Robert Royall, Charles Mayhew; front row: ?, James or Robert Annis, ?, ?, ?, Harry Percy Royall.

Robert Arthur Royall and his wife, Henrietta, in the porch at Welbeck Cottage, c.1915.

Young men of the village in Threadneedle Street in 1915. Left to right: Masters Woodrow, Stanley Shingles, Alec Stone, and Reggie Wall. The formal adoption of the name Threadneedle Street, previously a nickname, is as recent as the 1980s. At the time of the 1861 census it was called The Principal Street but by the time of the 1908 Ordnance Survey map it had been changed to The Street, and was an extension of the road that still retains that name (from Cooke's Road to Church Road). The name Threadneedle Street celebrates the fact that there were several seamstresses and tailors living on the road in the early-twentieth century.

This evocative image from the turn of the century is of Clara Dye and her dog. Clara was born in the village in 1895 and married Walter Cain, a Liverpudlian who came to nearby Langley in the First World War. They lived at Prospect Place where they raised two sons, Leonard and Ron. Clara was to become one of the key workers in Charlie Carver's fruit-picking team.

The Loyd family outside their cottage in Sunnyside, c.1912 (known as Green Shutters at the time of writing). Left to right: Levi, William, Elizabeth (née Turner), Hannah and Billy. William (1866–1930) was 18 years old when he began his duties as parish clerk and he performed them for 46 years. His father William (1826–1884) also did those duties for 24 years before him. Thus the family gave a remarkable total of 70 years in the service of Bergh Apton.

safeguarding sanitary conditions. The appointment of an overseer of the poor, and the parish constable, (hitherto chosen at the annual Vestry, the precursor of the Parochial Church Council meeting), were also made by the Parish Council. This body had to operate within the constraints of being unable to raise more than a 3d. rate to finance its activities.

It is of further interest that the franchise for the newly instituted local government bodies of 1889 and 1894 was extended to adult females who were ratepayers. At the Bergh Apton Parish Council meeting of 11 February 1895, it was agreed that all parishioners enjoying the relevant franchise were entitled to be admitted to its subsequent sessions.

References

[1] NRO: DN/VS 31/12

[2] NRO: DN/VS 54/6

[3] NRO: DN/VS 65/2, 84/10

[4] See Chapter X, p.75.

[5] TNA: HO107 756/3 f.14 p.23.

[6] TNA: HO107/1820 f.352 p.14.

[7] NRO: PD 497/13/1.

[8] E.C. Hopper, 'Church Plate in the Deanery of West Brooke', *Norfolk Archaeology*, (Norwich, Norfolk and Norwich Archaeological Society, 1910), vol.17.

[9] TNA: HO129/238 f.37.

[10] TNA: RG9/1229 f.114, p.8.

[11] Hopper, *op. cit.*

[12] NRO: PD 497/13/4.

[13] NRO: DN/TA 15.

[14] ESRO: ABE 37C.

[15] Sir B. Burke, *Landed Gentry (Harrison, 1875)*, vol.2; Vicary Gibbs (ed.) *Complete Peerage* (London, St Catherine Press, 1910), vol.1.

[16] TNA: RG10/1831 f.116, p.15.

[17] TNA: RG10/1831 f.120, p.20; RG11/1963 f.119, p.21.

[18] TNA: RG12/1541 f.101, p.1.

[19] Hopper, *op.cit.*

[20] Vicary Gibbs, *op.cit.*

[21] *Ibid.*

[22] *Ibid.*

[23] ESRO: ABE 37F.

[24] His late father's executors are named in Chapter XI, p.80.

[25] W. White, *History, Gazetteer and Directory of Norfolk* (Sheffield, William White 1836); W. White, *History, Gazetteer and Directory of Norfolk*, 2nd edn (Sheffield, William White 1845).

[26] I would suspect that the rebuilding took place a matter of months after the 1825 plan was presented.

[27] There is a copy of his will in the Denny-Cooke MSS in the NRO.

[28] TNA: RG9/1229 f.113, p.5.

[29] A copy of the conveyance is in the Denny-Cooke MSS in the NRO.

[30] A copy of Thomas Cooke's will is to be found in the Denny-Cooke MSS in the NRO.

[31] TNA: RG9/1229 f.113, p.5.

[32] There is a copy of Thomas Cooke's will in the Denny-Cooke MSS in the NRO.

[33] NRO: NCC 1826 f.232 Davy.

[34] There is a copy of Richard Cooke Denny's will in the Denny-Cooke MSS in the NRO.

[35] 41 George III 58

[36] E. Thomas (ed.), *Rural Rides* (London, J.M. Dent & Sons Ltd, 1912), vol.1, pp.19, 47–53.

[37] According to the Denny-Cooke MSS in the NRO.

[38] G. Bunting, *Parson Woodforde Society Quarterly Journal*, (Parson Wordforde Society, 1982), vol.15, no.1.

[39] NRO: NCC 1842 f.20.

[40] TNA: HO 107/756/3 f.6, p.6.

[41] NRO: DN/TA 407.

[42] NRO: DN/VIS 29a/2.

[43] See Chapter IV, p.23 and Chapter V, p.36.

[44] TNA: HO107/756/3.

[45] TNA: HO107/1820 ff.342–361.

[46] TNA: RG9/1229 ff.111–122.

[47] TNA: RG10/1831 ff.111–121.

[48] TNA: RG11/1963 ff.106–119.

[49] As an aside, with regard to Bergh Apton in particular, further investigation of this topic would appear desirable.

[50] Harrod's *Directory of Norfolk*, 1872.

[51] TNA: RG12/1541 ff.101–108.

[52] NRO: DN/VIS 54/6.

[53] NRO: DN/VIS 65/2.

[54] NRO: PD497/35.

[55] NRO: DN/VIS 75/2.

[56] NRO: PD497/36.

[57] NRO: C/ED 2/207.

[58] NRO: DN/VIS 75/2.

[59] Kelly's *Directory of Norfolk*, 1933.

[60] NRO: PD497/26.

[61] NRO: PD497/30.

[62] ESRO: ABE 30A.

[63] NRO: DN/VIS 84/10.

[64] NRO: SO 86/1.

[65] NRO: Denny-Cooke MSS.

[66] NRO: NPR Will 1871 no.268.

[67] NRO: NPR Will 1873 no.284.

[68] See Chapter X, p.84.

[69] Ordnance Survey evidence.

[70] 56 & 57 Vic. 73.

[71] NRO: PD497/28.

Chapter XIII

The Twentieth Century

The Census of 1901

The census taken on 31 March 1901 provides a detailed profile of the population of Bergh Apton at that time.[1] The parishioners, 418 in number, occupied 103 houses of which 37 had less than five rooms; there were also nine unoccupied houses of which six merely happened to be vacant on census night. As for the birthplaces of the population then, these may be summarised as follows:

Birthplaces of the population of Bergh Apton as given by the census of 1901					
Bergh Apton:	140	Nottinghamshire:	2	Shropshire:	1
Elsewhere in Norfolk:	232	Oxfordshire:	2	Somerset:	1
Suffolk:	7	Warwickshire:	2	Ireland:	1
London:	5	Cumberland:	1	South Africa:	1
Berkshire:	3	Dorset:	1	Not stated:	11
Lancashire:	3	Durham:	1		
Yorkshire:	3	Kent:	1		

Details of the 193 inhabitants, for whom occupations (or lack thereof) were declared in 1901, may best be summarised, under broad groupings, as follows:

Unoccupied		School Assistant:	1	Farmer	14
[Living on] Own Means:	2	Sub-Postmaster:	1	including 1 Farmer and	
Retired Farmer:	1			Market Gardener	
Retired Gardener:	1	**Tradesmen**		Farmer's Sons:	6
Retired Police Officer:	1	Blacksmith:	3	Fruit Grower:	2
		Bricklayer:	3	Gamekeeper:	2
Professional and Retail		Bricklayer's Labourer:	1	Gardener	4
Beerhouse Keeper:	1	Builder:	1	Gardener's Labourer:	1
Boot and Shoemaker:	2	Carpenter:	6	Horse and Stock Dealer:	1
Clerk in Holy Orders:	1	General Labourer:	1	Market Gardener:	8
Commercial Clerk and				Other Farm Workers:	15
Organist:	1	**Working on, or associated with,**			
Grocer:	2	**the Land**		**Servants and Service**	
Post Office Inspector:	1	Agricultural Labourer:	48	[Domestic] Servant:	28
[working as such in Norwich]		Agricultural Machinist:	1	Laundress:	5
Schoolmistress:	1	Carter:	2		
Pupil Teachers:	2	Farm Bailiff:	2		

Rectors of the Twentieth Century

Harvey William Gustavus Thursby

When the twentieth century opened, Harvey William Gustavus Thursby was serving as rector of Bergh Apton. According to the census taken on 31 March 1901, Revd Harvey Thursby was then occupying The Rectory with his wife, Margaret Emily, and three servants; in addition, their butler and his wife occupied four rooms over the Coach House.[2] Revd Harvey Thursby had two sons, John – known as Jack – and William. As for the Parish Church during H.W.G. Thursby's incumbency, his cousin Miss Sophia Charlotte Thursby had its south porch restored and a choir vestry added in 1902 at a cost of £357, this additional feature betokens a flourishing choir. Nine years later, in memory of her mother, Fanny Thursby, she had the east window replaced by one glazed by Charles Kempe; the old one was then placed in the north side of the chancel.[3] H.W.G. Thursby presented the parish with a hand-propelled funeral bier in 1910: this is no longer used for its original purpose, but was

Above: *Charlie and Rose Dye's bungalow in Threadneedle Street, at one time occupied by Ebeneezer Hindle. This photograph was taken in 1954, on completion of a major upgrade of the property.* **Left to right:** *Betty Dye, Charlie (Chubb) Dye junr, Charlie Dye senr, ?, Linda Tyler, Brenda Dye, Roy Tyler, Fred Dye (seated).*

Inset, right: *Charlie Dye, who retired from the Metropolitan Police and became a market gardener in Bergh Apton, with his granddaughters Greta Tyler (centre) and Vera Dye (barely visible, far right) at his packing shed on Mill Road in the early 1930s. Charlie was not the first generation of his family to join 'The Met', for his mother's brother Charles Henry Loyd (of the singular Bergh Apton spelling) had also served. Perhaps he had persuaded his nephew that it was a grand life, having himself served at Buckingham Palace at some stage in his service.*

Far left: *Jimmy Annis in Metropolitan Police uniform, c.1913. He was one of the many young men who left the village to make a career elsewhere and returned to set up their own market gardens.*

Left: *Harry Percy Royall who joined the Metropolitan Police in January 1914. Harry did not return to the village but completed his career in London.*

Taken outside the Hellington Bell, this photo captures the time around 1911 that the main road from Lowestoft to Norwich (now the A146) was first 'tarmaced'. The man sitting on the chimney is the engine's driver. The road gang appears to be taking a break in the company of some onlookers. This once tranquil spot is now a 60 mph commuter racetrack.

at least pressed into service as a prop in the scene recording the Black Death in the Millennium Pageant of 2000 (of which more later in the chapter). In 1917, the churchyard was again extended by two roods, this additional land was a further gift of Lord Canterbury of Seething Old Hall.[4]

At this point it should be mentioned that in 1901, Mrs Fanny Thursby, widow of the late rector, William Ford Thursby, gave the sum of £2,500 invested in the Norwich Diocesan Trust Fund, to the intent that the interest arising should be applied to maintaining a parish nurse. This was indeed done, with the following nurses' names established from the Parochial Church Council Minute Book: Nurse Steer, from or by 1922 to 1928; Sister Egan, 1930–1934; and Sister Haslam, 1934–1936.[5] Since the establishment of the National Health Service in 1948, the said interest has been applied at the discretion of the rectors and churchwardens. It should be stressed that Fanny Thursby's gift forms an endowment fund, not a charity.

Revd Harvey W.G. Thursby was one of Bergh Apton's most active rectors. He served as a magistrate upon the Loddon Bench, was an attentive supporter of Bergh Apton School, and (like his uncle, William Ford Thursby, before him) was an enthusiastic farmer of his glebe. In addition, he purchased two fields adjacent to The Rectory grounds called Spooner's and Sandigel's that had formed part of the Bergh Apton Manor estate prior to its sale in 1914.[6]

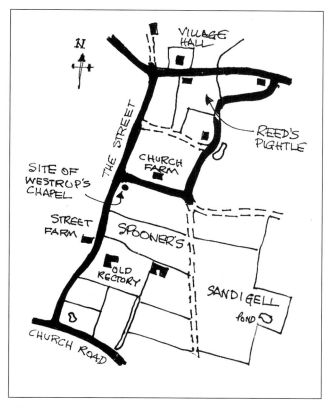

Fig.13.1. Field names in the centre of the village included Reed's Pightle (see p.62), Spooner's and Sandigel's (see this page). Westrup's chapel (see p.115) was located nearby until the early 1950s. The Village Hall on Cooke's Road was opened in 1953 (see Appendix II).

Sam 'Buck' Spooner snow-balling in 1916 with the Preston children whose father kept the Hellington Bell. Left to right: *Sarah Kate Preston, Sam 'Buck' Spooner, George Preston and Frances Preston.* It is said that Buck kept a live toad under his shirt next to his skin to ward off rheumatism.

The Hellington Bell, c.1923. The Bell was licensed only to sell ales and stouts. In the photo are Mr Preston the licensee, with his daughter Frances and her daughter Doreen. Sonny Preston (right), *a nephew, emigrated to Australia.*

Prospect Place, c.1910. This rare photo depicts the road between Loddon and Norwich before it was tarred. The houses in the background are at Prospect Place, an outlying hamlet of Bergh Apton.

George Barkley Raikes

George Barkley Raikes, who served as rector of Bergh Apton from Revd Thursby's retirement at Lady Day 1920 until 1936, did not share the latter's interest in farming. As a consequence, the church commissioners agreed to sell the outlying Bergh Apton glebe, that is other than The Rectory grounds and the churchyard, in 1921 for £637.10s., and this sum was invested in 3½ per cent War Stock.[7]

Bergh Apton church in the early 1920s, showing the new south porch and the radically altered south transept.

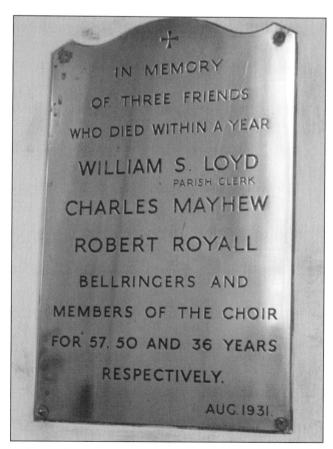

A brass plaque in the chancel erected in August 1931 to William Loyd (the parish clerk), Charles Mayhew and Robert Royall, friends who served in the choir and as bell-ringers for 57, 50 and 36 years respectively.

On 28 April 1930, the Revd Raikes reported to the Parochial Church Council that he had been left £100 by Canon John Alfred Laurence of Dilham, who had served as curate at Bergh Apton between 1860 and 1872, to be spent on useful parish work. At this time the need to have Bergh Apton's ring of six bells rehung had become urgent, and it was considered that Laurence's bequest might be applied to this work. In the event this money did not have to be spent thus, as a consequence of a faculty obtained in 1931 which permitted the church plate dating from 1675 and 1789 to be sold. The £200 arising from this sale in 1934, together with other sums collected amounting to £37, formed the exact amount needed to pay Messrs Gillett and Johnson to have the bells rehung in a metal frame with modern fittings.[8]

As for bell-ringers at Bergh Apton, a brass plaque on the north wall of the chancel records William Loyd, Charles Mayhew and Robert Royall who had served as such – and also as choristers – from the nineteenth century into the twentieth for the respective periods of 57, 50 and 36 years. These three had died by 1931, by which time the Lester and Boggis families were the chief providers of ringers in the parish.

Alexander St John Heard

Alexander (otherwise Alick) St John Heard served as rector of Bergh Apton from 1936 until 1941. He was a keen campanologist, and presented a set of hand bells to the church in 1937. In addition, the Parish Church possesses four handbells, which are believed to have been made at Lambourn, Berkshire, in the early-eighteenth century; how they came to be in Bergh Apton is not known.

Frederick William Martin

In 1941, the benefice of Bergh Apton with Holverston was united with that of Yelverton with Alpington, and was served from Bergh Apton Rectory by the Revd Heard's successor, Frederick William Martin. The latter's wife, Gladys, died in 1957, and in the following year he married the headmistress at Bergh Apton School, Miss Helen Catton. In 1959, a faculty was obtained which authorised the removal of the organ from the gallery to the south transept of Bergh Apton church.[9] Electricity was connected to the church and school in about 1957. The Revd Martin, who retired in 1959, was the last rector of Bergh Apton to occupy the historic Rectory, which property was sold to Keith Freeman in 1961 and has since been known as Bergh Apton Stud.

Frederic Mortimer Snellgrove

The church commissioners decided to build a replacement rectory at the south-west corner of Church Close, one more in keeping with the domestic requirements of modern clergy and their families. Frederic Mortimer Snellgrove, rector of Bergh Apton

111

Left: *Bell-ringers at Bergh Apton after ringing to celebrate the coronation of King George V in 1910. Left to right, back row: ?, ? Bracey, Robert Royall; front row: Albert Lawn, Billy Loyd and Harry Percy Royall.*

Below: *The bells were taken out of the tower in 1934 when the new frame was installed. The bell-ringers pictured here standing behind the bells in the churchyard are, left to right: Herbert Boggis, Harry Lester, Robert Lester, George Jermy and Alfred Boggis.*

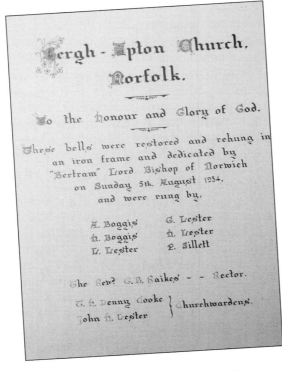

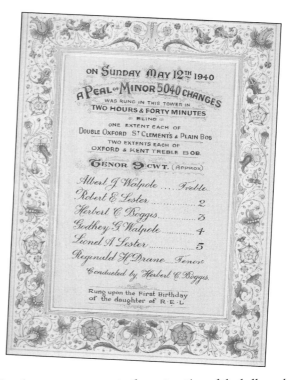

Above left: *This framed document hangs in the ringing chamber to commemorate the restoration of the bells and their installation in the new iron frame in 1934 during the time of Revd Raikes (1920–36). The bells were rededicated by Bertram, Lord Bishop of Norwich, on Sunday 5 August of that year. The ringing band that celebrated the occasion were Alfred Boggis, Herbert Boggis, Lionel Lester, George Lester, Harry Lester and Percy Sillett.*

Above right: *This peal board commemorates a quarter peal rung on Sunday 12 May 1940 to celebrate the first birthday of Robert E. Lester's daughter Alice. After the evacuation of Dunkirk later that month, church bells throughout the land were ordered to be used only in the event of enemy landings – a ban that was to remain in force until celebrations of the battle of El Alamein in November 1942. Alice returned to the tower 60 years later to help ring the half-muffled bells at the funeral of her uncle, George Lester, who had been sexton for over 60 years.*

Right: *Subscribers and ringers from when the bells were restored and rehung on 11 June 1890. There must have been some consternation when the board was unveiled as three names are wrong: R.F. Lloyd should read T.F. Lloyd; the Misses Leago were the Misses Seago; and Whall should be spelt Wall!*

Below: *The peal board in the ringing chamber that commemorates the peal rung on 24 May 1845 by William Scarlett, Samuel Scarlett, William Smith, Charles England, John Scarlett and John Dawson.*

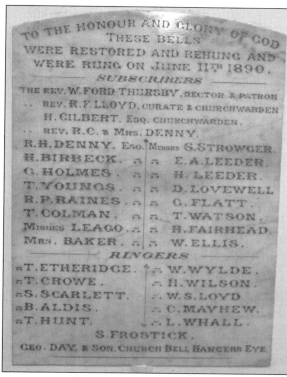

Above: *Bell-ringers of the mid-1970s. Left to right: Jimmy Forder, Herbert Boggis, ?, Norman Cossey and William Barratt.*

Left: *Ringers in the present band on the occasion of the marriage of Bergh Apton's Natasha Daniells to Richard Peachment on Friday 30 July 2004. Left to right: Bill Gates, Lizzie Burrage, Hilary Ling, John Burrage, Patricia Waters (tower captain) and John Ling.*

Bergh Apton church, c.1970. The battlements were taken down in 1958 during the incumbency of Revd Frederick Snellgrove. Inset: Revd Frederick Mortimer Snellgrove and Mrs Snellgrove in 1969.

from 1960 to 1972 and likewise rector of Yelverton first occupied this house. It was during his incumbency (c.1965) that Bergh Apton church choir ceased.

Michael Sydney Stedman

His successor, Michael Sydney Stedman, who occupied The Rectory from 1973 until 1985, held the newly-created office of team vicar in the Bramerton Group of 11 parishes; for in the former year Bergh Apton became an integral part of this – one of a number of such groupings pioneered within the Norwich Diocese. Other than Bergh Apton and Bramerton, the parishes concerned were Ashby St Mary, Carleton St Peter, Claxton, Framingham Pigot, Hellington, Rockland St Mary, Surlingham, Thurton and Yelverton – while the spiritual care of the church-less parishes of Alpington and Holverston also lay within this group's responsibilities.

Shortly after the establishment of the Bramerton Group, a bimonthly publication *Eleven Says*, was launched, which continues to provide a comprehensive news service for the parishes concerned. Subsequently, in June 1992, Eileen Lain-Rogers of Sunnyside, to supplement the news provided by *Eleven Says* and include items of more local and personal interest, founded the bimonthly *Bergh Apton Newsletter*.

Revd Michael Stedman in the early 1980s.

In 1984, Richard Cushing and his uncle, Lionel Lester, repaired the church clock. In 2004 Richard maintains the responsibility for winding the mechanisms of this clock and its chime once a week – a task that his uncle, George Lester, had previously carried out over a period of 45 years.

As a consequence of the departure of Michael Stedman in 1985, it was decided that there was no need for a clergyman serving the Bramerton Group of parishes to live in Bergh Apton, and The Rectory here was then sold as a private house with the authorisation of the church commissioners.

Bergh Apton Church in the Late-Twentieth Century

From 1985 until 1988, the actual living of Bergh Apton within the Bramerton Group was vacant, however, clergy from elsewhere within these parishes ensured that regular services and ministry were maintained here. From 1988 until his retirement in 1997, Gordon Ernest Jessup, rector of Thurton, where he resided, also served as priest in charge of Bergh Apton. Since 1997, Dr Peter Malcolm Knight, likewise rector of and living in Thurton, has similarly served Bergh Apton.

A final gift to Bergh Apton church in the twentieth century was of a Communion rail kneeler, presented by husband and wife Deryk and Pat Baylis who left

Revd Dr Peter Malcolm Knight, rector of Bergh Apton in 2004.

the village in 1999. Moreover, its organ was totally overhauled and restored in 2000, with the help of funding from the Bergh Apton Sculpture Trail (of which more later in the chapter); this work was completed so as to allow a 100-year anniversary celebration of the inaugural concert upon this organ to be held on the ninth of December then (see Chapter XII).

An Undenominational Chapel

In about 1923, Jonathan Wilfred Westrup of Church Farm purchased a war department hut for use as an Undenominational Chapel. He erected this on the site of a cottage at the corner of The Street and Dodger's Lane, once occupied by Isaac Browne,[10] and which had been demolished by 1905.[11] This chapel was removed about 1953.[12]

The Bergh Apton Manor Estate

In 1900 the joint Lords of the Manor of Bergh Apton were Richard Harrison Denny of Framingham Cottage, Framingham Pigot, and his younger brother, Thomas Henry Denny-Cooke of Richmond, Surrey; the latter, in his own right, was also Lord of the Manor of Washingford. As trustees of their late father Richard Cooke Denny, these brothers held the largest part of what had been historically the Denny and Cooke estates in Bergh Apton (and beyond), while Thomas Henry exclusively owned Washingford House and its farm. In addition, a part of this estate, including Bergh Apton Manor, was then mortgaged with James Henry Brooke Christie of Framingham Pigot Manor, father-in-law of Richard Harrison Denny; Bergh Apton Manor, under the provisions of Richard Cooke Denny's will, continued to be occupied by his widow, Jane Deeker Denny, until her death on 21 December 1913.[13]

According to the Duties on Land Values Schedules of 1910 for Bergh Apton, the manor estate as held by the trustees of Richard Cooke Denny was, at 554a.1r.37p., the most extensive in the parish. If one accrues to this the property then exclusively owned by Thomas Henry Denny-Cooke, 126a.3r.0p., and that mortgaged with James Henry Brooke Christie, 79a.1r.31p., the total of 760a.2r.28p. related to about three-eighths of the entire parish.[14] We take a further look at land ownership shortly.

James Henry Brooke Christie died on 20 September 1912, having left his estate to his son, James Archibald Christie, also of Framingham Pigot Manor and to whom probate was granted at London on the following 22 November. In the wake of their mother's death, the Bergh Apton Manor estate trustees put this, inclusive of the Washingford House property exclusively owned by Thomas Henry Denny-Cooke, and that mortgaged with James Archibald Christie (as his father's heir), up for auction in 26 lots on 4 July 1914.[15] It would appear

Weddings celebrated at Bergh Apton Church

The wedding of Ronnie Farrow and Barbara Dye in March 1952. Left to right: Rose Dye, Ronnie Farrow, Barbara Farrow (née Dye), Percy Wilson, Ethel Farrow, Vera Dye. Dimly in the background are Lenny Dye and Revd Martin.

Ivy Boggis and Wilfred Gibson, head gardener at Thelveton Hall, September 1935. (Ivy's father, Alfred John Boggis MM, was killed in October 1918.)

The wedding of John Lester and Joy Gooch in September 1955. Left to right: David Lester, Barry Cushing, Harry Lester, Anna Scarles, Edith Lester, John Lester and Joy Lester (née Gooch), Olive Scarles, Lily Scarles (the bride's mother) and Charlie Scarles.

Fred Littlewood, Revd Martin and Violet Littlewood (née Jermy) in August 1953.

Richard Peachment and Natasha Peachment (née Daniells) and the bride's mother, Jenny Daniells, on Friday 30 July 2004.

that the object of this sale was to raise sufficient funds to pay death duties and clear the mortgage on the estate; for as revealed two days later by the *Eastern Daily Press*, its core element Lot 1, being the manor-house with 34a.3r.38p., was purchased by the trustees' agent, Thomas H. Keith, for £2,000, while Lot 3, Washingford House farm with 304a.1r.34p. was withdrawn when the bidding reached £7,200. Indeed, as the Denny-Cooke manuscripts in the Norwich Record Office reveal, the trustees' mortgage with James Archibald Christie was cleared on 30 October 1914.

The role of lord of the Manor (as held jointly) of Bergh Apton, and that of lord of the Manor of Washingford, was to come to have little but symbolic importance from 1922. Given the pace of acquisition of copyhold property by the lords themselves, which automatically rendered it freehold, particularly since the Manor of Bergh Apton had been purchased by Richard Cooke Denny from Lord Abergavenny in 1869, and enfranchisement of copyhold property held by the dwindling number of other landowners in the parish, the income from entry fines and quitrents due to the lords had already fallen sharply. The provisions of the Law of Property Act, 1922, that required all property still held according to this form of tenure to be enfranchised in return for a once and for all compensatory payment to each lord concerned, brought an end to this ancient form of income.[16] Post-1922 lords of a few Norfolk manors have retained vestigial rights such as those concerning minerals, which may be discovered beneath them, or in respect of the management of surviving common land; but no such rights apply to the Manors of Bergh Apton and Washingford.

Between the First and Second World Wars, Mr and Mrs Thomas Henry Denny-Cooke of Bergh Apton Manor, which they had come to occupy in 1915,[17] contrived their house and grounds to serve as an independent holiday home for children from British boarding-schools who could not readily spend their vacations with their own families. One who enjoyed this accommodation was the noted actress, Dulcie Gray, as reported in the *Eastern Daily Press*, 18 March 2000.

Richard Harrison Denny, joint lord of the Manors of Bergh Apton and Washingford, died at his Sheringham home on 29 January 1944. His marriage had been childless, and consequently his brother Thomas Henry Denny-Cooke of Bergh Apton Manor was left as sole lord of these two manors. The latter was a dedicated, hard-working and popular resident squire of Bergh Apton, as the following quote from his obituary in the *Eastern Daily Press*, 15 September 1952 (two days after his death):

He had been a member of Loddon Rural District Council since 1916 and was vice-chairman of a number of committees. He served on the Housing Committee for 20 years and was also on the Sanitary, Highways and Assessments Committees. A Justice of the Peace, [he] was vice-chairman of Loddon Bench for many years and was also chairman of the Bergh Apton Parish Council. He was a churchwarden and a school manager, and for ten years up to 1946 he was also chairman of Loddon and Clavering Guardians Committee. During the First World War he was a special constable and a member of the Local Defence Volunteers, and in the Second World War was senior warden for Bergh Apton.... [He] was awarded the B.E.M. in the 1951 New Year Honours List.

Thomas Henry Denny-Cooke, and his wife who died at Bergh Apton Manor on 2 May 1960, had three daughters. The eldest of these, Beatrice Katherine, who was unmarried, sold the Bergh

Thomas Henry and Mrs Denny-Cooke in the garden of Bergh Apton Manor in the late 1940s or early '50s, not long before he died in 1952.

The marriage of Marjorie Chichele Denny-Cooke to Edgar Lamb on 8 June 1933. They are standing in the original iron-gated entrance to the churchyard where she is now buried.

This large body of the area Home Guard on parade in c.1943 included Bergh Apton's No.3 Platoon of No.1 Company 3rd Battalion Norfolk. They are in the grounds of Bergh Apton Manor (in what is called Monty's Meadow at the time of writing). Left to right, back row: *V. Pardon, Bertie Harwood, Cyril Dye, W.F. Howard, Peter Harvey, Reggie Carpenter, J. Gooch, Derek Stansby, Albert 'Doctor' Bloomfield, A.J. Holman, Sam Debbage, Billy Sewell, R. Rumsby, J.F. Cooper, W. Watkinson, Arthur Green, R. Utting, Bertie Kemp, C. Goldsmith, Eric Carver, A.W. Garrard, R. Brown, J.S. Vincent and Charlie Allum;* fourth row: *Cliffy Keeler, R.F. Harwood, C.W.A. Garrod, A.P. Garrard, R.C. Sadler, O.C. Taylor, G. Sadler, L. Codling, Basil Jermy, C. Sturman, Percy Martin, Ernie Panks, Leslie Catchpole, J.W. Stone, Alan Moll, Basil Sutton, Gily Beaumont, Frank Barber, H. Flegg, P. Cushion, Tom Baldwin, Jack Hoddy, Donny Carr, A.E. Beaumont, D. Vincent, G. Goddard, Jimmy Yallop;* third row: *S.A. Mallet, R.F. Bunnett, C. Scott, Charlie Forder, R. McLaughlin, G.L. Balls, R. Hoddy, C. Middleton, Reggie Barnes, D. Pitcher, G. Caley, J. South, C.V. Balls, Charlie Sadler, Carlos Glasspole, A. Saunders, Peter Keeler, Ronnie Moll, B. Basham, F. Brown, Fred Elwin, E. Mallet, Billy Frost, D.C.F. Naylor, B. Tuffs, Kenny 'Jericho' Keeler, P.G. Burgess, W. South;* second row: *Arthur Annis, Harry Sadler, L.Cpl Edwards, L.Cpl Gooch, L.Cpl Howell, L.Cpl Ernie Frosdick, L.Cpl Arnall Capps, Cpl Durrant, Cpl Kerry, Cpl Catchpole, Sgt Jack Loades, Sgt Lionel Lester, Sgt Walter Cain, Lt Herbert Betts, Lt Pullen, Lt Reggie 'Dodger' Drane, Sgt Ellis, Sgt 'Kimmo' Drane, Sgt Mayes, Sgt Coleman, L.Cpl Jack Frost, L.Cpl Gaff, L.Cpl Billy Drane, L.Cpl Green, L.Cpl Naylor, L.Cpl Cecil 'Trim' Alexander, L.Cpl Everett, L. Cpl Trett and G. Goodyear;* front row: *Jonny Hupton, Fred Kirby, F. Pearson, Arthur Loades, R.C. Gowen, Brian Tubby, Frank Thurlow, Ted Annis, Charlie Pitchers, R.K. Clare, Eddie Kiddle, J. Welling, B.I. Trett, E. Farrow, Frank Freestone, Charlie Winter, Ralph 'Chilly' Howard, R. Hallet, M. Adams, C. Downing, A.B. Oakley, Arthur Lovewell, W. Clarke, Clifford 'Joker' Frost, W. Trett and R. Cooper.*

The Women's Institute at a garden party in the park at Bergh Apton Manor in 1936. Left to right, back row: *Mrs K. Keeler, Mrs Margaret Lester, ?, Mrs Clara Cain, Mrs Lisa Frost, ?;* centre row: *Miss Nora Panks, Mrs Gedge, Mrs Williams, Miss Keeping, Mrs Freestone, Mrs Billy Panks, Mrs Clara Rackham holding Jennifer Lamb, Mrs Carol Seeley, Mrs Mitchell, Mrs Littleboy, Myrtle Matthews;* seated: *Mrs Lily Gooch (later Scarles) holding Joy, Mrs Tomlinson holding Rita (or Sheila), Alice (or May) Farrow, Mrs Anne Dye, Mrs London holding Kathleen, Mrs Matthews (formerly Mrs Debbage), Mrs Denny-Cooke holding Patricia, Mrs Dye, Mrs Bond holding June, Mrs Ada Lain holding Dennis, ?;* front group on grass: *Miss Betty Denny-Cooke, her sister Mrs Marjorie Lamb, Beryl Lester, ?, Doreen London.*

May Farrow, pictured here in the mid-1930s, at the Lodge on Threadneedle Street which was occupied by her family when her father David was coachman at Bergh Apton Manor. The cottage albeit enlarged is still redolent of this rural style of architecture at the time of writing.

including an involvement with both the church and the school.[19] Lord Canterbury had vacated Holly Lodge by 1933,[20] but was to be buried at Bergh Apton following his death at his Lyndhurst, Hampshire, home on 26 February 1941; he left no male heir and his title became extinct.

According to the Duties on Land Values Schedules of 1910 for Bergh Apton, property here was in the hands of 27 owners (including corporate bodies). The statistics of these may be presented more fully as follows:

No. of landowners	Area of land held
6	less than 1 acre
9	1–10 acres
6	10–100 acres
6	over 100 acres

As for the above statistics, the agglomerate of the three distinct ownerships of the overall Denny-Cooke estate as one, (see earlier in this chapter), there would be but five owners for each of the last two categories according to extent. In any case, the fall in the number of landowners here since 1841, when parallel statistics were extracted from the Tithe Apportionment Schedules[21] is marked. Yet, within a dozen years of the compilation of the Duties on Land Values Schedules, the number of landowners in Bergh Apton again rose, thanks to the following circumstances.

As a consequence of the Bergh Apton Manor Estate sale of 4 July 1914, as reported in the *Eastern Daily Press* two days later, other than two lots bought on behalf of the Denny trustees and six which were withdrawn and so retained by them, 18 were then

Apton Manor estate a year after her mother's death; Miss Denny-Cooke died on 20 June 1972, and was the last member of her family to be buried at Bergh Apton. The second eldest daughter, Constance Joan, married John Claud Fortescue Fryer of Chatteris, Cambridgeshire on 23 April 1919. He was subsequently knighted. Lady Fryer died in 1989, leaving as her heirs the two daughters of her younger sister, Marjorie Chichele who had married Edgar John Lamb of West Bridgford, Nottinghamshire, on 8 June 1933. The lordships of the Manors of Bergh Apton and Washingford, devolved upon the Lamb sisters, Mrs Patricia McLevie, a resident of Koorda, Western Australia, and Mrs Jennifer Findlay, who placed them on the market in the early 1990s. Their subsequent ownership has not been discovered, although it is known that no resident of Bergh Apton acquired them.

John Henry Manners-Sutton, 3rd Viscount Canterbury, inherited the Brooke Estate,[18] which included Bergh Apton Hall, Holly Lodge, Seething Old Hall, and (the then) Bergh Apton Cottage, from his brother-in-law, Henry Kett-Tompson, who died in 1872. Subsequently, a number of members of the Manners-Sutton family were to be buried at Bergh Apton, and have memorials in the church. This attachment to Bergh Apton is notable, given neither the 3rd, the 4th nor the 5th Viscount Canterburys actually lived in the parish; however, Charles Graham Manners-Sutton, the 6th Viscount, who inherited the title from his cousin, Henry Frederick Walpole Manners-Sutton, 5th Viscount, in 1918, made Bergh Apton his home for some years – the first lay peer known to have lived here. Directory evidence is that Lord Canterbury occupied Bergh Apton Cottage (later House) in 1922, and Holly Lodge from 1925 to 1929. Whilst living at Bergh Apton, Lord Canterbury and his wife played an active role in village life,

The only known photograph of one of Bergh Apton's principal citizens of the first half of the twentieth century – Charles Graham Manners-Sutton, 6th Viscount Canterbury (in the foreground wearing a hat) standing on the lawn of his home, Holly Lodge, which was in use as a bowling-green in the early 1930s. Lionel Lester, son of his agent John Lester, is standing to the left. He was Bergh Apton's District Councillor for 50 years.

The south aspect of Holly Lodge, principal home of the Canterburys during their ownership of the Brooke Estate from the 1870s to 1946.

purchased by nine individuals through bidding or by private contract.

The number of Bergh Apton landowners might have risen again five years later, for on 8 October 1919 the outlying portions of the Brooke Estate were auctioned at the behest of Lord Canterbury. However, as the *Eastern Daily Press* reported on the following day, the Bergh Apton lots – including Bergh Apton Hall, Bergh Apton Cottage, Bussey Bridge Farm, Holly Lodge and Holly Lodge Farm – were all withdrawn and retained by his lordship.

Street Farm

A property that did change hands in 1919 was Street Farm (later renamed Apton Manor), this then having been purchased from the Denny Trustees by the Norfolk County Council. This body had been empowered by the Small Holdings and Allotments

Little Street Farm, one of three prefabricated dwellings on the Norfolk County Council smallholdings established in 1920. This smallholding was first rented by Samuel Rayner then by Carlos Glasspole and finally by Fred Riseborough who bought the property when Norfolk County Council sold the houses and some of the land in the 1960s.

Act, 1908, to acquire land to alleviate rural unemployment and distress. It was to retain the ownership of this property, which was divided into smallholdings, until 1974.[22] To save confusion, I might add that the present-day farmhouse known as Street Farm is a modern house occupying what had been an orchard plot immediately north of the original Street Farm.

Pictured above: Frances Roper in the Land Army, c.1941, when her husband farmed one of the Street Farms owned by Norfolk County Council. They lived in the western half of Street Farm. At the time of writing her son Stuart still farms land in the village.

Town Farm

A property sale in Bergh Apton in the early 1920s, other than that of the outlying glebe (previously noted), concerned that of the larger part of Town Farm, including the farmhouse, on 25 September 1922. This sale was authorised by the charity commissioners at the behest of the Feoffees of this estate.[23] An outlying block of Town Farm land, extending to 11a.0r.8p. on the south side of Loddon Road, failed to attract a buyer in 1922, and continues to be let by the Tenwinter Trust as authorised by the Charity Commission.

Bergh Apton Hall

On 21 September 1929, at the instructions of Lord Canterbury, Bergh Apton Hall with its associated dairy farm, in all 196a.1r.16p., and a piece of land with a gravel pit by the church, were sold as lots 1 and 2. According to the *Eastern Daily Press* two days later, the former property was purchased by Mr G. Channell of London for £1,100, while the latter, extending to but 6a.0r.30p., was bought by Mr C.T. Sword for as much as £240 – particularly during a period of agricultural depression, gravel-bearing land was worth considerably more, acre for acre, than ordinary farmland.

Other Holdings

Taking individual holdings in Bergh Apton described in successive editions of Kelly's *Directory of Norfolk* from 1916 to 1937 as farms, smallholdings, market gardens and fruit and vegetable growers (or in a few instances under two of these heads), these rose from 24 to 30 between 1916 and 1925; as for the fruit grown here, cherries were particularly noted. Indeed, the property in Mill Road (known as The Garden in an Orchard at the time of writing) was planted as a commercial orchard in 1926 with apples, pears and cherries, and underplanted with soft fruit.[24] Maybe as a consequence of the agricultural depression which obtained for much of the 1920s and 1930s – admittedly ameliorated in and about Bergh Apton by the demand for foodstuffs including dairy produce and meat by the population of Norwich and its suburbs, and the steady increase in the production of sugar beet which was supplied to the factory at nearby Cantley – this total fell to 25 in both 1933 and 1937. That the larger part of Bergh Apton's agricultural land was used for arable farming is indicated on the Land Utilisation Map of 1931/2.[25] The outbreak of the Second World War in 1939 was to ensure that all manner of husbandry in Bergh Apton would flourish of necessity.

Further Property Sales

On 15 June 1946, the Trustees of the late Lord Canterbury, who died in 1941, auctioned the remaining portion of his Bergh Apton estate. The *Eastern Daily Press* reported two days later as to the principal properties concerned that Holly Lodge Farm and Washingford Bridge Farm, the latter admittedly largely in Mundham parish, duly acquired purchasers, while Bussey Bridge Farm was withdrawn – in the event it was to be sold by private treaty two years later.

At Michaelmas 1954, Michael William Armitage Harris of Holverston Hall purchased Washingford House and its associated farmland – including that which prior to 1882 had been farmed from Bergh Apton Manor – from the Denny-Cooke trustees.[26]

Agricultural Census Returns, 1967

The Ministry of Agriculture, Fisheries and Food agricultural census returns of 2 June 1967 provide a detailed picture of husbandry in Bergh Apton.[27] This data relates to all agricultural and horticultural holdings in the parish then, although not non-commercially run gardens.

No. of Holdings	Size of Holding
7	under 5 acres
5	5–15 acres
1	15–20 acres
5	20–29 acres
6	30–49 acres
5	50–99 acres
2	150–299 acres
2	300–499 acres

Holdings in Bergh Apton, as categorised in the 1967 agricultural census returns

With regard to the above holdings, the census returns did not declare how many were owner-occupied and how many were leasehold – or, as would have applied in some cases, part owner-occupied and part leasehold.

Cereals	Acreage
Barley	728a.1r.
Wheat,	186a.
Oats	77a.1r.
Rye	15a.
Root crops	**Acreage**
Sugar beet	152a.
Vegetables incl. potatoes for human consumption	118a.3r.
Beans, roots and kale for stock feeding	70a.2r.

Cereals and root crops recorded in Bergh Apton in the 1967 agricultural census returns

A significant element of Bergh Apton's farmland in 1967 was the 353a.1r. of permanent grass, about two-thirds of which (232 acres) was for grazing, and the rest for mowing; while rough grazing amounted to 37a.3r. In addition, clover, sainfoin and temporary grass extended over 55a.3r., all for mowing save 8a.3r. used for grazing.

Bergh Apton remained a noted fruit-growing locality in 1967, having 24a.1r. of orchard, and 22a.2r. of small fruit – 12a.1r. of the latter, judging from the statistics presented, grown under orchard trees. Hardy nursery stock, flowers (not under glass), and bulbs were grown on 15 acres.

Livestock	Total
Cattle	218
Pigs	748
Sheep	0
Poultry:	20,865

Bergh Apton's farm livestock in 1967 as categorised in the 1967 agricultural census returns

Population and Housing

The 1967 statistics also included the number of agricultural and horticultural workers in Bergh Apton (excluding farmers and farmers' wives): of regular employees, 30 were full-time and two were part-time; there were also ten seasonal workers.

The population of Bergh Apton as revealed by the 1901 census has been considered in some detail at the beginning of this chapter. Given the 'one hundred years' confidentiality rule' which obtains in respect of individuals enumerated in subsequent censuses, only broad statements will be made in the text which follows concerning the data they encapsulate.[28] The most striking feature they reveal is the near static population of the parish, viz.:

Year	Population
1911	424
1921	425
1931	414
1951	402
1961	430
1971	420
1981	410
1991	409

The Airey houses were built in Church Road after the Second World War. They were designed to last 20 years but it was over 40 years before they were eventually replaced. During the replacement the resident family of each house in turn was relocated to a mobile home on the site whilst their new homes were built. During the course of the operation the efficiency of South Norfolk District Council was praised.

These council-houses designed by the architects Tayler [sic] and Green were built on Church Road in 1956. They won an award from the Civic Trust in 1959 and from the Ministry of Housing in 1961.

While the total population of Bergh Apton changed but little throughout the twentieth century, there was growth in its stock of housing which deserves attention. Between the censuses of 1931 and 1951, the number of dwellings rose from 118 to 132: this rise is partly accounted for by the erection of two double-dweller council-houses on Church Road to the south of Town Farm in 1938/9, and otherwise by private houses in various locations. The rise in the number of dwellings from 132 in 1951 to 151 in 1961 essentially relates to the development of Loddon Rural District Council housing on Church Road opposite the south end of Bergh Apton Street, designed by the award-winning architectural partnership of Tayler and Green. Between 1961 and 1981, the number of dwellings in Bergh Apton only rose by four; however, from the latter year to 1991, the total rose to 175, most of the new houses having been built by or near Threadneedle Street on what had been Apton Heath prior to 1806.

A fuller consideration of the broad theme of population and housing in Bergh Apton during the twentieth century leads us to the following points. Firstly, in 1901, an average of just over four persons lived in each occupied house in the parish; while in 1991 there was an average of about two and one-third persons in each dwelling. Secondly, the data outlined reflects not only the demand for less-crowded living accommodation, but also the disappearance of the living-in servant class, and the trend towards smaller, often 'single-parent', families. The decline in the number of children here was to contribute to the closure of Bergh Apton School in 1981.

Bergh Apton School

Bergh Apton School was enlarged in 1905 at a cost of £400; while the average attendance in 1908 was 55, according to Kelly's *Directory of Norfolk* then. Much of interest concerning Bergh Apton School is recorded in its logbooks. The following entries have been extracted from that compiled between 1901 to 1927:[29]

24 July 1905:
Jack Alexander absent to have his tooth extracted (excusable).

24 June 1907:
Mrs Birkbeck's kind present of a book arrived by post on Saturday: 'Shock Headed Peter'.

20 December 1907:
The School closed this afternoon for the Xmas Holiday for 3 weeks as usual. A few games were indulged in in the afternoon, the girls had a knitting race (the toe of a stocking) and the Revd H. Thursby kindly gave and distributed some sweets.

Hannah Greenacre of No.4 Sunnyside at the rear of her cottage with children in the early 1950s. Hannah was one of the village parents to be bereaved during the First World War, losing her sons George and Charles.

Bergh Apton School in a production of The Mikado, *1934, produced by the headmistress, Mrs Williams, and her assistant Miss Hepburn. Left to right, back row: Tony 'Toetack' Hardesty, Vivian 'Sonny' Taylor, Lila Keeler, Irene Fisher, Jean Dean, Rosemary Boughen, Barbara Frost, Gerald 'Pimshie' Boughen; middle row: Eric 'Hoss' Hardesty, Ronald 'Duck' Appleton, Jack Lovewell, Brian Tubby, Evelyn Edge, Ivy Clarke, Josephine Hemmant, Doreen Edge, Arthur 'Dinkie' Edge; front row: Eric Caley, Rita Lutkin, Eva Taylor, George Freestone, 'Dickie' Bird.*

Bergh Apton School in 1912 with children outside on the road. The photograph includes: *D. Redgrave, E. Hipperson, Alice Farrow, Gladys Rope, G. Gooch, Alice Keeler, ? Annis, A. Rope, Dolly Norman, S. Kiddle, L. Loyd, Reg Wall or Ernie Keeler, Artie Kiddle, E. Read, Alec Stone, Billy Keeler, D. Stone, W. Loyd, Jack Royall, Lily Wall, P. Gooch, Ivy Boggis, T. Westrupp, Billie King, R. Wall, Harvey Eastell, Percy Keeler, Lionel Lester, R. Mayes.*

School play, c.1947 Left to right, back row: *Donald Self, Edward Frost, Albert Forder? Lambert Harvey, Charlie Flatt, Peter Parfitt, Kenny Hurrell, David Davison, ?, David Lester, Basil Brown, Peter Brown, Raymond Caley and Derek Littleboy (in front)*; middle row: *?, Nanette Thurlow, ?, Marjorie Glasspole, Eunice Dommit, Jean Littleboys, Ann Hurrell, Janet Mann, Brenda Elmer, Joyce Self, Ann Kemp*; front row: *Harry Forder, Michael Selby, Alan Self, Norman Carpenter, Jenny Carpenter, ?, Iris Fenn, Hazel Keeler, Gwen Davison, Sheila Fenn, Janet Kemp, Grace Forder, David Wood.*

Bergh Apton schoolchildren, 1920s. Left to right, back row: *Hubert Todd, Mary Purling, Heather Westrupp, Cybil Todd, Helen Drake, Grace Lester, Lila Purling, Millie Haynes, Maud Taylor, Ella Sutton, Kathleen Appleton, Hilda Appleton*; third row: *? Tolver, Dennis Rumsby, Eddie Rayner, Kenny Richens, Robert Freestone, Charles Cook, Jack Sutton, Leslie Jermy, Eddie Starman, Geoffrey Haynes, Ronald Rumsby, Wilfred Sillett and Joyce Lester*; second row: *Marjorie Fisher, Irene Fisher, Jean Dean, Rosemary Boughen, Amy Tolver, Rosemary Purling, ? Freestone, Nancy Rumsby, Ruth Purling and Ena Fisher*; front row: *David Rumsby, Sonny Taylor, ? Tolver, Ronald Appleton, Alfred Lovett, George (or Frank) Freestone, ? Tolver, Basil Jermy, Frank (or George) Freestone, Brian Tubby, Sidney Appleton, ? Tolver.*

Bergh Apton schoolchildren, 1948. Left to right, back row: *Miss Catton (headmistress), Eddie Frost, Donny Self, Albert Forder, Peter Parfitt, Charlie Flatt, Basil Brown, Kenny Hurrell, David Davidson, Peter Brown, Derek Littleboys, David Lester, Miss Hazel Hook (infants' teacher);* third row: *Raymond Caley, Mick Owen (or Bowgin), Joyce Self, Jean Littleboys, Margery Glasspole, Gwen Davidson, Hazel Keeler, Iris Fenn, Doris Elmer, Eunice Dommit, Brenda Elmer, Lambert Harvey, Alan Kiddle;* second row: *Diane Owen or Bowgin, Ann Kemp, Sheila Fenn, Muriel Thurlow, Gillian Forder, Grace Forder, Janet Kemp, Shirley Wood, Muriel Glasspole, Nanette Thurlow, Ann Hurrell, Janet Mann, Jenny Carpenter, Christine Carpenter (on Jenny's knee);* front row: *Tony Watkinson, Norman Carpenter, David Self, Harry Forder, David Wood, Russel Sutton, Alan Self, ? Brown.*

School ballet class, c.1950. Left to right: *Grace Forder, Janet Mann, Nanette Thurlow (hidden), Shirley Reeve, Elsie Jermy, Muriel Thurlow (hidden), Edna Jermy, Janet Kemp, Muriel Glasspole (hidden), Pat Banham, Gillian Forder and Evelyn Jermy.*

Children outside Bergh Apton church after the service that marked the closure of the school in 1981. The photograph includes Mrs Deller, Emma Coup, Donna Sillett, Stephen Hubbard, Guy Browne, Anthony Harris, Terry Burlingham, Susan Bransby, Elizabeth Andrews, Lisa Daniells, James Keywood, Julie Burlingham, Simon Loades, Jonathan Loades, Daniel Gifford, Matthew Ingram, Sarah Keywood, Deborah Norgate, Barry Wood, Gary Ingram, Simon Jermy, Fiona Hubbard, Jessica Folkes, Timothy Stedman, Tony Burlingham, Karen Daniells, Glyn Harris, Toby Browne, Sarah Wood and Mrs Aldrich (head teacher).

19 April 1909:
School reopened it having been closed since March 1st for whooping-cough.

3 December 1909:
Willie Keeler fell down on his way to School, his clothes were very wet therefore he could not attend today.

7 July 1910:
Four children living in Bergh Apton but who have been attending Thurton School were transferred to their own School and were admitted this morning.

27 June 1913:
General Report [re Religious Education]: 'This is a good School – well-taught with very good results. The children are attentive, keen and reverent – evidently interested.' Frederick C. Lee, Diocesan Inspector.

17 October 1913:
Medical Examination held this morning by Dr Waterworth.

22 October 1913:
Last Monday a rain-gauge was presented to the School by Revd H. Thursby – it is of great interest to the Children.

16 July 1914:
Whole Holiday given for Brooke Show. The Children – a team of 20 – entered for the Drilling Competition and won the Shield.

19 April 1915:
Primrose Day. Primroses sent to Hospital.

20 March 1916:
The three Lords were withdrawn this afternoon as their father – a sailor – was coming home for a few hours leave and wanted to have the children.

24 May 1916:
Empire Day. Children saluted Flag and sang patriotic songs. Revd H. Thursby visited in the morning and afternoon – and kindly read a patriotic story. Lessons given on 'Our Empire' and 'Our Empire Makers'.

27 November 1916:
Three Boggis' [sic] absent – Father home from Front. Tom Kiddle absent to help with thrashing [sic].

10 June 1917:
Mr Denny Cook [sic] called about War Savings Certificates.

21 October 1918:
The three Boggis children absent as Mrs Boggis heard on Saturday that her husband was killed in action on Oct 8.

11 November 1918:
Peace. The Armistice was reported signed during the morning. The boys redecorated the School gates with flags, flowers and bunting. The National Anthem and patriotic songs were sung.

31 October 1919:
The School closes this afternoon for a week: Peace Holiday.

19 March 1920:
Mr and Mrs Thursby came at 3.30 to say goodbye to the children, and was [sic] pleased with the two little gifts – a painting from the boys was presented to Mr Thursby, and a work-basket made and lined by the girls to Mrs Thursby.

24 September 1920:
Eight Choir Boys absent all day on account of their Outing to Yarmouth.

9 May 1921:
Report by H.M.I. Mr E.D. Fear: 'In many respects this is, and has been for many years a model village School. The tone, teaching and moral training continue to be excellent; but the attainments of the children do not reach the high level of former years through causes quite outside and beyond the Teachers' control. The whole of the village property changed hands last Michaelmas [an inexplicable exaggeration, at least as far as ownership as opposed to occupation was concerned], causing an abnormal exodus of the old Scholars [exaggeration], and an influx of a smaller number of indifferently trained [Scholars] from various distant places. In addition, there have been three closures due to epidemic sickness – nearly every child has been affected with one or other of the complaints; and the low vitality of the children and their long absence from School are quite sufficient in themselves to account for the apparent deterioration in the quality of the work'.

29 September 1921:
Dick Fairhead and Emily Lovett away sick, apparently from eating too many blackberries.

15 December 1921:
School Party at 2p.m. All parents with two exceptions present – several visitors from village also Lord and Lady Canterbury.

3 November 1922:
The organ tuned today.

22 December 1922:
Lord and Lady Canterbury invited all the children to a tea and Xmas Tree on Wed. Dec. 27. Only the children able to attend School [this] morning were allowed to come on Dec. 27 on account of whooping-cough.

1 June 1923:
The older children are going to see A Midsummer Night's Dream *at the Maddermarket Theatre tomorrow afternoon, through the kindness of Lady Canterbury.*

Unfortunately, as a consequence of conditions placed upon the deposition of such material in the Norfolk Record Office, the public cannot assess the logbook of Bergh Apton School from 1927 until its closure in 1981,[30] until the year 2031! This source would, for instance, have detailed matters concerning the evacuee children who were billetted in the village during the Second World War. Fortunately, some reminiscences were recorded in 2002 of Mrs Helen Martin – Miss Helen Catton until 1958 – who had taught here since 1941, and had been headmistress from 1949 until 1966, some of these follow.

Mrs Martin recalled that her principal objective was to bring out the full potential of each child in her care. Bergh Apton School was a happy one, and punishments were not meted out – offenders, such as the occasional boy caught swearing, were given a

Painting class in the late 1940s. Tommy Jermy in his wellington boots is up a ladder being held by Albert Forder. Miss Calton, Harry Forder and Grace Forder are examining paintings.

quiet talking-to, which Mrs Martin found sufficed. She introduced a uniform, the wearing of which was not made compulsory, but which became accepted by most pupils. She encouraged a love of culture, particularly manifest in a concert held each June. This included ballet performances – she having engaged a ballet teacher to give the necessary tuition – excerpts from plays, and poetry recitation; the role of Titania (*A Midsummer Night's Dream*) was particularly memorable. These concerts were very popular with parents, and in any case helped to raise money for 'extras' not provided for out of the official educational budget. On a number of occasions, dances were held, also to raise money for such 'extras'. Another annual event during Mrs Martin's time was the pre-Christmas concert; this was always a sell-out, and raised money to pay for the children's Christmas party.

Mrs Martin, who as Miss Catton had succeeded Winifred Bradbury as headmistress, left the School House with her husband upon her retirement. Mrs Margaret Isbell, who served as caretaker until the school's closure in 1981, and her husband Reginald then occupied the School House.

Other matters concerning Bergh Apton School are recalled by Barry and Richard Cushing. These include the monthly visit of the library van, the lunches cooked at the school for both this school and for a number of surrounding villages which were transported by Richard Wolfe of Bergh Apton Hall, and the – perhaps surprising in retrospect – fact that electricity was not provided until about 1957.

Until 1953, Bergh Apton School took pupils from the age of five until school-leaving age – by this time 15. Indeed, there are still a few villagers who received their entire education here. From 1953 until its closure on 24 July 1981, it took children between the ages of five and 11. It was then arranged for Bergh Apton children to attend Alpington School, which, according to the *Eastern Daily Press*, 6 November 1980, was to be expanded in two phases to cater for these extra pupils. From 1966 until 1980, the headmistress of Bergh Apton School was Mrs A.L. Aldrich; for the final year of the school's existence, Mrs Barbara Blake served as acting headmistress. Throughout the twentieth century, the school also had an infants' mistress: those recalled by Barry and Richard Cushing are Miss Betts, Mrs Mayne, Miss Weeks and, serving for over 20 years until closure, Mrs Hazeldene Deller.

Other than for purely educational purposes, Bergh Apton School frequently served as a meeting room for parish events prior to the building of the Village Hall. It was reported in the *Eastern Daily Press*, 26 April 1924 that a concert was held in the Schoolroom in aid of the choir and organ fund. Lord Canterbury gave a radio demonstration, this being the first occasion on which a number of parishioners had 'listened-in'.

A seaside outing from the village in 1935. Here we have Gilly and Edith May Littlewood with their children on the beach at Great Yarmouth. Left to right: Fred, Vera (now Mrs Ron Cain), Gilly, Edith May and Muriel (Chippie).

The Cain family at Prospect Place in the late 1940s. Left to right: Vera Weddup (née Dye), her son John, Walter, Clara and Derek (son of Leonard, see p.151).

Leisure

References to sporting activities at Bergh Apton include the Boys' Football Club, in existence in 1922, and the Cricket Club; both were noted in Kelly's *Directory of Norfolk* for 1922 and 1925. There is, however, photographic evidence for a Bergh Apton Football XI as early as 1910.

One facility for leisure that was closed in or shortly after 1933 was the Bergh Apton reading room at Glebe Cottage.[31]

Probably for the most part serving a somewhat different clientele, Bergh Apton's only public house, The Bell, closed on 11 July 1956; situated by the parish boundary at Hellington Corner, it was not readily accessible to many would-be imbibers in the village. The Thurton Red Lion, as mentioned in the last chapter, was just outside the Bergh Apton parish boundary but popular with many of its inhabitants. It closed in 1962.

An activity in which Bergh Apton folk have joined forces with those of neighbouring Thurton is drama. The Thurton and Bergh Apton Players were formed in 1978 under the direction of Ray Wharton, who remains the resident director. Their first production was *Sailor Beware*, and plays as such remained their annual proffering until 1985. Subsequently, one to four productions have been presented annually, with musicals and pantomime becoming noted features. Participation of young people has been encouraged, and the Young Players first performed – *Snow White* – in 1992.

The Bergh Apton Conservation Trust

It was during the 1990s that Bergh Apton became one of the foremost parishes in Norfolk, probably the foremost amongst those having a population under 500, in respect of innovative community activities. The Bergh Apton Conservation Trust (BACT) was founded in 1994, and was particularly formed to enable a group from the village to purchase four and a half acres of disused gravel pits behind the church (Church Plantation) to create a local nature reserve. English Nature helped to draw up the long-term management plan which sees the retention of open grassy areas, the gradual reduction of sycamore trees and their replacement with native species. Wide-ranging surveys have been undertaken by members of the trust on moths, butterflies, birds, mammals, invertebrates, insects, and flora both on the site and in the village in general. In addition BACT manages an extensive wildflower bank on the nearby closed landfill site owned by Norfolk County Council. It undertakes an annual programme of walks and talks to encourage a greater interest and knowledge of natural history and the importance of conservation. Finally BACT was responsible for initiating and directing the parish hedgerow survey of which more details were given in Chapter I.

The fête in 2003 at Bergh Apton Manor with the brand new conservatory on south side of house. The photograph includes: Alison Freeman, Trevor Myhill, Mary Debbage, Bob Kerry, Bob Debbage, Catherine Kerry, the sons and wife of Chad (an American visitor), Mrs Purple and Kenny Seely.

'The Bergh Apton Experience'

'The Bergh Apton Experience', a three-day festival, was given a prominent write-up in the *Eastern Daily Press*, 8 September 1994; it encompassed a church flower festival, concert, craft fair, art exhibition, teddy bears' picnic and open gardens. This event raised £3,300, which was apportioned between the Parish Church, the Village Hall, and Norwich Night Shelter.[32]

The Bergh Apton Sculpture Trail

The success of the event described above encouraged yet further innovation. The brainchild of Maria Phillips and Pat Mlejnecky, the Bergh Apton Sculpture Trail was planned, and then launched in 1997 by the Bergh Apton Community Arts Programme. A total of 17 gardens, together with the Parish Church, formed sites in which sculpture by prominent local sculptors, as well as some from rather further afield, placed examples of their work in such a way that these pieces both complemented and were complemented by their surroundings. This unusual venture was to attract considerable attention, not merely locally but nationally. The *Eastern Daily Press*, 25 July 1997, reported that the Sculpture Trail had raised in excess of £15,000, of which the Parish Church and the Village Hall were each to receive £5,000, the remaining profit being shared by six charities and certain local amenities. The Sculpture Trail was repeated in 1999, attracted between 8,000 and 10,000 visitors, and raised £29,000, which was distributed similarly to the money raised by the previous Sculpture Trail[33]. For its subsequent occurrences see p.141.

A New Millennium

Given the change of numbering the first digit of the New Year from 1 to 2, it was not surprising that many national and local institutions, groups and individuals, took the new millennium to start on 1 January 2000. Strictly speaking, this was not the case; for the correct date was 1 January 2001. Still, let us not cavil at an innocent, and indeed worthy, cause for celebration having been seized upon a year early! As for Bergh Apton, a millennium pageant was held on 29 July, and essentially took the form of 14 different time scenes being enacted, which reflected the history of the parish. To be sure, there is no proof that one of these, a battle between Romans and Iceni on White Heath, ever took place: nevertheless, all good fun.[34]

Transport

By the end of the nineteenth century, Bergh Apton was linked with Norwich and Loddon by carriers' carts. Such horse-drawn facilities were to continue to serve the village until the early 1920s.[35] Not far into the twentieth century, however, Bergh Apton folk had their first opportunity to travel to both Norwich and Loddon by motor omnibus, admittedly one that called at the very boundary of the parish at Hellington Corner. The stop was specifically advertised as 'for Bergh Apton'. The Great Eastern Railway Company inaugurated this service in 1905, and at the Norwich end of the route connected with trains at both Trowse and Victoria Stations. In 1908, there were four services each way on Mondays, three from Tuesdays to Fridays, and six on Saturdays; in 1912 and 1916, there were four each way on Mondays and Saturdays, three each way from Tuesdays to Fridays. While this facility was taken over by another, unspecified company in 1913, it continued to operate until 1916 when both Trowse and Victoria Stations were closed to passenger traffic as a wartime economy measure – the latter never to reopen as such.[36]

Directory evidence is that Walter Garrard Hayes of Seething ran an omnibus through Bergh Apton on Mondays, Wednesdays and Fridays in 1922, and on Mondays, Wednesdays and Saturdays from 1924 to 1926. One Carver operated this service in 1927. For at least the period 1929–1941, 'Nips' Bloomfield ran this bus, charging 1s. for a return to Norwich; he also

An Eastern Counties bus got stuck near Prospect Place on 26 February 1958 when the A146 was closed by snow-drifts. The girls sitting on the bonnet are Margaret Thurlow (left) *and Vanda Barley.*

drove the choirboys to Yarmouth for their annual treat, according to a letter[37] from Jimmy Rayner of Lavenham, a former Bergh Apton resident, to Bob Debbage of Alpington. In 1947, the Bergh Apton village to Norwich service was run by an operator called Bertie Lake.

The Cullings bus company of Loddon inaugurated a bus service through Bergh Apton village in 1948. The authorised route ran north from Seething over Bussey Bridge, and it was at Bussey Bridge Farm that the owner, Albert Kerry, agreed to demolish some of the roadside outbuildings there in order to make a wide enough passage for the bus.[38] It was noted at the parish meeting on 23 November 1970 that Cullings had written to the Parish Council to say that they were losing money on the service through the village. It was proposed at this meeting that Cullings should be permitted to raise their fares to cover the aforesaid shortfall. It was reported at the parish meeting on 21 May 1982 that Eastern Counties Omnibus Company had then recently taken over the route through the village. At the parish meeting on 4 May 1984, it was noted that the latter company received a subsidy from Norfolk County Council with regard to this route.

Other than buses running through the village, editions of Kelly's *Directory of Norfolk* list United Automobile Services Ltd as having served Bergh Apton on its Loddon to Norwich route at Hellington Corner in 1929 and 1933, and the successor Eastern Counties Omnibus Company Ltd likewise in 1937. The latter service, most recently operated by First, has continued ever since.

Telecommunication

The earliest recorded telephone subscriber in Bergh Apton parish was Major T.E. Bussell of Bergh Apton Cottage, one whose number was given in the *Norwich Area Telephone Directory* of 1924 as Brooke 12; a telephone at Bergh Apton Post Office – Brooke 17 – was not listed until the 1929 edition of this directory.

Electrification

Perhaps surprisingly for such a rural parish, the larger part of Bergh Apton was provided with electricity by Norwich Corporation as early as between 1928 and 1934. Some outlying parts of the parish had to wait somewhat longer for this facility: Bergh Apton Cottage (later Bergh Apton House), for instance, was not to be linked to the grid until 1947.[39] That electricity was not supplied to the Parish Church and the school until about 1957 has already been noted.

Water and Gas Supplies

A piped water-supply came to Bergh Apton in or shortly before 1954: the Washingford House farm Sale Particulars of 25 September 1954 reveal that the water main had then been laid 'recently'. Curiously, perhaps, there was no mention of this event in the Parish Council minutes. A gas main traverses Bergh Apton; however, the inhabitants do not use this form of power.[40]

Sewerage

The Bergh Apton Manor estate sale particulars of 1914 reveal that Bergh Apton Manor and Washingford House then had water-closets, which were apparently fed by pumps and emptied into sumps, but no bathrooms. It was not until 13 August 1986 that the Parish Council minutes reveal that survey work on a sewerage scheme was 'shortly to commence' on a part of Mill Road and The Street. This would appear to have been completed in 1987, according to the minutes of 27 May of that year. All the same, many inhabitants of Bergh Apton still make use of septic tanks for sewage and waste water disposal; while many older parishioners will recall – some doubtless with wry affection – the privies to the rear of their homes!

Bergh Apton Post Office

Bergh Apton Post Office, established in the nineteenth century remained in The Street until 1954. Arthur George Norman, sub-postmaster in 1922, also traded as a tobacconist; Frederick Walter Lock, sub-postmaster from or by 1933, also traded as a stationer. Mrs Savoy then served as sub-postmistress here until 1954. As a consequence of the latter's retirement, Mrs Grace Alice Cushing, who had run the shop opposite the Post Office since 1937 and prior to that worked for the owner of the shop Mr Williams from 1932, moved the large wooden structure she had acquired from Forncett sale ground which had been formerly used as a Barclays Bank and where she had run the village shop from 1948 situated in the orchard of the Annis family (Royston House) and had it erected alongside Cooke's Road at its present position. It was then fitted out to serve as the village Post Office and stores. Since Mrs Cushing's death her sons, Barry and Richard Cushing, have maintained both sides of the business.

Local Tradespeople

In 1922 Bergh Apton had two shopkeepers,[41] David Lovewell and George Wright; there were two firms of builders, Maurice Aaron Redgrave & Son, and Arthur Vincent & Son; also trading here then were Arthur Smith (blacksmith), Harry Wright (bootmaker), and Richard Last Sturman (jobmaster). Of those named in 1922, Arthur Vincent & Son, Arthur Smith and Harry Wright were still trading as such in 1937; while Richard Last Sturman was then described

Bergh Apton Post Office

Village commerce on wheels – Pointer's lorry with the village shop aboard in 1954. This was the start of its journey when it was moved 300yds from The Street (site of Orchard House in 2004) to its new home at Howgate Cottage on Cooke's Road.

Village commerce – Barry, Richard and Grace Cushing outside the shop and Post Office on Cooke's Road in 1982.

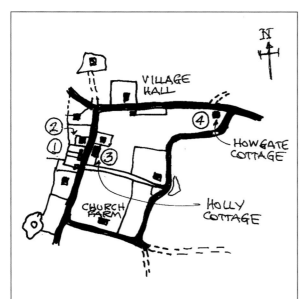

The village shop and Post Office in the mid-1990s.

Fig.13.2. Post Office and shop manoeuvres:

(1) 1937 – Grace Cushing bought the business on The Street, where she had worked since 1932.

(2) 1948 – Grace moved the shop to a wooden hut in an orchard a little further north.

(3) 1954 – The Post Office at Holly Cottage closed. Grace Cushing took over as postmistress and moved both the Post Office and her shop to Howgate Cottage on Cooke's Road, where her sons Richard and Barry Cushing still run it in 2005.

Richard and Barry Cushing in the village shop in 1999 with their aunt, the late Joyce Burgess. Joyce worked in the shop, first with her sister Grace Cushing and later with her nephews, for nearly 50 years until ill health forced her to retire only a short time before her death in 2002.

Grace Lester was 21 when she took over this shop in The Street in 1937. Her predecessor was Mr Williams, the husband of the head teacher at the school.

Holly House on Threadneedle Street, c.1980. This was both home and surgery to Dr Wardle before he moved to Mill Road and had a new surgery built there (John and Lizzie Burrage's North Court in 2004). Beatrice Denny-Cooke bought Holly House from Dr Wardle having moved out of Bergh Apton Manor on the death of her mother. According to one story, a man who was hardly ever ill entered Holly House by the front door and sat patiently in the front hall waiting for the doctor to call him into the surgery. It was only some time later, when someone (possibly Miss Denny-Cooke) discovered him sitting there, that he learned of the relocation of both Dr Wardle and his surgery some years earlier!

as a jobbing carpenter. Also trading then were Edgar Williams (shopkeeper), Charles Weeding (jobbing builder), Lionel Arthur Lester (jobbing carpenter), and Percy J. Keeler (haulage contractor).[42]

General Practitioners

Reference has already been made in this chapter to the post of parish nurse, which was maintained up to 1948 by the interest arising from Mrs Fanny Thursby's gift of 1901. In 1937, Bergh Apton's first general practitioner, Dr William Christopher Wardle, settled at The Hollies and used a room here for his surgery. A partner, Dr Bill Bellamy, joined Dr Wardle in 1953; however, from about 1960 when the latter retired, the former was to operate from a purpose-built surgery in Mill Road. His wife Joan, also a general practitioner, joined Dr Bellamy in 1965. For eight years from her husband's retirement in 1981, Dr Joan Bellamy continued to practise here in partnership with Dr John Sampson of Poringland. When Joan Bellamy retired in 1988, Bergh Apton's surgery sessions were transferred to the Village Hall, and continued there until 2000. (The Drs Bellamy kindly confirmed matters presented in this paragraph.)

Bergh Apton Parish Council

Much of interest concerning Bergh Apton in the twentieth century is to be found in the pages of the Parish Council Minute Book for 1928 to 1987. This not only records the deliberations of the Parish Council but also the annual parish meetings. Other than matters concerning buses serving Bergh Apton and utilities here, noted earlier in this chapter, and the parish charities, which are considered later in it, we next look at some extracts from this source.

Annual Parish Meeting, 12 March 1928:
There were six nominations for the six members of the Parish Council, hence they were all elected: T.H. Denny-Cooke, J.A. Lester, C. Mayhew, Revd G.B. Raikes, R.A. Royall and J.W. Westrup.

C.R. Cooper was nominated to serve as a parish constable, in addition to C. Weeding and D.H. Wiseman, nominated in 1928. I found no subsequent appointments to this position here, which was permitted in a parish in which the County Police Act (1839) had not been put into operation by the justices.[43]

Parish Council Meeting, 17 April 1931:
The clerk was to write to the Rural District Council to ask for the stretch of the road between Rectory Corner and Kiln Lane to be tarred.

Annual Parish Meeting, 5 March 1935:
It was resolved to give a tea and hold a sports (sic) for

Threadneedle Street from the west, near the Mill Road crossroads, showing Arthur Vincent's house and builder's workshops, c.1970. The dwellings Seven Bells and Oak Tree House occupy the workshop land in 2005. The oak tree is still there. Alan and Vera Weddup's daughter Julie is standing behind her father's car, parked outside the bungalow once occupied by her grandparents, Charlie and Rose Dye, Vera's parents.

Herbert Boggis on the stepladder is supervised by his long-time friend Billy Keeler in whose garden on Threadneedle Street they are picking apples, c.1994. Billy's attention to the job in hand may be explained by the fact that Herbert once missed an apple and it fell onto Billy's greenhouse, breaking some of the glass! This was the last year that Herbert, then 86 years old, did this job.

children aged until fifteen, and give each one a Jubilee mug. There was also to be a tea for parents of these children and old-age pensioners.

Annual Parish Meeting, 4 April 1938:
It was resolved to apply money left over from the Coronation celebrations in 1937 to start a fund for the provision of a children's playing-field.

The following persons agreed to act as air-raid wardens: M.A. Mace, Revd A. St J. Heard, L. Lester, R. Drane, Brigadier-General G. Dale, T.H. Denny-Cooke, A. Tubby and R.S. Batson.

Annual Parish Meeting, 11 April 1939:
It was stated that Norwich Fire Brigade now covered the village in an arrangement with Loddon Rural District Council.

Annual Parish Meeting, 11 April 1944:
The programme for 'Salute the Soldier Week' was discussed, and a target of £1,000 was fixed.

Parish Council Meeting, 4 December 1951:
Mrs Denny-Cooke brought to the attention of the meeting the need for an old people's club; she would speak to the old folks and report to the next meeting.

It was declined to take part in Loddon Rural District Council's invitation with regard to the collection of dry refuse.

Annual Parish Meeting, 30 May 1962:
It was agreed to support a 'Flag March' to be held in the parish on the following 4 September, in response to a letter from the Civil Defence Area Officer.

Parish Council Meeting, 15 May 1967:
It was reported that the parish sandpit had been sold for £675. The Parish Council had written to the Minister, asking for permission that this sum be put towards the provision of a playing-field for children and young persons, and were awaiting a reply.

Parish Council Meeting, 10 May 1968:
It was reported that the sum received for the sale of the parish sandpit had been reduced to £595.19s. following the payment of associated expenses.

Parish Council Meeting, 24 April 1981:
No objection was raised to the planning application to change the use of the School, which was to close in the following July, to residential property.

Charities

Bergh Apton's longest-standing charity, the Tenwinter Trust, dates back to the will of Christopher Tenwinter who died in 1599.[44] By far the larger part of his endowment, the Town Farm, was sold in 1922; the income which has since arisen has been derived from two sources: the money arising from the 1922 sale amounted in 1945 to £1,456.5s.8d. held in 4 per cent Funding Stock, 1960–1990, held by the Official Trustees of Charitable Funds, who passed the interest annually to the parish trustees, plus the annual rent – £10 in 1945 – for the 11a.0r.8p. of Town Farm land not sold in 1922. In anticipation of the new arrangement for regulating the trustees of the Tenwinter Trust – sealed 9 March 1945 – the Parish Council had, five months earlier, submitted the following names to the charity commissioners: the Revd F.M. Snellgrove, by virtue of his office as rector of Bergh Apton; T.H. Denny-Cooke and J.H. Lester, as co-opted trustees to serve for seven years; and J. Annis, F.W. Keeping and V.F. Kemp as representative trustees appointed by the Parish Council, of whom one was to be re-elected every two years.[45]

The Parish Council had the responsibility for administering the income from the fuel allotment, as initially awarded to the Guardians of the Poor in the Inclosure Award of 1806.[46] This land was let, and the income together with the interest arising from the invested Thursby Coal Trust money applied annually by the Parish Council to give eligible persons coal or, as had become the case by 1926, money with which to purchase the same. At the annual parish meeting held on 15 April 1952, it was agreed to raise the annual rent for the fuel allotment, by this time referred to as the poor land, from £21 to £26. At the annual parish meeting held on 9 March 1954, it was stated that 82 parishioners had been given £1 apiece for coal. With the authority of the charity commissioners, the poor land was sold and the proceeds then added to the invested Thursby Coal Trust money to form the Bergh Apton Parish Charity, as minuted at the Parish Council meeting of 24 November 1965. This new trust was to be managed by the rector for the time being, and four elected members, of whom two were to be parish councillors.[47] It is good to record the continued interest shown by the Thursby family in the affairs of Bergh Apton with Jack Thursby, son of Harvey W.G. Thursby, leaving the sum of £20,000 in his will of 1990 to increase the value of the Thursby Trust.

A Desideratum

Bergh Apton is inimitable, a special place with special people. Involved, concerned, active, there will always be more challenges for its inhabitants to grasp. As my text draws towards its close, may I propose – without wishing to presume upon the rights of property owners – the following desideratum?

Albeit a challenging task, it would be good to have Bergh Apton's 1,988 acres thoroughly field-walked. Who knows what may yet be added to such finds already detected on the surface by John Lester

End of an Era

It was almost the end of a farming era when Monty Seeley retired in April 1989. He had worked at Washingford House farm for nearly 40 years. Here he is, chaired by his co-workers to celebrate. Left to right: David Watkinson, Graham Harber, Monty Seeley, Kenny Seely, Arthur Smith and Neville Jermy. Both Monty and Arthur have died since this photograph was taken and none of the survivors are now employed as farm workers, but David and Graham still own and work land in the village, passed to them by Christopher Harris when he retired from farming in 1997.

Christopher Harris (right) presents an engraved tankard to Monty Seeley on his retirement in 1989. Monty started at Washingford House farm in the very early 1950s when he went to work for Billy Panks. He later worked for Christopher Harris's father Mike who bought the farm in 1954 after Billy died. Thus Monty's service on the same farm spanned almost 40 years.

(Chapter II)? There is the enigmatic King's Street of Edwin's will; did it indeed form a section of a hitherto unidentified Roman road? Was there indeed a farmhouse destroyed long ago by fire on the Tithe Map plot called Burnt House Yard? Surely there are artefacts to be uncovered relating to the earliest recorded village alehouse, the demolished former Adam and Eve, subsequently known as The Hare? And what about the sites of the houses by the edge of Apton Heath, abandoned as a consequence of the Inclosure Award of 1806?

Bergh Apton is special; its sometimes eccentric boundary must have tales to tell which its documented history has not revealed, or can probably never reveal. This boundary must be preserved in its entirety: we owe it to Aelfric and to Edwin; indeed we owe it to all those, known and unknown, who lie within the Parish Church of SS Peter and Paul and its graveyard, and within the abandoned but not forgotten site of St Martin's, Apton.

References

[1] TNA: RG13/1858 ff.87–95.
[2] TNA: RG13/1858 f.91, p.9.
[3] NRO: PD497/28.
[4] NRO: DN/TA 15.
[5] NRO: PD497/29.
[6] Deed evidence.
[7] Glebe Terrier evidence.
[8] NRO: PD 497/29 and PD 497/13/6; P. Cattermole, *Church Bells of Norfolk Part 1 The Hundred of Clavering* (Aylsham, Golden Ball Press, 1991).
[9] NRO: PD 497/13/10.
[10] See Chapter XII.
[11] Ordnance Survey evidence.
[12] Personal comments: the late Aubrey Arthur Forder Parfitt.
[13] NRO: Denny-Cooke MSS.
[14] NRO: P/DLV/1/286.
[15] NRO: BR122/315.
[16] At least lords of manors no longer had to pay their stewards to act on their behalf in recording the conveyance of copyhold property and related matters.
[17] Registers of Electors evidence
[18] See Chapter XII, p.102.
[19] Extracts from the school logbook are quoted later in this chapter.
[20] Kelly's *Directory of Norfolk*, 1933.
[21] Chapter XII.
[22] NRO: C/VES/66, 89.
[23] Town Farm deeds evidence.
[24] According to the *Eastern Daily Press*, 6 September 2003
[25] This based upon the 1 inch to 1 mile Ordnance Survey Sheet 67 (Norwich and Great Yarmouth).
[26] Personal comments: the late Christopher Armitage Harris.
[27] TNA: MAF 68/5041, Norfolk (Part 1), No.386.
[28] Given the circumstances of wartime, the census was not taken in 1941.
[29] NRO: C/Ed 2/210.
[30] NRO: C/ED 2/211.
[31] See also Chapter XII.
[32] *Eastern Daily Press*, 20 September 1994.
[33] *Bergh Apton Newsletter*, no.44, August/September 1999.
[34] Reported in the *Eastern Daily Press*, 31 July 2000.
[35] Inferred from directory evidence.
[36] Kelly's *Directory of Norfolk* 1908, *Directory of Norfolk* 1912 and *Directory of Norfolk* 1916; C.J. Allen, *Great Eastern Railway*, 5th edn (London, Ian Allen Ltd, 1968).
[37] Published in the *Bergh Apton Newsletter*, no.44, August/September 1999.
[38] Personal comments: Tony Kerry.
[39] Personal comments: Derek Blake.
[40] Personal comments: Derek Blake.
[41] Kelly's *Directory of Norfolk* 1922.
[42] *Ibid*, 1937.
[43] W.E. Tate, *The Parish Chest*, 3rd edn, (Chichester, Phillimore, 1969) p.177.
[44] Chapter VIII.
[45] NRO: PD 497/34; Parish Council minutes.
[46] See Chapter XII, p.93.
[47] Personal comments: the late Christopher Harris; Parish Council minutes.

Bergh Apton Looks Forward

This epilogue was written on behalf of the Bergh Apton Local History Group by one of its members but with the input of others to cover the years 2000–2004.

The Millennium Pageant

The first major community activity of the new century was the presentation of a pageant involving over 80 of us ranging in age from five to 70 plus. It was written to celebrate the village's long recorded and imagined history and included glimpses of significant events in our national and local life of the past 2,000 years bringing in turn joys and sadness to those who lived here before us.

It took place on the evening of Saturday 29 July 2000 in the clearing of Christopher and Liz Meynell's young plantation on the south-facing slope of the Chet Valley just above Bergh Apton Hall. It was an extraordinary day of lows and highs. The lows of the afternoon consisted of torrential rain that flooded roads and fields and the wind that blew so fiercely that it demolished a tent erected to protect the after-pageant supper of a spit-roasted hog – the project seemed doomed! But the highs were the determination of the producer and cast to do it anyway, the quite beautiful evening of still and sunset that emerged from the storm, and the sensation we all felt that the spirits of past generations of Bergh Apton folk were abroad, and that they were watching us as we portrayed something of their times.

When it was over we held hands and took our bows feeling that we had united the past and the future of this village. What we sensed was expressed in the closing words of the narrator:

So our history is told and we are now its story. A new century lies before us with all its opportunities and possibilities. One of the themes running through this pageant, spoken and unspoken, has been 'they loved this place'. What we, your pageant-makers, hope is that our attempts to recapture some of the people and events in our past will, in the words of T.S. Eliot, reveal that 'the end of all our exploring will be to arrive where we started and to know the place for the first time'.

As he spoke the cast unfurled a banner that read 'and all shall be well' and that is what we trust as we close this book. Through Geoffrey Kelly's words we have looked back to where we come from. But where shall we go? And how shall we get there?

The Pageant of July 2000. The Anglo-Saxons are arriving to settle the land. Left to right: *Rachel Parfitt, Barney Mewton, Suzanne Mayes, Paul Rainbird, Linda Davy, Jessica Butterworth* (partially hidden), *Ashley Myhill, Joy Munden, Abbie Rolfe, Michael Rolfe, Frances Hubbard, Rebecca Parfitt, Derek Guy, Stephen Mitchell, William Gates and Elizabeth Kerry.*

Agriculture

Geoffrey Kelly's text identifies Bergh Apton as an ancient community whose lands, even before they were settled, were passed over by hunter-gatherers whose arrowheads and other artefacts are still being found. He has shown us a community developing gradually, shaped by religion, politics and the land itself.

The old existence and dependence on that land are no more. The point is no better illustrated than by Geoffrey Kelly's observation that only four of Bergh Apton farmhouses are lived in by those who farm their land. For the record they are Martin and Carrie Holl at Hillside Farm, Tony and Kate Kerry at Bussey Bridge Farm, Richard and Gillian Loades at Beech Farm and Derek and Jill Harvey at Street Farm. And, living just on the borders of the village in Alpington at Garden Farm are Bob and Mary Debbage, much of whose land lies in Bergh Apton.

As well as the farmers, gone too are the fruit pickers and farm workers whose evocative photographs appear in earlier chapters. They have disappeared in the great change in the food-supply chain of England. The apple and cherry trees in the orchards which they cultivated and harvested have been grubbed up and the fruit is flown in from countries whose produce is cheaper and more uniform, but not better in taste. The comradeship of the men who tilled the land and stooked the sheaves at harvest time and who worked with horses has gone too. Agriculture has been replaced by agri-business whose huge machines make economic sense but are too big for our country lanes, too heavy for much of our land and make lonely men of their operators.

The key element of this change is the speed with which it has taken place. In 50 years or less the old agricultural life – almost 1,000 years old albeit with

Behind: *The first ever issue of the current series of the* Bergh Apton Newsletter, *published in June 1992. The issue of affordable housing, its principle topic, has returned in 2004!* In front: *The October 2004 issue of the* Bergh Apton Newsletter.

significant modification along the way – has gone. Families whose roots go back generations are in the minority, and the old ways of sharing work and play, and going to church every Sunday, have also largely disappeared, along with the life that fostered them.

But change is part of life and, whilst we may be saddened by the passing of the agrarian idyll, we should not be carried away by thinking it was perfect, for it wasn't and great hardships and deprivation often accompanied it. Life has moved on and is now more affluent and more comfortable. The great majority of people who live here work outside the village rather than in it. Most work in and around Norwich, but they live here happily and feel at home with the land they live in and travel through on the way to work and home again.

The Farm Shop at the modern-day Street Farm (not to be confused with the Street Farm which was renamed Apton Manor). The photograph of the interior of the shop was taken two days before it closed on 31 July 2004.

It is this latter sense that will secure our future. It is what makes Bergh Apton work well as a community rather than as a dormitory for Norwich, as one may gather from the 18 A4 pages of the village newsletter published every two months, recording activities, news and opinion. Within the last year the village website (www.berghapton.org.uk) has been launched, which features an electronic version of the newsletter.

Geoffrey Kelly tells us that the census of 2001 recorded a population of 420, a rise of 11 over the 1991 total. The number of dwellings also rose by 12 to a total of 187. Thus the twentieth century trend towards smaller households continued right up to the millennium. The houses built in the last decade of the twentieth century have been built almost entirely in the area of the pre-Inclosure Apton Heath, that is to say Threadneedle Street, Mill Road and Church Meadow Lane.

Many villages around Norwich, including the neighbouring village of Poringland, have seen great changes in their way of life through expansion, which we in Bergh Apton have watched with at best awe and at worst alarm. Whilst there is some opinion in favour of similar growth here we are protected for the time being by a planning decision from the 1990s that there will be no new houses until the infrastructure exists to support them. Recent debate at Parish Council meetings demonstrates that the great majority does not wish to see any expansion other than limited and essential housing for village people who would otherwise have to leave.

The Parish Council

The Parish Council that considered the above question was elected in May 2003. It is the first on record to have been elected in a contested election. That does suggest a healthy state of village affairs in what should be seen as the bedrock of government rather than its lowest form. The members of this council are: Alison Freeman (chairman) of Holly Lodge Farm, Loddon Road; John Ling (vice-chairman) of Watermeadows, Bussey Bridge; Derek Blake of Broomfield, Loddon Road; Jean Bobbin of the Old School, School Road; Chris Johnson of Jays Cottage, Bussey Bridge; Sally Leigh of Willow Cottage, Langley Road, Chedgrave; David Skedge of Brambly Hedges, Cooke's Road. The clerk is Philippa Fuller of The Old Stables, Brooke, who has recently taken over the duties from Lorie Lain-Rogers of Oak Cottage, Sunnyside, who succeeded Vicky Dalgleish of Cooke's Road in 2002.

The Village Sign

The same Parish Council completed the valuable work begun in 1998 by its predecessors to create Bergh Apton's village sign. It was unveiled by Peter Annis of Orchard View on The Street, in the presence of nearly 100 people on 29 September 2004, and was dedicated by Canon G. John Phillips of Mere Farm, Whiteheath Road.

The council asked Peter to unveil the sign because his family has probably lived here longer than any other, with many gravestones in the churchyard and an uncle on the war memorial. Peter was our postman for many years and works the land of a market garden that he inherited from his father.

Chris Johnson, the village tree warden, planting a young Scots Pine on Sunnyside in 2003. The tree replaced one of the four original trees that have featured in many photographs taken in this southerly area of the village.

The unveiling of the village sign on 25 September 2004. The sign was unveiled by Peter Annis and dedicated by Canon G. John Phillips. All involved in the design and production of the sign were thanked by Alison Freeman (chairman of the Parish Council). The ceremony was attended by 92 residents.

Members of the working group that is looking at proposals for modifications to the church. Left to right: *John Phillips, Dennis Moye, Pat Waters, John Ling, Maria Phillips* (seated), *Lorie Lain-Rogers, Audrey Harvey, Christopher Meynell, Revd Peter Knight, Trevor Price, Roy Flowerdew.*

Members of the Bergh Apton Conservation Trust on holiday at Kardamyli on the Peloponese Peninsular, Greece, in 2003. Left to right: *Bob Fox, Barbara Fox, Daphne Vivien-Neal, Linda Davy, David Lester, Biddy Collyer, Lorie Lain-Rogers, Annelise Savill, Tony Davy, Hilary Ling and James Savill.* (Missing is John Ling who took the photograph.)

A typical scene at the Bussey Bridge tea stop on the Sculpture Trail of 1999. The tractor and trailer are part of the park-and-ride transport system.

'The Burghers of Apton' created by the late Verena Murtagh after the 1997 Sculpture Trail that also provided a seat on the green in Church Road.

Mark Goldsworthy carving his oak sculpture of St Martin for the 1999 Sculpture Trail, near the site of the vanished church that bore this saint's name.

'Hare' by Anne Richardson on the 1999 Sculpture Trail in the garden at Howgate Cottage.

The fact that three generations of his family watched Peter pull the Union flag away to reveal the sign is an indication that they shall be here for many a year yet.

Those that gathered to watch included the sign-maker Ivan Soanes of Norwich and a representative of East Coast Castings Ltd of Carbrooke near Watton, who cast the sign in aluminium alloy. Village people included families who have lived here for more than one generation and others who have moved here recently. We had among us Scots, a Czech, Irish and Germans, all of whom have made this community their home. That is probably the key to our future – the fact that we live comfortably together, enjoy our neighbourliness and come together from time to time to do something for the benefit of the community and our neighbours rather than simply for ourselves.

Societies and Organisations

The village has some key societies and organisations that make that possible. They are the Parochial Church Council; the Parish Council; the Village Hall management committee; Bergh Apton Conservation Trust and the Bergh Apton Community Arts Trust.

Each recognises that its future is subject to change. The Parochial Church Council, having held open door 'brainstorm' sessions to ask what the community needed from its church building, has formed a working group that is now considering how to provide what was agreed to be important. The Parish Council will soon have completed its 'Parish Plan' that does the same thing for the services and facilities of the village so that it may argue its case for changes and improvements at District and County level from a position of knowledge. The Village Hall management committee has formed a small sub-committee charged with recommending what must be done to the hall, a building now showing signs of its age, to meet the future needs of the community. The Conservation Trust is actively looking to manage more land so that the beneficial effects of conservation may spread to other parts of the village.

Bergh Apton Community Arts Trust

Bergh Apton Community Arts Trust (BACAT) deserves special mention. Geoffrey Kelly's chapter on the twentieth century covered the first two biennial Bergh Apton Sculpture Trails organised by BACAT but it was the third, scheduled for the summer of 2001, that tested the mettle of the group. Just as the tempo of planning was reaching its height, and expenditure on programmes, logistics, loos and the like was about to be committed, an outbreak of foot and mouth disease brought the English countryside to a grinding halt. BACAT had to consider the options of cancellation, postponement or constraint (limiting the trail visitors to the roads rather than footpaths), all of which would have affected the

expenditure of quite large sums of the money. The decision was made to postpone until the following year. It was not, in the end, a difficult one to make for the roots of the event are in the countryside and its success depends on the agricultural community to turn out and help. It could do no other than abandon something that might imperil that community's livelihood with unintentional contamination imported by a visitor.

The decision demonstrated that the trail works on a three-year cycle as well as two. The generic formula of a Sculpture Trail is not new but this one sets its stall out on a loop of country lanes and footpaths measuring more than 7 miles, with a free park-and-ride system and bikes for hire. It drew more than 8,000 visitors to the village in 2002. What seems to have caught the imagination of the public was its practice of setting the work of nationally recognised professional sculptors in private gardens.

The trail is also interesting because of the wide diversity in the personal objectives of those that plan it and provide the army of volunteers that execute it. Some want a wider understanding and appreciation of the arts, and see the trail as a means of achieving that. Others are keen to benefit projects, mainly in the village but including some international elements too, through the distribution of funds raised on the trail. Others want simply to enjoy the experience of helping to make an exciting project work, and to see others having fun and learning something new.

As *The Book of Bergh Apton* goes to press the plans for the next trail, in May and June of 2005, are already well advanced. The Village Hall has rung to the shrieks of laughter and cries of delight on two Saturdays in October 2004 as almost 200 village people gathered to create models of themselves in clay for a set piece entitled 'The Little Bergers of Apton', a fond nod, perhaps, in the direction of Anthony Gormley's 1991 work 'Field'.

When the 'Little Bergers' are exhibited on the trail they will both delight and amuse. But they will also impress, because the standard of both artistic approach and modelling skill is really rather good, and support the belief contained in one of BACAT's tenets that the artistic spirit of Everyman will flourish if given the opportunity, and that BACAT's role is to provide that opportunity.

Local Groups

The village's social structure includes other less formally constituted bodies. Amongst them are regular users of the Village Hall including the Bowls Club, Bergh Apton and District Society, Youth Club and Baby and Toddler Group. The key element of all of them is that they were formed by people who wanted to provide some form of service or entertainment, and just got on with it. They are recognised as being important to the well-being of our community.

The Post Office/Village Shop

No revue of Bergh Apton would be complete without reference to our village shop and Post Office that now, with the closure of other local Post Offices, also serves the neighbouring villages of Hellington, Holverston, Ashby St Mary and Thurton. Geoffrey Kelly has dealt with its history but we should also record just how greatly it is valued as a meeting place, an exchange for news and gossip and a symbol of our health as a community. One rarely emerges without something in addition to the items on the grocery list – most often a smile. One always gets a friendly welcome from Barry and Richard Cushing and probably a bit of gentle leg-pulling as well. Their shop is a jewel to be treasured. But it must be used as well because it cannot survive without our custom either as a shop (proudly vaunted by its adherents as 'the Harrods of the East'!) or as a Post Office.

The decision by the government to abandon the practice of paying pensions and benefits via the Post Office has not helped the survival prospects of rural Post Offices. Not only has the income from the government for performing the service gone but so, too, has the additional income that derives from purchases that recipients might make while they were collecting their entitlement. More than that, though, the change has meant the end of their weekly visit to this lively meeting place by many people to whom it was, consciously or unconsciously, a valuable part of their lives.

Communication

Mail services may well be another reducing service with the coming of rapid electronic communication through the fax machine, a bewildering variety of cheap phone services and now e-mail and the Internet that has recently become available in the village on broadband.

It is the way of the world that any threat is also an opportunity and the use of these fast and instant communications services is a case in point. E-mail and the Internet have made it possible for us to establish a relationship and exchange information and pictures with families all over the world whose roots are here in Bergh Apton. That would not have been possible to the same extent had we had only the traditional mail services.

Let us take just one example in the publication of this book. John Madden, a direct descendant of the Revd Wyndham Carlyon Madden, used the Internet to send us the image of the rector that appears on p.88, taken from a portrait that hangs on a wall in his home in British Columbia, Canada. We also corresponded at length by e-mail to his cousin the late Hugh Wilkinson, also in Canada, about their ancestor. In the same way we also communicated with an Australian descendant of Thomas Hase Blake, transported in the 1800s. George Pilbrow is

Dolly Wood fulfilled a childhood dream at the age of 80 when she saw her village from the air. She took a helicopter ride over Bergh Apton with Kip Bertram in June 2003, just before he and his wife Alison (not in picture) flew down to Ascot races. Kevin Parfitt of Church Farm, who brought Dolly from her home at Church View on Church Road, is on the left.

another Canadian contact. His ancestor John Sharman emigrated in 1830 and went on to organise charter voyages on which others from this village and from other villages in Norfolk took the same path to a new life.

These are some examples of long-range communication but we speak and write to many other people closer to home too, who have family associations with the village. The names Royall, Rayner, Athow, Lord, Leeder, Matchett and Kett all appear in one or more places in Geoffrey Kelly's text, and we speak to or write to people of those families today. Other names on our contact list are Rope, Middleton, Blaza and Greenacre. The importance of these associations is that, a long time after their direct association with the village has disappeared, they are interested in us and we are interested in them. This is strong cement that should ensure that we do not lose touch.

The Community

So where are we, and where do we go from here? Bergh Apton is a lively village whose people have a broad range of interests and jobs to occupy them and to provide their livelihood. Farming and market gardening are no longer the dominant force that they were, but the community still values its surrounding countryside as its heritage and its environment. As the book goes to press new interests are being fostered, just two examples being an archery club and a reading discussion group. We have little commercial employment in the village, but our residents have a wealth of skills and enterprise that the village may call on to serve its cause when they are needed.

The Bergh Apton Local History Group commissioned this history of the village so that we may all learn about our past. We hope also that the protection and value of our future may be made stronger by what we have learned.

The most important lesson may well be that, having emerged from its first 2,000 years in good heart, this small Norfolk community will thrive in the future if we work together to maintain a sense of community and make this a good place to live.

The War Dead of Bergh Apton
1914–18 and 1939–45

By John Ling

Introduction

Today, the events of the First World War are but flickering sepia-tinted images on our TV screens but it was real and tragic for the wives and children of the 20 Bergh Apton men who died, and those of the five more who died in the Second World War.

In a small farming community that relied heavily on a large army of farm workers these losses were economic as well as tragic. In the years after the First World War Bergh Apton's economy suffered because we lost one man in every four who went away to fight (Town & County column of the *Eastern Daily Press*, 6 August 1919).

There is no one left in the village to tell us at first hand of these men who did not return from the 1914–1918 war and very few who knew those who died between 1939 and 1945. It is thus our responsibility to write down what we know of every man so that those who come after us may also know. This appendix is a summary, that reflects the information we have gathered for the village archive on each man whose name is carved on the war memorial.

My own interest in this subject came from the friendship between my father and Jim Hollowell of the 4th (TA) Battalion of the Suffolk Regiment, who died in the fighting that preceded the fall of Singapore in February 1942. Jim's battalion and the 4th (TA) Battalion the Royal Norfolks landed in Singapore only weeks before it fell, equipped for fighting in the Sahara Desert but diverted at the last moment to defend Singapore. They were ill prepared and poorly-trained to fight the Japanese. Jim Hollowell was killed in that fight but my father never knew how he died.

It was only in the year 2003 that, through a chance remark by the late Jerry Hunt of Brooke, I learned that he had served with Jim and had seen his Bren gun carrier receive the direct hit that killed him. Jerry died of cancer only a few weeks after he told me, and I am so grateful that we made that vital connection when we did, for Jerry filled a gap in my knowledge of a man whom my father mourned every Remembrance Day until his own death in 1996. I was less than a year old when Jim went away so I never knew him. He was my godfather.

Bergh Apton's war memorial on which the names of its 25 fallen soldiers are carved. The memorial stands in the churchyard of the Parish Church, just to the north-west of the tower.

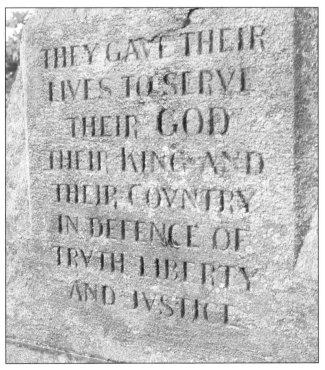

The south face of the war memorial.

Above: *Remembrance Day, Sunday 9 November 2003. Ena Smith of The Street in Bergh Apton plants a small cross to honour one of the fallen while Frances Hubbard, her neighbour, waits to do the same for another.*

Right: *Walter Alexander, 1915.* (NORFOLK COUNTY LIBRARIES AND INFORMATION SERVICE)

Acknowledgements

A great number of people have helped in the research for this appendix. It is always a risk to name names for fear of offending those one omits, but I need to make the attempt because I could not have got this far without their support.

Peter Rope provided details of his uncle Alfred Rope's service record, as did Anna Stratton and Joy Lester about their uncle Clement Wall. Leonard Cain's brother Ron has helped hugely with Len's story and photographs. Bob Kerry and Ashley Price brought back photographs of cemeteries and memorials in France and Belgium, and my sister Ann Ball visited UK memorials on my behalf. I am also indebted to Lorie Lain-Rogers, the keeper of Bergh Apton's archive, for her advice and encyclopaedic knowledge of where to look in our records for vital pieces of information. Chris Johnson, himself the author of a book on his father's war, has given freely of his time and experience in

Some pupils of the Hewitt School in Norwich went to the Western Front in 2001 to learn about the First World War. Here they are at the Tyne Cot Memorial, Zonnebeke, on Remembrance Day, where they laid a wreath in memory of Robert Beaumont whose name is on the memorial. Left to right: *Daryl Burt, Alice Roberts, Ashley Price.*

research, and my knowledge of Alfred John Boggis MM is indebted to Di and Bernie Webb.

My thanks are also due to Dan Breen, a Calgary-based Canadian researcher. Dan was absolutely invaluable in my research into the service records of Walter Alexander of the Newfoundland Regiment, and I would not have found Dan without the help of both the Canadian students who staff the Newfoundland Memorial at Beaucourt Hamel on the Somme and the people in St John's, Newfoundland who manage the memorial.

Photographs and information arrive even as I write the final elements of this appendix and I hope that I may slot them all into the final version. If I have omitted the names of donors through the press of time upon me I ask their forgiveness. Our gratitude is great for their help albeit that it is, through my own shortcomings, anonymous.

I must also pay tribute to the Commonwealth War Graves Commission that maintains the resting-places and memorials to those who died. Its website (www.cwgc.gov) is essential reading for those who seek information on family and friends who fell in these conflicts. Its care for the cemeteries and memorials of the fallen makes them places of great tranquillity and reflection on the awfulness of war.

Finally, a note on our county regiment in which the majority of these men served. This text refers to both the Norfolk Regiment and the Royal Norfolk Regiment but they are one and the same body that was honoured with the 'Royal' prefix in 1935 by King George V on the 250th anniversary of its formation as the 9th Regiment of Foot. The regiment is said to have gained its nickname 'The Holy Boys' during its campaign in the Peninsular Wars under Wellington where the enemy troops took its Britannia cap badge to represent the Virgin Mary. Through several amalgamations since 1968 the regiment is now a part of the Royal Anglian Regiment.

The Menin Gate. No memorial has the power to move people as does the Menin Gate in Ypres, unveiled in 1927. It is probably the most famous of all the First World War memorials. Leonard Rope is remembered amongst the men of the 31st (Alberta) Infantry Regiment on the gate.

Memorials and Cemeteries for Bergh Apton Men in France and Belgium

Ypres   Menin Gate
            Tyne Cot, Zonnebeke
            Railway Dugouts, Zillebeke
            Menin Road South
Etaples, Le Touquet
Bucquoy, Arras
Loos, Pas de Calais
St Pol sur Ternoise
Beauval, Amiens
Thiepval, Bapaume
Louverval, Cambrai
Guoy, Cambrai
Villers-Bretonneux, Amiens
St Saveur, Rouen
Bayeux

This is the Thiepval Memorial, the huge structure designed by Sir Edward Lutyens and unveiled by The Prince of Wales in 1932. It lies 14km east of the main Autoroute from Calais to Paris, a little to the south of Arras, and stands on the site of a small French village that was totally destroyed in the fighting. The names of Aubrey Stone and Sidney Kedge are among the 73,412 listed on its walls.

Memorials and Cemeteries for Bergh Apton Men in England

Chatham, Kent
Runnymede
Portsmouth Harbour

Men Remembered on Memorials and Cemeteries Outside Europe

Ramleh, Palestine
Basrah, Iraq
Cairo, Egypt
El Alamein, Libya

The Men of Bergh Apton Who Died

We have recorded here all we know about the Bergh Apton men who died. The Military Medal was awarded to Corporal Alfred John Boggis in the First World War. During the course of the actions in which two men died, Private Ernest Albert Leeder in 1917 and Private Leonard Cain in 1944, the Victoria Cross was awarded to one of their comrades. All of them are in our thoughts at times throughout the year but particularly in early November as Armistice Day approaches and then on the nearest Sunday when we gather at the war memorial to pay our respects.

Walter Ernest Alexander
(1504, Lance Corporal, 1st Battalion, Royal Newfoundland Regiment)

Walter died on Wednesday 5 July 1916, aged 24 and is buried at Beauval, near Amiens. Fortunately for us his mother Annie applied for a pension from the Army to replace the money that Walter had contributed to the family. The plea was rejected, but it had caused the gathering together of papers investigated during the case. This archive, held in Ottawa, helped me to build quite a clear picture of Walter and his circumstances, which are worth spending a little time on here.

When he signed on at St John's, Newfoundland on 30 April 1915, Walter Ernest Alexander was a 23-year-old fireman in Boswarlos, on Newfoundland's Port au Port peninsular. He was 5ft 5in tall, weighed

Annie Alexander and her daughter Eva (christened Edith) at Verandah Cottages in Bergh Apton at some time before Walter was killed in July 1916. By the time that awful news arrived they had moved to Mereside in Brooke.

129lbs (58.5kg) with brown hair and grey eyes. He gave his next-of-kin as his mother, Annie Alexander of Bergh Apton, Norfolk, England.

Walter's enlistment papers have an entry 'Previous service: 12 months Special Reserves, 3rd Batt. [Battalion] Norfolks [sic]' and that may have assisted his promotion to Lance Corporal within a few months of joining. His battalion was shipped to England in mid-1915, and thence to Marseilles on 3 April 1916.

His service records, sent to us by Dan Breen, tell us that he received a head wound from shell shrapnel on 2 July (the second day of the First Battle of the Somme) and died of his wounds in a casualty clearing station three days later on 5 July.

The Canadian Memorial website tells us something of the carnage of these events:

The total [British] casualties sustained on the opening day of the Battle of the Somme alone totalled 57,470, of which 19,240 were fatal. No unit suffered heavier losses than the Newfoundland Regiment, which had gone into action 801 strong. When the roll call of the unwounded was taken next day, only 68 answered their names. The final figures that revealed the virtual annihilation of the Battalion gave a grim count of 255 killed or dead of wounds, 386 wounded, and 91 missing. Every officer who went forward in the Newfoundland attack was either killed or wounded.

There can be little doubt that Walter was one of those who did not answer that roll call on that next day.

The Canadian archive documents relating to Walter, of which copies are now held in Bergh Apton's archives, deal with unsuccessful attempts, over the next few years, by his mother Annie to obtain a small war pension (to replace the small sum

The Newfoundland Memorial at Beaucourt Hamel in what is now a memorial park to the men of the Newfoundland Regiment who died in the First World War. The huge losses on the Somme were tragic for such a small island population.

The Danger Tree at Beaucourt Hamel on the Somme. It still stands at Beaucourt Hamel in the area where the Canadians attacked on 1 July 1916. It was so named because, standing alone (and remarkably surviving!) in 'No Man's Land' between the front lines, its range was known by the enemy, and any man near it was in danger from sniper fire.

Annie and Robert Alexander (centre, in dark clothes) in the garden of the house at Holly Hill on Sunnyside where they spent their later years. Walter's sister Eva is between them in the back row. The others are all members of the Pentin family, Annie's relations on her parents' side. The photo was taken by Charlie Pentin in 1934 or 1935.

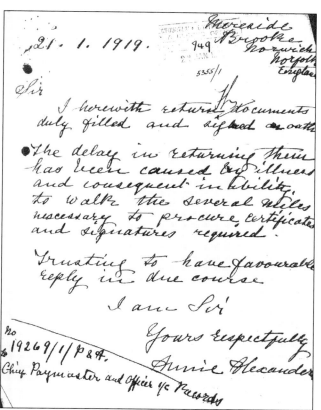

Annie Alexander's letter of 21 January 1919, one of several she wrote to the Canadian authorities in her firm strong and educated hand, seeking a war pension.

that her son sent her during his lifetime). They tell us something of him and of his family, and include the telegram sent to his mother on 14 July 1916, the day that the War Office in London received the news of his death. It reads 'Regret to inform you that 1504 Lance Corporal Walter Ernest Alexander 1st Royal Newfoundland Regiment died of wounds in France on July 5th'.

They also include his will dated 29 June 1916 – only three days before he was fatally wounded – reflecting Army recommendations to its soldiers, before going into battle, that they organise their affairs against the risk of being killed. Walter left his entire estate to his mother.

The personal possessions returned to his mother are noted on a receipt dated 10 May 1917. Her signature on the receipt is clear and strong but what must she have felt as she signed for the final possessions of her son? They comprised his kitbag, sent from Ayr, and a packet of items sent back from France. The receipt detailed the contents of the packet as 'a leather pocket book, some letters and photos, a Bible, a lock of hair, a pamphlet, 5 foreign coins, a pipe and tobacco pouch and a cotton bag'.

At the time of Walter's death his parents lived at

Mereside in Brooke where they had moved from Verandah Cottages in Bergh Apton shortly before-hand. By the time the government drew up the records of the Commonwealth War Graves Commission (in 1920/21) they were back in Bergh Apton living at Holly Hill on Sunnyside, where they continued to live for many more years.

In the years that followed Walter's death it is clear that the Alexander family was going through hard times. Annie wrote to the Army asking if they might pay her a pension as she had partly relied on Walter's pay for the past eight years to supplement her husband's meagre wages (he was paid about 25s. (£1.25) per week as a woodman on the late Lord Canterbury's estate).

Her submission included an affidavit signed by Harvey W.G. Thursby, rector of Bergh Apton at that time, that told of her husband Robert's failing health and the inability of her sons Robert and Harry, both now with small children to feed, to help her. Sadly it was all to no avail. The Army wrote to tell her that it was unable to pay her a pension because she had not been wholly reliant on Walter for support.

(As I researched Walter's family I realised that Walter's brother Harry was the same age. A check on local records confirmed that they were twins, registered on the same day in Loddon in the December quarter of 1891. The census of 1901 also shows them living with their parents, their half-brother and their sister at Verandah Cottages in Bergh Apton.)

Arthur W. Annis (3/7182, Private, 7th Battalion, the East Yorkshire Regiment)

Arthur died aged 34 on Monday 24 July 1916 and is buried in St Sever Cemetery, Rouen. He was the son of Samuel and Rosetta Annis of Bergh Apton. The fact that he is buried at St Sever, in the bend of the River Seine as it passes just to the south of the centre of Rouen, tells us that he had probably been wounded and evacuated to a base hospital near the coast where he succumbed either to his wounds or one of the diseases that were widespread amongst the sick in the conditions of those days.

At the time he was wounded the Battle of the Somme was into its second week. His regiment was in the thick of it in the Fricourt/Mametz sector of the Front from the time of the first attack on 1 July until they were withdrawn on 11 July. We have yet to establish what happened to Arthur in the confused conditions of that battlefield.

His details on the village war memorial demonstrate the importance of double-checking apparently reliable records for his name is given as Arthur James Annis whereas in Commonwealth War Graves records he is Arthur W. Annis. Bergh Apton baptism records confirm that the CWG records are correct for he was baptised Arthur William in our church.

Happily James Annis, another of Rosetta Annis's sons, survived. Nine year's Arthur's junior he had been with the Metropolitan Police before the war and served with the Royal Flying Corps. After the war he returned to 'The Met' before returning to Bergh Apton to run a market garden on The Street, of which much of the land is still cultivated by his son Peter.

Robert George Beaumont (42033, Private, 22nd Battalion, the Manchester Regiment)

Robert died, aged 29, on Thursday 4 October 1917 but his body was never recovered. He is remembered on the Tyne Cot Memorial, Zonnebeke, Belgium. He was the son of Robert and Jane Beaumont of Sunnyside, Bergh Apton, and husband of Ellen who lived at 2 Kimberley Street, Norwich.

Robert died on the first day of an action known as 'The Battle of Brooseinde' in which the Manchesters suffered very heavy casualties, losing 281 men of all ranks either killed, missing or wounded in the fighting with German opposition that made very effective use of machine-gun fire from a position known as Joiner's Wood.

Alfred John Boggis MM (18279, Corporal, 9th Battalion, the Norfolk Regiment)

Alfred died aged 37 on Tuesday 8 October 1918, only a month before the end of the war. He is buried in Prospect Hill Cemetery at Gouy, near Cambrai. He was married to Rosa and was the son of Alfred and Sabina Boggis of Yelverton. He himself had three children, Alfred, Herbert and Ivy. The electoral roll of 1915 shows that his home, with Rosa and his children, was in The Street in Bergh Apton.

Amongst Alfred Boggis's papers that are now in the care of Di and Bernie Webb, having been kept by his son Herbert until his own death in 2002, is a letter from what was then known as the Imperial War Graves Commission to Rosa Boggis in 1920. It told her that the men in the war cemetery at Brancourt, where Alfred had been laid, had been moved to Gouy.

In a map-search for the location of Brancourt we were directed to the village of Brancourt en Laonnias, more than 35 miles south of Gouy. But then we spotted Brancourt le Grand no more than 5½ miles to the east of Gouy. Here, we believe, we have found the place where Alfred Boggis was killed.

A scroll, signed by King George V, went to every household that had lost someone in the First World War. This is the label on the one sent to Rosa Boggis for her husband Alfred John Boggis MM, in April 1920.

Rosa Boggis and her children, 1917/18. Rosa raised Alfred, Herbert and Ivy by herself after her husband was killed just a month before the end of the First World War.

Wilfred Gibson and his wife Ivy (née Boggis) at her mother's cottage in Threadneedle Street in the mid-1940s. Also pictured are: Herbert, Rosa and Alfred Boggis.

This studio photo must have been taken before the promotion and award of the military medal that Alfred Boggis won on 28 April 1917, as it shows neither badges of rank (he was a full Corporal when he died) nor the ribbon of his award.

Herbert Boggis at his father's grave at Prospect Road Cemetery, Guoy, in France, 1997. Herbert died three years later, aged 91.

The family of every man who died received a bronze plaque (sometimes called a 'Death Penny') to honour his death. Many have been lost or have been polished so much that they have lost their detail but this one, still in its original wrapping, is in mint condition. The plaque was originally sent to Rosa Boggis, but was passed on to Herbert and is in the possession of Di and Bernie Webb at the time of writing.

There is also a letter dated 16 October 1918 written to Rosa by Chaplain Wilkins of the 9th Norfolks. It is the original, scrawled in pencil and now very faded. It includes the words:

I am just writing to express my deep sympathy for you in the death of your husband in action on Oct 8th... He was thought very highly of in this Battalion and I am glad to think of him as one of my friends for a long time.

At the age of 37 Alfred John Boggis was a mature man, and one of proven bravery. One senses from the padre's letter that he had attributes of steadiness and loyalty, and they will have been a great help to many younger soldiers in their teens and early twenties who served with him.

(Charles) W.W. Bracey (883DA, Deck Hand, Royal Navy Reserve)

Bracey was the first of our men to die, and the youngest. He was 19 when he sailed on the trawler *Eyrie* as part of a minesweeping flotilla to clear a German minefield laid in the Humber at the very start of the First World War. The ship sank when a mine hit it on 2 September 1914. It was less than a month after Britain entered the war on 4 August.

The quest for details of this young man was complicated because the Bergh Apton War Memorial and the Commonwealth War Graves Commission information does not tally. The memorial refers to him as Charles W.W. Bracey but the only commission record was for a Wilfred Bracey whose father Frederick is recorded as living in Claxton. The register of births finally revealed that the names he was given were Walter Wilfred. He was the son of Frederick Bracey of Bergh Apton, who moved to Claxton after the death of his son. Walter Wilfred is also remembered on the Royal Navy War Memorial on the heights above Chatham's Royal Navy Dockyard where his name is carved simply as Wilfred.

The incident that led to his death is told in a paper written in 2001 by Len Barnett entitled 'Trial & Error – Royal Navy and Mine Countermeasures 1904–1914' from which the following is an extract.

Under orders from HALYCON, the minesweeping torpedo-gunboat SPEEDY sailed on August 31st with ten steam-drifters: initially shooting their nets on September 1st. Nets were similarly deployed the following morning. At the centre, but behind the nets EYRIE struck a mine, carrying away her stern and sinking in three minutes. Compatriots sent their boats off and picked up survivors. Immediately after the first detonation, another mine exploded in the next boat's nets.

Coming so soon after the beginning of the war the

Chatham Royal Navy Memorial. Wilfred Bracey is named on this memorial overlooking the former Navy dockyard in Kent. There is another, similar in design and size, in Portsmouth on which the name Jack Mayes is recorded. Together these memorials record the names of the 43,500 Royal Navy personnel who were lost at sea. A total of 18,500 died in the First World War and 25,000 in the Second World War.

sinking of the *Eyrie* was covered in some detail by the *Eastern Daily Press*. Of more interest to us was the newspaper's round-up of news from Norfolk villages on 24 September 1914 in which was reported that he was the first man from the village of Bergh Apton to die, and that the condolences of the whole village were tendered to Mr Bracey by the rector, H.W.G Thursby at Harvest Festival.

Leonard Walter George Cain (5773757, Private, 7th Battalion, the Royal Norfolk Regiment)

Leonard was 24 when he was killed on Tuesday 8 August 1944 as the British Army advanced through Normandy following the D-Day landings. He died during an action that pitted the 7th Royal Norfolks against tanks of the 12th SS Panzer Division outside the village of Grimbosq some 17km south of Caen on the River Orne. The action lasted over 36 hours and the bravery and determination of the 7th Battalion has become recognised through the award of the Victoria Cross to Major David Jamieson who commanded Leonard Cain's company.

The website of the Royal Norfolk Regiment, the Britannia & Castle (www.norfolkbc.fsnet.co.uk), describes the action and concludes with the words:

their [SS Panzer's] heavy losses caused the Germans to withdraw. By evening, when the 12th SS Panzer Division finally gave up, the Coy [Company] position was largely intact, ringed with German dead and burnt-out tanks.

Leonard and his fellow soldiers who fell in that battle are buried in Bayeux Cemetery. He was the husband of Miriam, father of Derek and the son of Walter and Clara Elizabeth Cain of Prospect Place, Bergh Apton. Leonard's brother Ron Cain, who has been a faithful visitor to his brother's grave and to Grimbosq over many years, lives in The Street in Bergh Apton.

The collar badge of the Royal Marines Light Infantry that Chris Johnson unearthed in 2003 while digging his garden at Bussey Bridge where Victor Gillingwater lived.

Victor George Gillingwater (CH/1473(S), Private, 1st Battalion, Royal Marines Light Infantry)

Victor was born in Mundham and worked as a woodman before he enlisted with the Royal Marines Light Infantry (RMLI). He died aged 20 on Saturday 17 February 1917 and is buried in Queen's Cemetery, Bucquoy, near Arras, only a couple of kilometres from where he was killed.

Victor Gillingwater was one of 64 marines who

Part of Bucquoy War Cemetery where Victor Gillingwater and many of his comrades of the Royal Marines Light Infantry are buried, having been killed in the battle for the sunken road at Miraumont in February 1917.

died in a battle that was intended to give the British a view of German activities in the the upper valley of the River Ancre in which the marines attacked Germans defending a sunken road running from Grandcourt to Miraumont. General Douglas Haig, Commander in Chief of British forces, referred to the action in a despatch to Parliament of May 1917, as follows:

At the same time [as the main thrust] arrangements were made for a smaller attack... designed to seize a portion of the sunken road lying along the eastern crest of the second spur north of the Ancre and so obtain control of the approaches to Miraumont from the west. Our assault was delivered... on both banks of the Ancre at 5.45 am on the 17th February by the 2nd, 18th and 63rd Divisions.

A year before I read this account of the battle, on a visit to Victor's grave, I had approached Bucquoy from Grandcourt via Miraumont. Knowing what I know now, I realise that this was the very road attacked by Gillingwater and his comrades.

Chris Johnson of Bussey Bridge uncovered a metal object while digging his garden in 2003 that proved, when cleaned, to be an RMLI collar badge. It was only some time later, when we had established that Victor's parents, George and Mary Gillingwater, had lived at Bussey Bridge, that the significance of the find became apparent. There can be no doubt that it belonged to Victor Gillingwater, but whether he lost it when home on leave or it was lost at a later time we shall never know.

(See also the connection between Victor and Alfred Rope in the latter's story on p.155).

151

Charles William Greenacre (16520, Private, 2nd Battalion, the Norfolk Regiment)

Charles died aged 23 on Saturday 22 April 1916 in the Middle East where he is remembered on the British War Memorial in Iraq, that was originally erected in Basrah, but moved to Al Nasiriyah in 1997 on the orders of the Iraqi government. It was badly damaged in the Iraq War of 2003 but has been restored and rededicated.

He was born in Westwick in north Norfolk but his mother Hannah (née Loyd) was a Bergh Apton girl who was living with husband William and family on Sunnyside in her home village when both Charles and his brother Henry (q.v. below) were killed.

Charles and many young Norfolk men died when almost the whole of the British Army's 6th Division surrendered following the Turkish Army's 143-day siege of Al Kut. Following the city's surrender the Turks marched the British troops 100 miles to Baghdad in 120 degrees of heat with little food and water, resulting in the death of most of the 10,000 prisoners who set out from Al Kut.

We don't know if Charles died during the siege or on the march, or if he died from wounds or from one of the many diseases prevalent in the area at that time.

This infamous event was part of the British Army's Mesopotamian Campaign against both the Turks and dissident Arab forces that is calculated to have cost more than 40,000 British, Indian and West African lives (CWG website).

Henry George Valentine Greenacre (15008, Private, 1st Battalion, Coldstream Guards)

Henry was killed aged 24 on Monday 27 March 1916, only 26 days after his brother Charles died in Iraq. He is buried in the Menin Road South Cemetery at Ypres in Belgium.

Henry was baptised in Bergh Apton on 13 March 1890, the only one of Hannah Greenacre's six children to be born in her native village. His wife Louisa

The Kerry family from Hellington Corner visited various First World War cemeteries and memorials in 2000. Henry Greenacre was one of the men whose grave they visited to pay their respects. Here they are at his grave in the Menin Road South Cemetery.

This is Hannah Greenacre, the mother of George and Charles Greenacre, both of whom fell in the First World War. She lived on Sunnyside in Bergh Apton for many years into her old age. Her close neighbours were Annie and Robert Alexander who lost their son Walter.

The Menin Road South Cemetery, just a few hundred yards east of the great Menin Gate in Ypres, where Henry George Valentine Greenacre is buried.

(née Keeler) was living in Brooke when he was killed but on the electoral roll of 1939 she is recorded as living with her parents at the Hellington Bell public house in Bergh Apton where her father was landlord. She is buried in Bergh Apton's churchyard.

Sidney Richard Kedge (G/4148, Private, 6th Battalion, the Queen's (Royal West Surrey) Regiment)

Sidney was killed, aged 21, on Saturday 8 July 1916. His body was never found and he is remembered on the Thiepval Memorial.

There are no details about him or his connection with Bergh Apton as we go to press with the *Book of Bergh Apton* but we have found a man of the right age and the same age who was born in Eynsford in Kent whose father Richard Kedge was a farm labourer.

That might mean that his work may have brought him to Bergh Apton. We shall keep searching for him in the records in the next phase of the research on the war memorial.

Sydney George Keeler

We had thought that Sydney George Keeler on our war memorial was the Sidney Keeler who is included on the Royal Navy Memorial at Chatham, killed on Tuesday 22 September 1914 on board HMS *Aboukir* when the German submarine *U-9* sank three large but ancient British cruisers off the Dogger Bank. It was one of the greatest tragedies in the entire history of the Royal Navy, in which 1,459 men died in less than half-an-hour.

That link may prove to be wrong given the recent find of the birth record of the only man in the UK with the names Sidney George Keeler, registered in Loddon in June 1899 to parents John and Martha Keeler of Cooke's Road, Thurton. He would have been only 16 years old in 1914 – too young to be the man on the Chatham Memorial who was a Royal Fleet Reservist, which implies that he would have been aged in his 30s or 40s.

It's back to the drawing-board in this instance, to find out how such a young man's name is on the memorial in our churchyard.

Ernest Albert Leeder (5133, Private, 11th Battalion, Australian Infantry)

Ernest died on Monday 16 April 1917 but his body was never recovered and he is remembered on the impressive Australian Memorial at Villers-Bretonneux near Amiens.

He enlisted in the Australian Army on 24 January 1916 in Bunberry, Western Australia and was trained in the huge infantry depot at Blackboy Hill in

Jack Lovewell, photographed when training as a Rear Gunner in Canada amid winter snow in 1942. He died when his bomber was lost during a raid. Herbert Boggis described him as 'a personable young man' and told Bernie Webb of the time during the Second World War when someone asked Jack about his future. 'Rear Gunners don't have a future' was his prescient reply.

The Australian war memorial at Villers Bretonneux looks out over rolling countryside to the north of the River Somme that claimed so many thousands of lives so far from home.

Jack Lovewell and his fellow trainees, 1942. They were training to fight in Bomber Command, with the white flash on their rakishly tilted forage caps identifying them as cadets. Jack Lovewell is the fourth from left on the third row. (The reverse of this photo carries the signatures of all the cadets. We would very much like to hear from anyone who recognises any of these men.)

Western Australia, where over 32,000 men were trained before joining the Australian Infantry in the First World War.

His enlistment papers tell us that his brother farmed at Town Farm at the time of his enlistment, and his mother was Sophia Maria Leeder of the neighbouring Valley Farm on Welbeck Road who had lost her husband Edmund only the year before she lost this son.

When he had completed his training he was sent to the war as part of reinforcements that embarked at Freemantle on the troop ship *Shropshire* on 31 March 1916. He passed through Egypt and close to the Dardanelles where his battalion had previously been mauled by the Turks at Gallipoli and landed in France in May 1916 where he was sent to his unit, the 11th Infantry Battalion

We have no record of how he died but we know the activities of his battalion on the day he died. We may reasonably conclude that he was lost in an action where the Australians, many of whom were killed as they ran out of ammunition, were in a fierce fight at the village of Lagnicourt, in which Lieutenant Charles Pope was awarded a posthumous Victoria Cross.

Jack Edmond Lovewell (1333957, Sergeant, 75th (RNZAF) Squadron, RAF Volunteer Reserve)

Jack was killed aged 21 on Monday 16 August 1943 but his body was not found. He is remembered on the RAF Memorial at Runnymede.

He was the son of Arthur and Ethel Lovewell who ran the village shop on Threadneedle Street, owned much of the land around the crossroads where Threadneedle Street and Mill Road meet in Bergh Apton, and are buried in our churchyard.

Archibald Russell Mayes (C/J/12120, Leading Seaman, Royal Navy)

Archie was killed on Wednesday 19 February 1941 while serving on board HMS *Warspite* in the Mediterranean and is buried in Ramleh War Cemetery in Palestine, near Tel Aviv. We understand that this is a different place from Rameleh in Palestine where so much destruction has taken place in the ongoing conflict between Palestinians and Israelis.

Whilst we have yet to trace an official record to link him to Jack Mayes (q.v.) we know from Ron Cain's first-hand evidence as a neighbour of the wartime years that he was brother to Jack Mayes (q.v.). Their family lived at Prospect Place in Bergh Apton on the A146.

Sidney Herbert Marks (350568, Private, 1st Bn, the Essex Regiment)

We are confident, but as yet it is not proven, that this is the man recorded on our memorial. He was killed on 8 October 1917 and that date fits with an entry in Bergh Apton Parish Church's register of services recording a memorial service held for Private S. Marks on 2 December 1917.

The Commonwealth War Graves Commission records that his wife lived in Norwich, only 6 miles away, so the next step in research will begin there.

A note in the CWGC record says that he was 'employed by the late Captain Lord Richard Wellesley, Grenadier Guards' which may be a reference to employment before military service. This may give us something else to go on in further researches into Sidney, one of only two people who remain a mystery to us.

Harry Samuel Mayes (13004, Private, 7th Battalion, the Norfolk Regiment)

Harry was killed Friday 1 October 1915 but his body was never found. He is remembered on the Loos Memorial at Lens, in the Pas de Calais. Commonwealth War Graves Commission records have only one soldier killed by this name so we are confident that this is the man on our memorial.

By sad coincidence, when researching his details in the record office, we noticed that his birth was recorded on the same page of the registry of births as that of Walter Wilfred Bracey (q.v.) who also died in the war.

The St Pol extension to the original War Cemetery. This is the burial place of Albert Parker.

John Arthur (Jack) Mayes (P/M 38591, Petty Officer, Royal Navy)

Jack Mayes served in the destroyer HMS *Cossack* and was killed aged 38 on the night of Thursday 23 October 1941 when the Tribal class destroyer was torpedoed and sank in the Mediterranean with the loss of 158 lives. His body was not recovered and he is remembered on the Royal Navy Memorial in Portsmouth. He was the brother of Archie Mayes (q.v. above).

Albert William Parker (220779, Pioneer, 392 Road Construction Company, Royal Engineers)

Albert was killed on Friday, 9 February 1917 and is buried in St Pol Communal Cemetery Extension at St Pol sur Ternoise in the Pas de Calais.

He was the husband of Rose Parker and lived at Hellington Corner in Bergh Apton. There is an interesting footnote here, in that the Unknown Warrior who is buried in Westminster Abbey to represent all the dead of the First World War was taken from this cemetery.

Herbert Charles George Podd (1474624, Gunner, 74th Field Regiment, Royal Artillery)

Herbert was killed aged 26 on Sunday 28 June 1942, serving with the 8th Army in the Western Desert and is remembered on the Alamein Memorial in Egypt, having no known grave. His family was from Norwich but parents Herbert and Rose rented a house on Threadneedle Street in Bergh Apton during the war having been bombed out of their house in the city.

Herbert Podd's sister Pauline came to Bergh Apton in the late 1990s looking for her friend Ena Smith who lived near her during the war, but Ena was away from home for the day. We are very keen to make contact with Pauline or anyone in the family.

Alfred Hubert Rope (CH/1472(S), Private, Royal Marines Light Infantry)

Alfred Rope died aged 23 on Saturday 5 May 1917. He is one of 10,769 soldiers buried in Etaples Military Cemetery close to the British Expeditionary Force's main base for the support of its war machine. Its facilities included a military hospital complex where, even ten months after the final armistice, in September 1919, three hospitals and the Queen Mary's Army Auxillary Corps convalescent depot remained to treat men seriously wounded in battle.

Left: *Etaples War Cemetery. Hilary Ling of Bussey Bridge, Bergh Apton, at the grave of Hubert Rope in the summer of 2003.*

The Etaples War Cemetery. Only a small part of this huge burial place for thousands of British soldiers can be glimpsed through a camera lense. Those buried here include Hubert Rope, who died in one of the base hospitals in and around this town that was a key depot for British Expeditionary Forces during the First World War.

Alfred Rope was one of the two sons of Aaron and Ellen Alice Rope of Holly Farm on Loddon Road. Both sons were to be killed within a little over a year of each other.

His birth certificate records him as Alfred Hubert while on the 1901 census he is listed as Herbert and on his CWGC record he is Hubert Alfred. We can, however, be confident that he was called Hubert in the village as that was the name used by the Revd Harvey Thursby when he recorded his memorial service on 8 June 1917.

We know nothing yet of how and where Alfred was wounded. His evacuation to Etaples obscures clues that one often gets by checking a burial site with known battles in which a man's regiment was involved. However there may be a sad clue in his enlistment record. It tells us that he volunteered for the Royal Marines on exactly the same date and at the same London recruiting office as his near neighbour Victor Gillingwater (q.v.) whose service number is consecutive to his. Victor lived at Bussey Bridge – literally a few hundred yards from the Rope farmstead – and we realised that these two young men almost certainly went to London together as friends to enlist for the great adventure.

They died within three months of each other in 1917, and it may well be that Alfred Rope was mortally wounded in the same Royal Marines assault in which his friend and neighbour was killed.

Leonard Godfrey Rope (80227, Private, 31st Battalion, (the Alberta Regiment) Canadian Infantry)

Leonard was killed at St Eloi aged 27 on Friday 7 April 1916 but his body was never found. He is remembered on the Menin Gate at Ypres in Belgium.

His parents Aaron and Ellen Alice Rope farmed at Holly Farm on Loddon Road. He enlisted as a volunteer in Calgary Alberta on 8 April 1915 – his 27th birthday – but we have few details of his travels between Bergh Apton and western Canada except that he left this village in about 1912.

He joined the 31st Battalion (Alberta Regiment), part of the Canadian Army's 5th Brigade that became known as the 'Iron Fifth' for its exploits under the command of Lt Colonel (later Brigadier General) Ketchen.

We know a lot about Len from his Army records

sent to his nephew Peter Rope from the National Archives of Canada, and will use them to illustrate his story.

He was 5ft 9in tall and weighed 11st 6lb (72.5 kg). He wore a size 36in jacket and had light-brown hair. His medical record on enlistment says that his physical development was 'good' – as one might expect from a farmer in the prime of life. We may even suppose that he was right-handed, for he had been vaccinated in his left arm.

The 31st Battalion sailed to England from Montreal on 15 May 1915 and then on to France. They arrived in Boulogne on the morning of 19 September and went straight to the Front – into the trenches at Kemmel in Belgium.

Life in the line apparently settled into a pattern about which we know quite a bit from a book entitled *History of 28th Battalion* (a sister battalion, fighting alongside the 31st) by G.E. Hewitt. Hewitt writes that each battalion would spend between four and eight days in the line and then rest in the nearby village of Locre. The nuns of the Convent in Locre gave the men hot baths at a cost of 1 franc – soap and towels not included! – and meals that must have been a welcome break from Army victuals.

Leonard's pay, from whence came that franc for a bath, was modest. A Canadian Regiment volunteer got $1 (Canadian) per day with an extra 10 cents 'field allowance'. His records show that, when the battalion was in the line, he drew only a small amount every month (usually about $2.50) to pay for baths, café meals and 'baccy', but in December 1915 he drew $16.56 (perhaps to spend during a spot of local leave?).

In the spring of 1916 the 31st Regiment moved to St Eloi, near Voormezeele close to the Belgian border. It relieved a British unit in trenches that had recently seen fierce fighting and where mine explosions had formed huge boggy craters, filled with mud and rainwater. Hewitt describes the situation thus.

St Eloi – The 31st and 27th Battalions man the newly taken line, still full of British dead and wounded, with the (mine) craters between their front line positions and the support trenches where the 28th Battalion was positioned.

That was the situation in which Leonard Rope and his 31st Battalion pals found themselves on 1 April, 1916. He had only six days to live.

We don't know how he died, but we can be confident that we know when and where. On the night of 7 April, his Battalion was involved in confused and ferocious fighting. Here's what Hewitt says:

April 7, 1916. An attack was made during the night of April 6–7 on craters 4 & 5 by bombing parties from 25th, 28th and 31st Battalions led by Lt Murphy of

25th Battalion. They reported that, despite heavy rain and shellfire, they got quite close to the craters before being repulsed. In fact, they lost their way in the dark and occupied a group of craters north of crater 4 and, though they captured several small German patrols, they had failed to even identify their objective correctly... The following night, April 7–8, the 6th Brigade was relieved after suffering 617 casualties in the preceding four days of fighting.

It is probable that Leonard was amongst the 617 men who died in the fighting in one of those raiding parties. It had been the eve of his 28th birthday.

You will find his name on the Menin Gate in Ypres, amongst those of thousands upon thousands of men whose bodies were never found. He may have sunk into the awful mud of those huge craters to lie there still, beneath the poppy fields of Flanders.

Aubrey Samuel Stone (14304, Lance Corporal, 9th Battalion, the Norfolk Regiment)

Aubrey was killed on Sunday 17 September 1916 but his body was never recovered and he, too, is remembered on the Thiepval Memorial.

The Commonwealth War Graves Commission records do not include his next-of-kin but we know that he was the son of John and Mary Stone in The Street, and that he was one of 11 children. His mother's maiden name was Bracey so he may also have been related to Walter Wilfred Bracey (q.v.). Aubrey's nephew, John Clemence, lives at Davy Place in Loddon.

Aubrey Stone's family on the beach at Great Yarmouth. We don't know when this photograph was taken, but it was at a time when bathing-machines, seen in the background, were still in use. The soldier in the middle of the front row is Charles Clemence who was later to marry Mabel Stone (in the hat). Thus he became Aubrey's brother-in-law and father of John Clemence who gave us the photograph.

Clement Sidney Wall (14334, Private, 8th Battalion, the Norfolk Regiment)

Clement worked for Mr Redgrave, the builder, who lived at The Beeches in Threadneedle Street. We have a picture of him as an athletic man from his niece Anna Stratton who told us that he was a runner of some reputation who would often pay small children a ½d. or 1d. to time him on training runs. On one occasion he ran to Denton to take part in a race, won the race, and ran home again. The round-trip distance he ran just to take part was over 36 miles!

Clement was one of four brothers who fought in the Great War. He was killed aged 29 on Saturday 11 August 1917 and is buried in the Railway Dugouts Burial Ground at Zillebeke near Ypres. He was the son of Leonard and Anna Maria Wall of The Street in Bergh Apton, and uncle to Joy Lester of this village, Anna Stratton of Thurton and to Olive Hudson of Harleston. His parents and his sister, Lily Scarles, are buried in Bergh Apton churchyard.

Charles Daniel Weddup (10405, Private, 1st Battalion, Coldstream Guards)

Charles was one of two village men to die in the service of this famous Regiment raised in the Scottish borders. He was killed on Sunday 17 October 1915 but, like so many, has no known grave. He is remembered on the same Loos Memorial as Harry Mayes who died only two weeks before him.

We have no details yet of his family but we still have to check the birth of a Charles Daniel Weddup, entered in the Norwich register for the June quarter of 1895. It may link him to Annie Weddup who was living in The Street in Bergh Apton at the beginning of the war.

James Robert Wright (P/7989, Lance Corporal, Military Police Corps)

James, 33 years old, died of fever on Tuesday, 17 December 1918, over a month after the armistice aboard a hospital ship in Alexandria harbour. He is buried in Cairo War Memorial Cemetery. His parents Robert and Elizabeth Wright of Sunnyside, Bergh Apton are buried in our churchyard. His wife Annie Elizabeth Wright is also buried here.

Those Who Returned

There is now no one left who survived the First World War and returned to the village to take up life in a small community again. Many did and they deserve our thanks and recognition but, sadly, we know too few of their names and they are all gone. Those that greeted them when they came home have also gone so there is no one left to tell us who they were. Pat Waters and Lorie Lain-Rogers remember Lionel Lester speaking with feeling at one remembrance service about each man whose name is carved on the war memorial but, sadly, we have no record of what he said that day to help us continue in that knowledge.

But we do have a very detailed record of their homecoming, in the form of a report in the Town & County column of the *Eastern Daily Press* of 6 August 1919. It tells us what the people of the time did to celebrate the return of the living who came through the First World War and to pay their respects to its dead:

The parishioners of Bergh Apton entertained their returned sailors and soldiers to a welcome home in The Rectory grounds by permission of H W G Thursby on Tuesday 31st July. A Thanksgiving service was first held at the Parish Church after which an adjournment was made to The Rectory where a long programme was then carried out. The first item was athletic sports open to all parishioners including contests for ladies and schoolchildren. This was succeeded by an excellent dinner served in a marquee. 57 invitations had been sent out and 32 were able to be present. The Rector proposed the health of our guests which was responded to by Captain C E Norgate. A Toast to those who had fallen in the service of their Country was proposed by Mr T H Denny-Cooke who mentioned that out of a population of 400 Bergh Apton had contributed 80 men to the defence of their country of whom 20 had made the great sacrifice and in whose honour the parish are about to erect a Memorial Cross in the churchyard as a token of their gratitude and thanks. The Toast was honoured by the company rising and standing in silence. During the dinner tea was provided for all parishioners and this was followed by a variety of entertainment by the 'The Dandies'. After Lady Canterbury had distributed the prizes for the sports and cheers had been accorded to Lady Canterbury, Mr [sic] and Mrs Thursby and the Sports Committee, dancing on The Rectory lawn to the music of the Norwich Co-operative Band brought to a close the successful entertainment.

From this report we may judge that 60 men came home. The difference between life and death in battle is often a matter of standing a few inches to the left or right of the path of a bullet. Thus, whilst this appendix is about those who were killed in the two wars, it has been equally important to develop a better knowledge of those who returned safely. There is not enough space to tell their story here but I have set myself the task of writing it for the village archive as a future project. At this early stage in that process I need to record my thanks to, amongst others, Prebendary Arthur Royall of Worthing, John Armiger of Chedgrave, Peter Annis, Sybill Holl and Connie Ducker of Bergh Apton and Bob Debbage who is now of Alpington but is a son of Bergh Apton. All have already given much to, or have agreed to help in, this endeavour.

Some Who Returned

Arthur Robert Royall of the Royal Irish Regiment, c.1918. Arthur survived the First World War, despite having been posted as killed in action. He lost an eye in battle but served in the Royal Irish Regiment for four years after the war ended, until it was disbanded.

Harry Percy Royall in 1914/18. The 'flashes' of his uniform identify his regiment as the Machine Gun Guards. Harry survived the war to rejoin the Metropolitan Police (see also p.108).

Another brave man, Jimmy Seeley MM (Military Medal), c.1980. Jimmy's experiences of the fighting around the River Somme led him to give extra names to his son Ted. He added the names Montaubon Thiepval in memory of two French villages that he would have passed through or fought over.

Jimmy Annis in Royal Flying Corps uniform, at some point before 1918. Jimmy survived the war and came home to raise a family on his market garden on The Street, (see also p.108).

Leonard Royall, c.1917. Leonard survived the war in which he was twice decorated for bravery with the award of Distinguished Conduct Medal and Bar.

Roll of Honour

First World War

Walter E. ALEXANDER   5 Jul. 1915
  1st Bn, Royal Newfoundland Regt
Arthur W. ANNIS   24 Jul. 1916
  7th Bn, the East Yorkshire Regiment
Robert George BEAUMONT   4 Oct. 1917
  22nd Bn, the Manchester Regiment
Alfred John BOGGIS   8 Oct. 1918
  9th Bn, the Norfolk Regiment
Walter Wilfred BRACEY   2 Sept. 1914
  Royal Navy Reserve
Victor G. GILLINGWATER   17 Feb. 1917
  Royal Marines Light Infantry
Charles W. GREENACRE   22 Apr. 1916
  2nd Bn, the Norfolk Regiment
Henry G.V. GREENACRE   27 Mar. 1916
  1st Bn, Coldstream Guards
Sidney Richard KEDGE   8 Jul. 1916
  6th Bn, Queen's Royal West Surreys
Sydney George KEELER   Nothing yet known
Ernest Albert LEEDER   16 Apr. 1917
  11th Bn, Australian Infantry
Sidney Herbert MARKS   8 Oct. 1917
  1st Bn, the Essex Regiment
Harry Samuel MAYES   1 Oct. 1915
  7th Bn, the Norfolk Regiment
Albert William PARKER   9 Feb. 1917
  392nd Company, Royal Engineers
Alfred Hubert ROPE   5 May 1917
  Royal Marines Light Infantry
Leonard Godfrey ROPE   7 Apr. 1916
  31st Bn, Canadian Inf (Alberta)
Aubrey Samuel STONE   17 Sept. 1916
  9th Bn, the Norfolk Regiment
Clement Sidney WALL   11 Aug. 1917
  8th Bn, the Norfolk Regiment
Charles Daniel WEDDUP   17 Oct. 1915
  1st Bn, Coldstream Guards
James Robert WRIGHT   17 Dec. 1918
  Military Police

Second World War

Leonard CAIN   8 Aug. 1944
  7th Bn, the Royal Norfolk Regiment
Jack Edmond LOVEWELL   16 Aug. 1943
  Royal New Zealand Air Force
Archibald Russell MAYES   19 Feb. 1941
  Royal Navy
John Arthur (Jack) MAYES   23 Oct. 1941
  Royal Navy
Herbert Charles George PODD   28 Jun. 1942
  74th Field Regt, Royal Artillery

The Price That Was Paid

A total of 25 Bergh Apton men died in the two world wars. The 20 who were lost in the first one represented something like a quarter of the male working population.

Thomas and Agnes Mayes of Prospect Place lost sons in both world wars. Harry Samuel was killed in 1915 at the age of 20 and both Archie and Jack were killed in 1941 when in their late 30s.

William and Hannah Greenacre lost the eldest two of their five sons in the First World War when Henry and Charles died within less than a month of each other but a continent apart. The loss to Aaron and Alice Rope was, if anything, more tragic as they lost the only two sons they had when Alfred and Leonard were killed just over a year apart in April 1916 and May 1917.

Rosa Boggis brought up three young children Alfred, Herbert and Ivy on her own after their father Alfred John died with only a month to go before the end of hostilities.

Four times we lost two men on the same battlefield. Henry Greenacre and Leonard Rope fell in the fighting around Ypres in the Spring of 1916. A little over a year later, in autumn 1917, Robert Beaumont and Clement Wall died in much the same area. Sidney Kedge and Aubrey Stone are remembered on the same huge memorial at Thiepval. Charles Weddup and Harry Mayes were killed in the same battle within a fortnight of one another and are remembered on the memorial at Loos.

Great was the price our village forebears paid. Many were the homes cast into grief so that we might do what we do this day in freedom.

When you go home, tell them of us and say 'for your tomorrow we gave our today'

EPITAPH ON THE KOHIMA WAR MEMORIAL, INDIA AND ON THE BASRAH WAR MEMORIAL, NASIRIYAH IRAQ, JOHN MAXWELL EDMUNDS (1875–1958).

Poppies, the symbol of the war dead, grow on the roadsides of Bergh Apton in equal profusion as they do in the fields of Flanders where so many young men died.

The Village Hall

By John Ling

This second appendix to Geoffrey Kelly's history of Bergh Apton is about the Village Hall (Fig.13.2, p.131). My own interest in the subject started when Hilary, my wife, agreed to become hon. secretary in 2003 and arrived home from the meeting laden with boxes containing papers on its history. The minute book made fascinating reading and is the basis for this appendix. Where I have made comments on any specific point that has come only from the minute book itself, or that confirms what has otherwise been told to me, I have made reference to the date on which it appears in the minute book.

This is not a learned work. There will be errors and omissions caused by both my lack of first-hand knowledge on the Village Hall and my failure to dig deeper into some aspects of it. But I hope that it is a fair summary of what can be gleaned from writings and stories about the building and its people. First in hope, then in planning and finally in being, it has been for almost 70 years part of the lives of many people who live in or have had an interest in this parish.

Much of my original research was done for a small exhibition that was part of the golden jubilee celebrations of the opening of the Village Hall, held on the day itself – 2 June 2003. The rest emerged from further research when the decision to write the appendix was taken. I am very grateful indeed to the many kind people of Bergh Apton who have patiently listened and then responded as best they may to my questions and probings on things in the minute book that needed clarification. Their help has ensured that the appendix is as free as reasonably and humanly possible from sins of both omission and commission. Trevor Sillett, Fred Littlewood, Kevin Parfitt and John Phillips, past chairmen in times of change and before Hilary and I finally settled in the village in 1997, have been particularly helpful in this process and I give them my thanks.

The Original Committee

The story began in 1938 when residents of Bergh Apton met at the school under the chairmanship of Thomas Denny-Cooke of Bergh Apton Manor and agreed to set in train the building of a Village Hall. The minute book tells it thus:

A Parish Meeting was held at the School on 19 January to discuss the question of building a Village Hall for Bergh Apton. Mr Denny-Cooke took the chair. There

was a large attendance of Parishioners and it was decided with only one dissentient [sic] to proceed with a scheme and form a Committee to deal with it. The following persons were elected, T H Denny-Cooke Esq, Brigadier Gen. Dale, J Annis, C Carver, W Keeler, F Keeping, V Kemp, W G Panks, A Tubby, A Vincent, Mrs Denny-Cooke, Mrs Freestone and Mrs Tubby.

The minute was written by Fred Keeping of Welbeck Road, the Norwich Union insurance agent in the village who was to serve as secretary until May 1949.

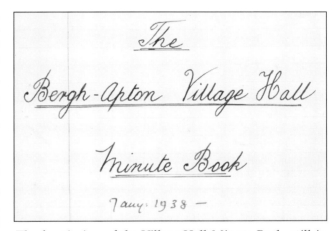

The frontispiece of the Village Hall Minute Book, still in use at the time of writing, to record annual general meetings.

Fund-Raising

The present-day Bergh Apton fête was born in these early days of Village Hall fund-raising, and first appears in the minute of a meeting on 23 March 1938 when Thomas Denny-Cooke offered the grounds of Bergh Apton Manor on Whit Monday when the sum of £30.5s.4d. was raised. That may seem rather modest when set against today's revenue of £3,086.68 (2004) but it was, in fact, a very tidy sum in those days.

Progress was threatened soon after that first fête by a little local difficulty that began when, at the annual parish meeting on 4 April, those present agreed 'to apply money left over from the Coronation celebrations in 1937 [for King Edward VIII] to start a fund for the provision of a children's playing-field'. Geoffrey Kelly also refers to this minute on p.134 of this book.

The protagonists of the Village Hall project argued that these surplus funds amounting to £6.5s.2d. ought to have been donated to the Village Hall building fund. A debate on the issue took place on 26 April 1938 and, judging from the evidence of the minute (Village Children's Playing-Field minute book), it was stormy.

It even involved a lively if short-lived altercation between Thomas Denny-Cooke and Brig. Gen. Dale of Holly Lodge on Sunnyside, over procedure. One may imagine the atmosphere in the school-room as the General had the temerity to silence Thomas Denny-Cooke who was not only the long-established seigneur of the village and owner of much of its land, but a Justice of the Peace to boot!

When calm returned to the meeting, the playing-field committee agreed to consider an offer made by Mr Denny-Cooke to provide a piece of land for the playing-field.

A little more drama was to come. At its next meeting a few days later, the committee rejected Mr Denny-Cooke's offer on two grounds: the land he offered was too far from the school; and he proposed to restrict access to the months between October and March (perhaps to take the hay off it in the summer?).

Despite their irritation the members of the playing-field committee then proved themselves to be pragmatists by agreeing to transfer the surplus funds to the Village Hall project. They recognised that the latter had more support in the village and would win any battle for funds. In the words of the minute dated 3 May 1938:

This [the handing over of funds] would enable them to complete the Village Hall this year in all probability. The necessity of raising money for the hall would disappear before the end of the summer and we should be free to gather funds, not only almost alone in the field but with a united and friendly village to help us.

Ah, if only life was so simple! It was not that summer but the one 15 years hence that the Village Hall opened its doors. The intervening time was spent battling with bureaucracy, rising prices, apathy and the Second World War to raise the funds needed to build. The story of the struggle is told in great detail in the minutes of a committee whose determination to succeed will win the respect of anyone who has the time to read of their efforts.

The War Years

Despite the Second World War wreaking havoc with their plans, the minute book shows that the committee made what contribution they could to the war effort. At a public meeting in the school on 25 July 1940, soon after the fall of France and the retreat from Dunkirk, the village carried unanimously a proposition by Brig. Gen. Dale (now vice-chairman of the hall committee)

and seconded by Mrs George Freestone:

That the interest received on the amount invested for the Parish Hall in Defence Bonds be handed back to the Government for the duration of the war as a small contribution from the parish of Bergh Apton.

When this motion was made and carried the funds stood at £170.9s.10d. of which £150 was invested in Defence Bonds.

Things got no better with the cessation of hostilities in Europe in May 1945. Progress was frustrated by material shortages and the consequent rising prices, linked with a lack of government resources to make grants and loans for such projects.

A Donation of Land

Things were not always easy in the relationship with Mr Denny-Cooke who, you will remember, promised in 1938 'to give the land for a Village Hall and convey the same free of cost'. On 19 September 1949 he confirmed that offer but less than a fortnight later he told the committee that he did not feel justified in giving an acre because, as is recorded 'the car park

This poster dates from 1949, when fund-raising for the building of the Village Hall was the objective of the fête.

and bowling-green were unnecessarily extensive'. He agreed to give an area measuring 60yds by 60yds on which the committee decided that they would ask the architect Frank Dewey to draw up plans for a building measuring 50ft by 28ft (minute of 7 October 1949).

The site that Denny-Cooke gave was originally livestock grazing on the manor estate owned, until the 1960s, by his family. For some time before this he had permitted its use for football and cricket matches for which the teams used the reading room (Maddie Smith's Glebe Cottage on the other side of Cooke's Road in 2004) as their changing room and equipment store. It is very probable that this was the field he had in his mind when he offered land to the playing-field committee in May 1938.

If previous observations suggest that the Village Hall committee's relationship with the Denny-Cooke family was poor it would be wrong, for they had been consistent supporters and leading members of the project throughout. The difficulty over the size of the plot seems to have been some point of principle that must have been resolved six months later, for Mr Denny-Cooke gave a further quarter of an acre to the project (minute of 19 May 1950).

Costs and Funding

The situation in late 1952 was bleak indeed. Building costs continued to rise and various sources of funding seemed to clash, as one required one thing and another required the opposite to approve funding. Arthur Vincent advised that the lowest price he could give them for a simple hut with no internal divisions was £1,045 and they had only £846.10s.0d. in funds. They also heard that any plans to close the school would not be taken for another ten years so that was not an available option. It was not a good time.

The breakthrough came when the Denny-Cooke family made a generous gesture that enabled the committee to press the 'go' button. On 17 November 1952 the then chairman Sandy Newman Sanders, one of Anglia Television's announcers who lived at St Martin's Acre (White Willows in 2004), told the committee that Mrs Denny-Cooke had given a donation of £200 to the fund in memory of her husband Thomas who had died in September.

Let us not sniff at this apparently modest amount. Government statistics on its website (www.eh.net/hmit) give its value in 2004 as £3,109 so it was not a small sum. If Mrs Denny-Cooke calculated that this figure would give the committee confidence to go ahead with construction, she was right, for they agreed there and then 'to unanimously approve a proposal to erect a Dri-Crete hut as Village Hall at a cost of £1,035' (minute of 17 November 1952).

That was Arthur Vincent's price to build what is

Sandy Newman-Sanders, chairman of the Village Hall committee in 1952. During that same year, the decision was made to build the hall. Sandy was a well-recognised personality from Anglia Television, in the very beginning of independent television broadcasting in East Anglia. He lived at St Martin's Acre (known as White Willows in 2004) on The Street. (ANGLIA TV)

basically the Village Hall we still use at the time of writing. We know precisely what was agreed as it is recorded in the minutes of that meeting:

The Hall to be erected with 'Dri-Crete' blocks in natural cement shade, 66 feet x 24 feet (inside 22 feet 6 inches) with concrete [?], £915. This sum to include £25 for electrical wiring. Plain deal floor extra £120 approx.

Suddenly all was activity. Local and national government and other bodies agreed to make grants and loans for both the building and the contents (including a radiogram for village dances!), Mrs Denny-Cooke undertook to find the guarantors necessary to secure the loans, and construction began.

The Opening of the Village Hall

At last, on the day of Queen Elizabeth's coronation on Tuesday 2 June 1953, the Village Hall opened when Revd Frederick Martin (chairman of the Village Hall committee) and Mrs Denny-Cooke performed the ceremony that included a dedication service conducted by Mr Martin. No details of the day are officially recorded but Grace Forder remembers that her brother Harry won the prize in the 'Bowling for a Pig' contest. He took home to Bussey Bridge a live pig that the family named Isabel after the donor Mr Isbell of Town Farm.

Extensions and Improvements

Much has happened in the first 50 years of the Village Hall's existence including three major extensions and many more modest but important improvements such as the replacement of the original 'Elsan' chemical toilets with flushing ones in the 1960s!

The first major work in 1985, at a cost of some £1,900 (minute of AGM 17 April 1985) provided a new kitchen on the south-east corner of the hall to replace the original one at the north-west corner. The cost of this project was kept down to a reasonable figure by dint of Barney Curtis and Tony Knights doing the major work but with a lot of the manpower provided free of charge by members of the bowls club.

Then in 1992 two major changes took place at the same time. The small stage at the north end of the hall was removed to make way for a new theatre-style stage complete with proscenium arch, built into the area that housed the original kitchen and store/meeting room. At the same time, the 1985 extension on the east side of the hall was further increased to provide a committee room, access to the garden on the east side, wings for the stage and a

The Village Hall some time after 1985 when the new kitchen was added, but before the slide was removed in late 1989 or early 1990.

new emergency exit. All this created a much-improved venue for the Thurton and Bergh Apton Players, recently arrived from their original venue in Thurton & Ashby Village Hall, to put on their ambitious and popular musicals. All these improvements were completed under the chairmanship of Trevor Sillett (1985), Fred Littlewood (1986) and Canon John Phillips (1992).

The Girl Guides celebrating Christmas 1955 in the Village Hall with their leader June O'Riorden of White Willows. Left to right, standing: *Maureen Elwin, Beryl Cushion, Wendy Rackham, June Sutton, June O'Riorden, Evelyn (Evy) Jermy, Ann Howard, Elsie Jermy, Margaret Winter;* seated: *June Ellis, Beryl Bradley, Rosemary Bloomfield, Margaret Brown, Janet Kemp and Judith Bloomfield;* kneeling: *Monica Savory, Olive Elmer, Olive Scarles, Sheila Gilbert, Valerie Littleboy, Shirley Littleboy.*

The Committee

Having introduced three officers of the committee responsible for the operation of the Village Hall, we should look at the constitution that orders their doings. It was first considered in detail in 1949 when the conveyance of the land donated by the Denny-Cookes was being finalised. The committee agreed that control of the building should be non-political and non-sectarian (minute of 16 May 1949) and that these conditions should be incorporated into the conveyance being prepared by the Loddon solicitor Mr Gilbert.

Ownership, on payment of the sum of £10, was finally conveyed to a trust on 20 March 1950 of which the Revd Frederick William Martin and Captain Philip Theodore Symonds of Town Farm were the original trustees. The trust deed specified that the hall be used as follows:

... for the purposes of physical and mental training and recreation and social moral and intellectual development through the medium of reading and recreation rooms, library, lectures, classes recreations and entertainments [sic] or otherwise as may be found expedient for the benefit of the inhabitants of the parish of Bergh Apton.

Management was vested in a committee of 17 people of which six are elected at the annual general meeting. Another eight are nominated by eight local organisations that use the hall on a regular basis. Those active in the early 1950s, defined in the conveyance were the Parish Council, School Managers, Women's Institute, Royal British Legion, Red Cross, Girl Guides, Women's Voluntary Service and the committee of Bergh Apton Flower Show. The final three places on the committee are for people whom the elected and appointed committee members may co-opt.

That management structure remains in place at the time of writing but the nominated bodies, with the approval of the charity commissioners, have changed with the changing pattern of village life and society. The only body that remains on the committee in its original form is the Parish Council.

Others represented on the committee today are Alpington and Bergh Apton Voluntary Aided School (which most of our juniors now attend), Bergh Apton Community Arts Trust, Bergh Apton & District Society, the flower arranging group, the Parochial Church Council and the Thurton and Bergh Apton Players who have members representing both senior and junior sections.

Events and Functions

Having met the management it is time to look at the people who use the hall. It has been the scene of many happy occasions both corporate, when the management committee or other Bergh Apton body

Fred and Violet Littlewood's wedding reception was the first private function at the Village Hall in August 1953. Before they got married Violet (née Jermy) lived on Church Road. Her family had moved there from Threadneedle Street where young Fred and his family had been their neighbours.

arranges events, and private, when the hall is hired by families or organisations to hold their own functions. The very first of these private functions in August 1953, only two months after the hall was opened, was the reception following the marriage of Fred Littlewood of Threadneedle Street and Violet Jermy of Church Road in Bergh Apton's Parish Church. Fred and Violet went on to keep a very close association with the hall through Fred's chairmanship of the management committee in the 1980s when Violet was his vice-chairman and through their interest in the bowls club of which they are both leading lights to this day.

The Bergh Apton and District Society, formed in 1993, uses the hall for its monthly 'home' meetings when it is not away on its adventurous programme that includes overseas weekends and, in the inimitable terminology of its founder and chairman Lynton Johnson, 'retail therapy trips'.

The fact that two funeral services have been held in the hall causes one to reflect that the proper rhythm of life in a small community brings both happiness and sorrow in their turn.

Earlier reference to the bowls club reminds me to mention the numerous sports and social clubs that

Christmas Dinner in the Village Hall with the Good Companions, c.1960. The photograph includes: Revd Frederick Martin, Mrs Ives, Lavender Alexander, Sarah Kate Dew, Jimmy Dew, Mrs Forder, Rose Dye (wife of Charlie) and Libby Dye.

Above: *The Thurton and Bergh Apton Players have been performing in the Village Hall since 1988 with Ray Wharton's celebrated promise that each show will be 'bigger better and even more spectacular!'. Here is part of the crew and cast for* Anything Goes *of March 2003. Left to right, back row: Lynton Johnson, David Buckle, Paul Bassenthwaite, Clive Parsons, James Crabtree; middle row: Diane Ellis, Sandra Curston, Ray Wharton, Simon Peck, Audrey Chapman, Maria Andrew; front row: Thomas Robinson, Steven Robinson.*

Left: *Members of the Bergh Apton Society during an evening of old-fashioned entertainment in January 2003. Left to right: Jenny Daniells, Shelagh Yallop, Heather Perfitt, Poppy Annis, Evie Sayer, Eileen Goody, Audrey Harvey and Jill Harvey.*

The Good Companions on a visit to Fred Lutkin's 'Lambs Court' in Claxton in the 1960s. The photograph includes: Lilian Howes, Betty Denny-Cooke, Fred Lutkin, Ada Lain, Lally Farrow, May Farrow, Mr Howard from Nichols Corner and Sarah Kate Dew.

have used the hall. The bowls club itself first appears in the minutes in April 1984 when Neville Sutton reported that the club 'was in a league and at present were the top of the league'. He also reported that the club hoped to obtain a second bowls mat for which the Parish Council had already agreed to grant £100 of the £376 required. In 2004 the club meets in the hall every Tuesday evening and most Fridays evenings and has had success in competitions far beyond its walls, for its trophy cabinet seems to fill up every year with prizes and trophies from all over East Anglia.

The hall was home to the Good Companions for many years and a rifle club moved here from Alpington in 1984 (but there is no record of how long it stayed). Josie Whiting's famous whist drives were a regular feature of the hall's bookings diary from the very beginning until 1991, and its card tables still form a vital part of the equipment deployed each year at the annual village fête.

The Fête

This last point prompts me to deal with Bergh Apton's fête in a little more detail. We know from newspaper archives that there was once a fête held in The Rectory

The first fête that was jointly organised by the Village Hall and the church in the grounds of Bergh Apton Manor was in 1983 and was the idea of Major Colin Mackenzie. Here, on the steps leading from the house into the garden, he looks on as Lady Anne receives a bouquet from Lorie Lain-Rogers on behalf of the fête committee. Chairman Fred Littlewood is holding the microphone. The costumes worn by the committee and helpers mark this as the fête of 1985, which had an Edwardian theme.

garden but there is no record of its lifespan. In its present form it has been going since 1938 with interruption only for the Second World War and the year of the Village Hall's silver jubilee in 1978 (secretary's report for year 1978/9) and is held at the manor in a tradition begun by Thomas Denny-Cooke and carried on by his successors as the manor's owners, Mr and Mrs Morse, Major and Lady Ann Mackenzie and, since 1990, Kip and Alison Bertram, with daughters Verity and Felicity. The fête was initially a means of raising funds to build the Village Hall but Major Mackenzie introduced the concept of sharing both the work and the proceeds between the Village Hall and the Parochial Church Council. That co-operation between the only two public buildings in the parish continues happily to this day.

At one time the fête programme had an evening dance, a sports programme and games that included the 'Bowling for a Pig' competition in which Harry Forder won his pig in Queen Elizabeth II's coronation year. Peter Annis, during one mardle I had with him this summer, told me that he won the same prize a few years later. Today's fête is a little tamer and the prize is an uncontroversial hamper of food. Other present-day activities focus much more on stalls that sell a variety of produce and products, serve the famous Bergh Apton fête cream teas and Kevin's Kitchen specialities of crêpes suzette and Buck's Fizz.

Health Matters

The Village Hall has also been used to keep a check on the health of Bergh Apton residents and those in neighbouring villages and Geoffrey Kelly has already referred in Chapter XIII to the doctor's surgery that operated in the hall from 1988 until the millennium.

Norfolk County Council's health department also ran a monthly children's clinic in the hall that they described as an 'infant welfare centre' or 'child health clinic' during its lifetime of 14 years between 20 September 1955 (NCC Public Health Department letter of 8 August 1955) and 3 July 1969 (letter of 4 July 1969). An article in the *Eastern Daily Press* at the time of the clinic's opening says that it served the villages of Alpington, Ashby, Bergh Apton, Hellington and Yelverton. Thurton is notable for its absence from the list but may have had other arrangements for the care of its children.

A letter written to Beatrice Denny-Cooke, hon. secretary, by the county medical officer on 28 January 1958 gives a human touch to this contract. It complains that 'the Village Hall is not too warm when the Infant Welfare sessions are held' and goes on to ask that 'the fires be lit in the morning in order that the room may be warm enough for undressing the children by 2.00 pm'. Those of you who know how cold the hall can be on winter days will surely appreciate the validity of this request!

The Village Hall in 2004

It isn't possible in an appendix to include every organisation that has used the space in or around the Village Hall – there are too many. But, as a snapshot in time, the schedule of regular users in 2004 may suffice to show its diverse usage. The list includes the village youth club, baby and toddler group, painting class (will it one day produce such quality that we will be famed for the Bergh Apton Colourists!?), the bowls club, a yoga class, the Thurton and Bergh Apton Players, Bergh Apton & District Society, the flower club and, as one would expect, the Village Hall management committee itself.

The Parish Council uses the hall for most of its monthly meetings that are well supported by the public and attended by our councillors who are, at the time of writing, John Fuller (South Norfolk District) and Adrian Gunson (Norfolk County). Events include the annual parish meeting, the AGM of both the Conservation Trust and the Local History Group and the AGM of the Village Hall itself.

The annual village Christmas lunch, an event of quite recent beginnings, grows in strength as each year passes. It caters for nearly 100 guests who either live alone or are of an age when it gives pleasure to their younger neighbours to act as their hosts in the Village Hall in December.

It is the epitome of a little adage that my brother-in-law the late Geoffrey Ball told me about the pomp and ceremony of the City of London, in whose affairs he was much involved. He defined the progress of a popular event thus: Its first year is its inauguration. In its second year it is 'part of a great tradition' and by its third year its origins 'are lost in the mists of time'. The Bergh Apton Christmas lunch is now of that maturity and is fondly regarded and eagerly anticipated equally by those who cook it and serve it as well as by those who eat it.

Another even more recent but increasingly popular lunchtime project is an annual pot-luck lunch organised by members of the Parish Church to follow Harvest Festival. Everyone brings enough to eat for themselves and one other, and we sit down to catch up with each other's news relieved of the responsibility of mass catering.

The hall is the venue for concerts arranged through the Bergh Apton Community Arts Trust and for its own arts workshops. The concerts are part of a programme financially supported by Creative Arts East, a Wymondham-based arts catalyst that books high quality professional artists to tour rural Norfolk communities. BACAT's workshops fulfil part of its constitutional objectives, bringing artists in many media to the village to share their skills and experience with local people. The latter meet some of the costs of these events but they are underwritten and shared by a BACAT fund created from Sculpture Trail income.

This list of hospitality events in the Village Hall

Members of the Village Hall management committee, 2004. Left to right, back row: John Ducker, Lynton Johnson; middle row: Maddie James, Evie Sayer, Hilary Ling (secretary); front row: Jenny Daniells, Sandra Sillett, Shelagh Yallop, Maggie Smith (chairman). Missing from the photo are Poppy Annis, Kate Kerry, Simon Peck, Heather Sarsby, David Skedge and Ray Wharton.

'Kevin's Kitchen' on the morning after the Sculpture Trail of 2002. The photograph includes: Trevor Sillett, Richard Cushing, John Ling, Kerry Avery, Jean Flowerdew, Audrey Harvey, Tim Rolph, George Harvey, Sandy Schröder, Barbara Marshall, David Skedge, Mary Debbage, Malcom Robinson, Kevin Parfitt, Lesley Smith, Dennis Moye, Tony Cooper, John Hughes, Carrie Kerry, Sandra Sillett, Lorie Lain-Rogers, Madge Farrer, Janet Pring, Hilary Ling, Nicky Butterworth, Elizabeth Robinson, Paul Butterworth, Teresa Parfitt, Bob Debbage, Janet Skedge, Max Avery, Nina Avery, Caitlin Avery, Tom Butterworth, Catherine Kerry, Elizabeth Kerry, Georgie Butterworth, Jessica Butterworth, Johnny Parfitt, Bob Kerry, Maggie Smith and her son Jordan. Madge Farrer (in white trousers) was 99 years old at the time. She went on to reach 100 and achieve celebrity status as the village's first recorded centenarian.

would not be complete without including the occasional breakfasts laid on by Kevin Parfitt and his team of cooks, servers and washers-up, all in the guise of 'Kevin's Kitchen'. These wonderful social occasions are a development of Kevin's catering stall at the annual fête and occur at such times as the end of the Sculpture Trail and New Year's Day. At that time in particular the quality of the bacon and eggs and the fizz of champagne in the Buck's Fizz restores the constitution of many a jaded village reveller.

The only sad note of this review is that the Village Hall committee nowadays rarely organises public dances as it once did. Social change has meant that these events cost more – even a modest live band rarely gets out of bed for less than £400 – and their supporters are a diminishing number, perhaps because of the pressure of other demands on people's time. The result is that income simply cannot offset costs.

But that earlier list of events suggests that the hall is alive and kicking, and filling the role foreseen by that group of village people who gathered in the school way back in January 1938.

The Play Area

And what of that other group of 1938, the Village Children's Playing-Field Committee, whose aims were never fulfilled? The playing-field was never provided and probably never will be. The minute book does record a proposal by Mrs Lawrence that a grant be sought from the Playing-Fields Association (PFA) to provide a see-saw, two swings, two seats and a sand pit (AGM of 28 March 1961). However the PFA advised (letter dated 19 April 1961) that only 50 per cent of costs would be offset by a grant and the committee deferred the proposal in the light of their earlier decision to put their fund-raising energies into a village-wide effort of that year to restore the Parish Church.

Not until 1971 were a slide and some swings installed but they were removed in the late 1980s when their design and condition no longer met the standards of modern equipment safety regulations (minutes of AGM 3 April 1989).

Almost ten years later two young mothers, Karen Myhill of Loddon Road and Suzanne Mayes of Gravel Pit Lane, decided to take the initiative to replace them. They applied for funding from South Norfolk Council, grant-making trusts and other bodies, and organised fund-raising events in the village to meet the costs of erecting a new integrated play area in the grounds of the Village Hall.

They achieved their target of £19,281.75 when Bergh Apton's Tenwinter Trust and BACAT, the oldest and the newest Bergh Apton benefactors, made grants to the project so that work could begin. Our County Councillor Adrian Gunson formally opened the play area, which was then given into the safekeeping of the Parish Council, on 8 September 2002.

The play area is the latest improvement in a long line of alterations and extensions to adapt the Village Hall. As *The Book of Bergh Apton* goes to press, the management committee is looking at the next phase of modifications (or even a complete re-build) to meet the changing needs of the community. Change is also demanded by an increasingly rule-bound society to meet all the laws and regulations that aim to give risk-free and equal access to absolutely everyone.

This latter objective imposes both personal and

Prize-winning pirates celebrate their 'best-in-class' victory at the celebrations of the Village Hall's golden jubilee on 2 June 2003. Left to right: Sophie Thurtle of Sunnyside, William Kerry of Bussey Bridge Farm, ?,?,?.

The evening celebrations of the Village Hall's golden jubilee on 2 June 2003. Kip and Alison Bertram arrived from Bergh Apton Manor in true 1953 style in Kip's veteran Austin Seven, dressed for the occasion and ready to dance!

corporate liabilities on the people who run rural facilities like Bergh Apton's Village Hall. At times the committee – all unpaid volunteers – must be tempted to walk away from the struggle. And it is, indeed, a struggle these days to comply with the growing burden of regulation and legislation and still provide a small community with simple facilities for modest activities at a reasonable cost.

But it is the nature of small villages to rise to challenges. Modern Bergh Apton will arrive at a satisfactory outcome, to alter or rebuild, and to comply with regulations, just as its forebears did in 1938, when initial differences of opinion turned to common purpose. It is a very Bergh Apton way of doing things.

Village Hall Committee Members

From the start of the project in 1938, the minute book of the Village Hall committee has recorded the names of village people who planned it and then ran it. In that time a dozen amongst them have served as chairmen and chairwomen:

Chairmen and Chairwomen of the Village Hall Committee	
1938–1948	Thomas Denny-Cooke JP, Bergh Apton Manor
1949–1950	Captain P. Symonds, Town Farm
1951	Beatrice Denny-Cooke, Bergh Apton Manor (and later The Beeches)
1952	Sandy Newman-Sanders, St Martin's Acre, The Street
1953–1955	Revd F.W. Martin, The Rectory
1956–1970	Monsey Vincent, The Villa, Threadneedle Street (Laurel House in 2004)
1971–1975	Josie Whiting, Church Road
1976–1983	Kevin Parfitt, Church Farm
1984–1985	Trevor Sillett, Church Road
1986–1989	Fred Littlewood, Seven Bells, Threadneedle Street
1990–1995	Canon John Phillips, Mere Farm House, White Heath Road
1996 on	Maggie Smith, Church Road (of Cock Road, Hardley in 2005)

Many more people have given their time and energy as committee members. Up to 1992 the minutes were hand-written with varying degrees of legibility and that may have created some errors in transliteration. The following list, culled from the minute book and in alphabetical order, includes everyone (other than the chairmen listed above) whose name appears therein, with the year that his or her name first appears:

Members of the Village Hall Committee

C. Alexander (1945), Maria Andrews (1993), Ted Armiger MM (1983), Lavender Alexander (1950), James Annis (1938), Poppy Annis (1959), Mr Barnes (1954), Mrs Barnes (1951), Bill Boardman (1969), Mrs Alfred Boggis (1951), Jill Browne/Emms (1976), Nicky Butterworth (2000), Miss Byatt (1952), Jean Bobbin (1994), Charlie Carver (1938), George Carver (1952), Miss Catton (1949), Mr Catton (1945), Audrey Chapman (1995), John Claydon (1994), Kevin Clow (1998), Dianne Corbin (1976), Joe Corbin (1969), Jean Cracknell (1964), Stephanie Crome (1987), Hilary (Brenda) Culbertson (1987), Brig. Gen. Dale (1938), Jenny Daniells (1980), Sam Debbage (1952), Mrs Denny-Cooke (1938), John Ducker (2002), Mrs Elmer (1952), R. Fairhead (1938), Paul Farrow (1984), Roy Flowerdew (1991), David Ford (1966), Sylvia Ford (1966), Grace Forder (1958), Harry Forder (1958), Mrs Forder (1965), Alison Freeman (1990), John Freeman (1990), Jessie Freestone (1938), Mrs Alan French (1955), Mr and Mrs Frosdick (1954), Stanley Gilbert (1954), Carlos Glasspole (1949), Miss Haines (1950), Mike Harris (1956), Milton Harris (1976), Audrey Harvey (1990), Revd Heard (1938), Geoffrey Holmes (1953), Mrs Jeffree (1945), Lynn Jermy (1978), Mrs Jermy (1954), Lynton Johnson (1994), Billy Keeler (1938), Mrs Keeler (1951), Fred Keeping (1938), Miss Keeping (1951), Mrs Kemp (1938), Victor Kemp (1938), Gillian Kent (1976), Kate Kerry (2002), Carol Keywood (1971), Eileen Lain-Rogers (1988), Mark Lake (1988), Mr and Mrs Lawrence (1957), Sally Leigh (2001), Ruby Leist (1951), Mrs Lewis (1953), Hilary Ling (2002), Violet Littlewood (1979), Mrs Locke (1945), Mrs Lucas (1966), Janet McGill (1987), Mrs Newman-Sanders (1952), Billy Panks (1938), Theresa Parfitt (1995), Simon Peck (1994), Miss Poppy (1951), Martha Rayner (1951), Lisa Reeve (2000), Chris Roe (1976), Heather Sarsby (2002), Evie Sayer (1985), Mick Sayers (1997), Mrs Dot Seely (1959), David Seeley (1976), Florence Sillett (1963), George Sillett (1975), Melissa Sillett (1998), Sandra Sillett (1981), Wilfred Sillett (1954), Ian Smith (1987), Leslie Smith (1996), Shirley Smith (1988), Revd and Mrs Snellgrove (1961), James Steggles (1989), Linda Sturman (1981), Mrs G. Sturman (1978), Dennis Sutton (1958), Mrs Ethel(?) Sutton (1954), Helen Sutton (1979), Neville Sutton (1978), A. Tubby (1938), Mrs Tubby (1938), Arthur Vincent (1938), Miss M. Vincent (1945), Mrs Vincent (1951), Mick Waller (1982), Lynne Ward (1981), Derek Ward (1982), Mr and Mrs A. Weddup (1955), Ray Wharton (1988), Jack Whiting (1958), Betty Wood (1980), Shelagh Yallop (1981), Mr Youngs (1950).

Index

Subscribers

Kathleen Andrew (née Catchpole), Pulham St Mary

Peter R. Annis, The Street, Bergh Apton

Barbara M. Appleton, Hardley, Norfolk

Garry and Kerry Avery, Bergh Apton

Nigel and Paris Back

Simon J. Bailey and Hailey Loveday, Bergh Apton, Norfolk

Mr Richard Baker, born in Bergh Apton

Ann Ball, Shoreham, Kent

Patricia Irene Banham, Bergh Apton, Norfolk

Judith Barber, (Greenacre), Felpham

Elsie E. Barker (née Jermy), Bergh Apton, Norfolk

John E. Barmby, Kirstead, Norfolk

Jill Barton (née Rogerson), formerly of Holly Lodge

Felicity Bertram, The Manor, Bergh Apton

Kip and Alison Bertram, The Manor, Bergh Apton

Verity Bertram, The Manor, Bergh Apton

Janice M. Bibby, Watton, Norfolk

Miss Eileen B. Bircham, Thurton, Norfolk

Derek J. Blake, Bergh Apton

The Blazer Family, Bergh Apton

June and Bill Boardman, Bergh Apton

Bernie and Jean Bobbin, Bergh Apton

Mr and Mrs P.A. Booth

John W. Bracey, Sprowston and Surlingham, Norfolk

P.J. Brompton, Alpington, Norfolk

Cherry and Elyshia Brooks

Edna B. Brooks (née Jermy), Bergh Apton, Norfolk

Sandra Brunton (née Dye), Geneva, Switzerland

David Buckle and Diane Ellis, Musical Director, Thurton and Bergh Apton Players

Bobby and Debbie Burlingham, Beccles, Suffolk

Bob and Vera Burlingham, Bergh Apton, Norfolk

Tony, Tracey, Daniel, Shannon and Harley Burlingham, Topcroft, Suffolk

Elizabeth and John Burrage, Bergh Apton, Norfolk

Ian Burrage, Seething, Norfolk

David Buxton, Thurton

Ron C. Cain, Bergh Apton, Norfolk

Mrs Vera Campbell-Walls, Wimberly Circle, Bristol, Tennessee, USA

Barry D. Carpenter, Brooke, Norfolk

Diane Carpenter, Chedgrave

The Carrick Family, Bergh Apton, Norfolk

Jonathan M. Cary, Thorpe St Andrew, Norwich

David Catchpole, Ashby St Mary

Audrey Chapman, Thurton, Norfolk

Audrey Chappell, The Old Forge, Mill Road, Bergh Apton

Lynda J. Chilvers, King's Lynn, Norfolk

John Anthony Clemence

Benjamin Crome, Bergh Apton

Stephanie and Richard Crome, Bergh Apton

William Crome, Bergh Apton

Paul Crowe, Henfield, West Sussex

M.P. Cubitt

Lila Cunnell (née Purling)

Bernard and Maureen Curtis

Barry and Sara Cushing

Brenda Cushing (née Dye), Poringland, Norfolk

Richard Cushing, Bergh Apton

Jennifer Daniells (née Carpenter)

Ian, Debbie and Rachel Davey, Bergh Apton

Mr and Mrs Davey, Upminster, Essex

David G. Davidson, formerly of Bergh Apton, Norfolk

A. Louisa Davy, Wickhambrook, Suffolk

Tony, Linda and Bryony Davy, Flint Cottage, Bergh Apton

James Debbage, Bergh Apton, Norfolk

Robert J. Debbage, Alpington

Muff Dudgeon, Chagford, Devon

Jean and Michael Dulieu, Alpington

Cyril Dye, Bradwell, Norfolk

Derek Leonard Charles Dye, Rockland St Mary, Norfolk

Stephen Dye, Burgh St Peter, Norfolk

Mrs Vera M. Dye, Norwich, Norfolk

Ruby R. Eastell, Sprowston, Norfolk

Myrtle Edge, Kirstead

Ron A. Everson, Seething, Norfolk

John and Lisa Farrant, Bergh Apton, Norfolk

Mr and Mrs J.F. Farrer

Charles and Jack Farrow

David and Susan Farrow

Paul Farrow

Mr R. Farrow, Ipswich, Suffolk

Ronald and Barbara Farrow (née Dye)

Jennifer Findlay, (Denny-Cooke Family), Australia

Sharon Finn, Greystanes, NSW, Australia

Irene Fisher, Norwich

Roy and Jean Flowerdew, Bergh Apton

Jessica Folkes, Halvergate, Norfolk (Bergh Apton School 1974–81)

Marion and Alan Folkes, Brooke, Norfolk

Sylvia and David Ford, Alpington

Albert and Rodney Forder, Bussey Bridge, Bergh Apton

Mr and Mrs E. Forder (The Stone Family of Bergh Apton)

Gillian Forder, Bussey Bridge, Bergh Apton

Grace Forder, Bussey Bridge, Bergh Apton

Harry Forder, Bussey Bridge, Bergh Apton

Mair Shelley Forder, Gloucestershire

J.H.R. Forman

John and Alison Freeman, Holly Farm, Bergh Apton

Thomas Freeman, Holly Farm, Bergh Apton

William (Griff) Freeman, Holly Farm, Bergh Apton

Reggie, Alice, Joy and Gillian Frost, Mill Road, Bergh Apton

John Denny Fryer, Branscombe, Devon

John Palmer Garratt, grandson of Palmer Leeder

David Gifford, Ditchingham, Norfolk
Eric Gooch, Bergh Apton, Norfolk
Eileen Goody, Bergh Apton, Norfolk
Mark Gosling, Bergh Apton, Norfolk
David Gould, Alpington, Norfolk
John Gray, Costessey
John R. Green, Warren View, Loddon
Edmund Greengrass, Bergh Apton, Norfolk
The Greens, Boundary Farm, Yelverton
Himu Gupta, Norwich, Norfolk
Dr Anna Guy, Bergh Apton
Mrs Elizabeth Hall, Lidgate, Suffolk
A. and S.H. Hampton, Little Thetford, Cambridgeshire
Mr G., Mrs K., Miss J. and Miss E. Harber
Mrs Gwen Harber (née Davidson)
Tony Hardesty, Bergh Apton School 1930–36
Christine Harris (née Balls)
Milton and Ruth Harris and family, Town Farm, Bergh Apton
Derek and Jill Harvey, Street Farm, Bergh Apton, Norfolk
George and Audrey Harvey, Bergh Apton
Mike, Sarah and Jen Hassnip, Bassingham, Lincoln
Sue Hill, Sunnyside, Bergh Apton
The Holl Family, Hillside Farm, Bergh Apton, Norfolk
Malcolm Holman, Norwich, Norfolk
Mr Robert Horgan, Witney, Oxfordshire
Olive and Clive Hudson, Harleston, Norfolk
Sarah Hunt (née Woods), Stoke Holy Cross, Norfolk
Emma Elizabeth Hurn, Bergh Apton, Norfolk
Mrs Jessie Elizabeth Ibbott (née Parfitt)
Paddy Imeson, North Wales
Lewis Ingram, Norwich
Reg Isbell, Rockland St Mary, Norfolk
Reg Isbell and daughter Jill
Mrs W.D. Jenner, Maidenhead, Berkshire
E. Pippa Jennings, London
The Jermy Family, Bergh Apton, Norfolk
Neville Jermy
Shane A. Jermy, Bergh Apton, Norfolk
Mr Simon T. Jermy, Bergh Apton, Norfolk
Terry Jermy, Bergh Apton, Norfolk
Mr Thomas A. Jermy, Bergh Apton, Norfolk
Mr and Mrs C.D. Johnson, Bergh Apton, Norfolk
Lynton C.J. Johnson and Mr Ray T. Wharton, Thurton
Mr Brian Joscelyne, Braintree
Ann Keeler, Bergh Apton, Norfolk
Colin W. Keeler, Bergh Apton, Norwich
Daphne Keeler, Bergh Apton, Norfolk
Gerald Kelly, Norwich
Mrs E. Kennedy
Christopher Kent, Seething, Norwich
Gillian Kent, Bergh Apton
Ronnie, Susan and Tine Kent, Bergh Apton
Eileen Rodi Kerry, Bussey Bridge Farm, Bergh Apton
The Kerry Family, Hellington Corner, Bergh Apton
Tony and Kate Kerry, and sons Jamie and William, Bergh Apton, Norfolk
Vic and Carol Keywood, Bergh Apton, Norfolk
Harriet King BVSc, MRCVS, Holsworthy, Devon

Maurice King, School of Architecture, University of Bath
Roxanne and Graham King, Bell House, Hellington Corner (the former Hellington Bell)
Verity King BA (Cantab.), London SE1
Revd Dr Peter and Mrs Christine Knight, Thurton, Norfolk
Billy Lain-Rogers, Ashby St Mary
Eileen Lain-Rogers, Norwich, Norfolk
Lorie Lain-Rogers, Bergh Apton, Norfolk
C.R. and D.L. Langford, Scarning, Norfolk
Mrs Eileen Leathers (née Todd), Thurton
Timothy A. Leeder, Thurton, Norfolk
Mrs Sally Leigh, Parish Councillor, Editor of Bergh Apton Newsletter
David R. Lester, Hellington Corner
John C. Lester, Spixworth, Norfolk
John and Joy Lester, Bergh Apton
Michael J. Lester, Broome, Norfolk
John and Hilary Ling, Bussey Bridge, Bergh Apton, Norfolk
Jean Littleboy, Thurton, Norfolk
Carolle A. Littlewood, Norwich
Fred and Violet Littlewood, Bergh Apton
Michael E. Littlewood, Bridlington, East Yorkshire
Diane M. Loades, Langley, Norfolk
Edgar Loades, Thurton, Norfolk
Stephen Lord, Market Harborough, Leicestershire
Timothy R. Loades, Bergh Apton, Norfolk
Mrs Vanda P. Lowe, Old Costessey, Norfolk
Mr and Mrs N. Lutkin, Thurton, Norfolk
John C. Madden, Vancouver, Canada
Magic Pot, Poringland
Keith and Ann Etta Mann, Red Lion House, Lion Lane, Bergh Apton
Jean M. Marchant, Coventry, West Midlands
John and Barbara Marshall, Bergh Apton
Roger Martyn, London NW5
Muriel J. Maynard (née Thurlow), Seething, Norfolk
Patricia E. McCormack (Matchett), Drouin, Victoria, Australia
Mrs Robyn McGreggor, Sydney, Australia
Patricia McLevie, (Denny-Cooke family), Australia
Ed and Phyll Mendelsohn, Alpington, Norfolk
G. Francis Meynell
Joshua and Zanna Meynell
Liz and Christopher Meynell
Mark and Rachel Meynell
The Middleton Families, Bergh Apton
Diane E. Miller, Brooke, Norfolk
Philippa Millington (née Snellgrove), London
The Mitchell Family, Threadneedle Street
Clover Moore, Thassos, Greece
Jim and Joy Moore, Shotesham, Norfolk
Judith Moore (née Keeler)
Peggy Moreton (née Fryer), born at The Manor, February 1920
M.J. Morter, Wymondham, Norfolk
Dennis Moye
Joy L. Munden, Bergh Apton, Norfolk
Karen, Trevor, Shaun, Martin, Ashley and Hannah Myhill, Bergh Apton, Norfolk

Geof and Ingrid Nelson, formerly Bergh Apton/now Calgary, Canada

The Rt Revd The Lord Bishop of Norwich

Valerie E. Nutter (née Peake)

Bernard O'Brien, Yelverton

Jonathan William Parfitt, Church Farm, Bergh Apton

Rachel Louise Parfitt, Church Farm, Bergh Apton

Rebecca Jane Parfitt, Church Farm, Bergh Apton

Russell C. Parfitt, Bergh Apton, Norfolk

Kenneth D. and Heather M. Perfitt, Bergh Apton, Norfolk

The Revd G.J. Phillips and Mrs Maria Phillips MBE, Bergh Apton

Trevor, Sue, Ashley, Daniel and Lucy Price, Bergh Apton, Norfolk

Dawn Pullan, Brooke, Norfolk

Beryl and Derek Ranwell, Chet Cottage

Phyllis Ride, Bergh Apton, Norfolk

Mike, Shirley, Chris and Tim Rimmer, Bergh Apton

Margaret Roebuck (née Hoddy), Ashby St Mary

M. and J. Rolfe, Beckholme, Bergh Apton

Richard T.A. Rope, Harrow, Middlesex

Victoria H. Rope, Thorpe St Andrew

Stuart Roper, Hardley, Norfolk

The Revd Prebendary A.R. Royall

John William Rudd, Bergh Apton, Norfolk

Louise R. Rynkewicz (née Lester), USA

Dr John Sampson, Poringland, Norfolk

Heather E. Sarsby, Bergh Apton, Norfolk

Christine Saunders (née Reeve), Claxton, Norwich, Norfolk

John Savill, Norwich, Norfolk

Mark Savill, Norwich, Norfolk

Evelyn G. Sayer (née Jermy), Bergh Apton, Norfolk

Mrs Sandy Schröder, Bergh Apton, Norfolk

The Scott Family, Kirstead, Norfolk

Janet Seeley, Bergh Apton, Norfolk

Linda J. Seeley, Bergh Apton

Michael Seeley, Bergh Apton

Eric J. Seely, Bergh Apton, Norfolk

Suzanne E. Sewell, Brockenhurst, Hampshire

Gillian Dodie Sharman Appel, B.C., Canada

Nancy Georgina Sharman Lanyon, B.C., Canada

Robert Sharman Pilbrow, P.Q., Canada

Percy Sillett, Bergh Apton, Norfolk

Sandra and Trevor Sillett, Bergh Apton, Norfolk

The Sim Family, Athelstone, South Australia, descendants of John Blaza (1747), Bergh Apton

David and Janet Skedge and Family

Barrie Smith, Norwich, Norfolk

L.A. and M.E. Smith, Hardley, Norfolk

Sarah and Simon Smith, Bergh Apton, Norfolk

Brian Snellgrove, London

Martin and Pam Snellgrove, Hope, Flintshire

Arthur and Mary Southgate, Bergh Apton, Norfolk

Ethel Audrey Stansby (née Rope), Australia

The Revd Michael and Gillian Stedman, Framlingham, Suffolk

John, Fiona and Emma Steggall, Holly Lodge Barn, Bergh Apton

James and Emma Steggles, (formerly of May Cottage, Bussey Bridge)

Anna and Chris Stratton, Thurton, Norfolk

Eileen Sunderland, Bergh Apton, Norfolk

Geoffrey R. Sutton, Hellington Corner, Bergh Apton

Sheila Tattersall, Leire, Leicestershire

Elizabeth Thompson, New Zealand

Samual Thrower, Hellington Corner, Bergh Apton, Norfolk

Sam Thrower, Hellington Corner

Keith W. Thurlow, Dersingham, Norfolk

Kevin, Caroline, Robert and Sophie Thurtell, Sunnyside

Liz and Peter Tubby, Bergh Apton

Dr Gunter and Renate Turk, Apton Manor, Bergh Apton

The Vivian-Neal Family, Brooke

Mark and Ann Walker (née Farrow)

Phil Wallace, Bergh Apton

John F.W. Walling, Newton Abbot, Devon

Jenny P. Warner (Forder), Gloucestershire

Tony and Brenda Warren, Washingford House, Bergh Apton

Patricia Waters, Valley Farm

The Waters Family, Royston House, Bergh Apton, Norfolk

Diane and Bernard Webb, Hardley, Norfolk

Alan Weddup and Vera Weddup (née Dye)

John and Jeanette Weddup, Sudbury, Suffolk

Alf Weeks, evacuee with Mr and Mrs Freestone, Valley Farm

Michael J. Whiting, Bergh Apton, Norfolk

Michael and Jill Willcox, Holly Lodge, Bergh Apton

Nicola and William Wilson-North, Appletree Cottage, Threadneedle Street, Bergh Apton, 1990–97

Nigel Wimhurst

Mrs D.J. Wincott (née Preston), Blofield

David J. Wood, Bergh Apton

Dorothy Wood, Bergh Apton, Norfolk

Nanette Woodrow (née Thurlow), Seething, Norfolk

Ann Woods (née Reeve), Bergh Apton, Norfolk

Jeremy Woolsey, Burgh St Peter, Norfolk

Dr David Wurr, Harbury, Warwickshire

Yallop, Whiteheath Road, Bergh Apton